DEPORTATION

DEPORTATION

THE ORIGINS OF U.S. POLICY

TORRIE HESTER

PENN

UNIVERSITY OF PENNSYLVANIA PRESS

PHILADELPHIA

Published by
University of Pennsylvania Press
Philadelphia, Pennsylvania 19104-4112
www.upenn.edu/pennpress

Printed in the United States of America
on acid-free paper
1 3 5 7 9 10 8 6 4 2

A Cataloging-in-Publication record is available from the Library of Congress
ISBN 978-0-8122-4916-3

Contents

Abbreviations

AR-CGI U.S. Department of Labor, Bureau of Immigration, *Annual Report of the Commissioner General of Immigration* (Washington, D.C.: Government Printing Office, 1894–1924).

CAN Immigration Branch, RG 76, National Archives of Canada, Ottawa, Ontario.

CCF-AZ Criminal Case Files, 1869–1911, Arizona Territorial Court, Third Judicial District, Records of the District Courts of the United States, RG 21, National Archives, Pacific Region, Laguna Niguel, Calif.

CCF-CA Criminal Case Files, 1907–1929, Southern District of California, Southern Division (Los Angeles), Records of the District Courts of the United States, RG 21, National Archives, Pacific Region, Laguna Niguel, Calif.

ChEx-AZ Chinese Exclusion Case Files, 1897–1911, Arizona Territorial Court, Fourteenth Judicial District, Records of the District Courts of the United States, RG 21, National Archives, Pacific Region, Laguna Niguel, Calif.

DF Central Decimal File Subjects 1910–1949, Central Files 1910–January 1963, U.S. Department of State Records, RG 59, National Archives, College Park, Md.

DS Diplomatic Correspondence, Central Files of the Department of State, 1778–1963, RG 59, National Archives, College Park, Md.

FRUS U.S. Department of State, *Foreign Relations of the United States* (Washington, D.C.: U.S. Government Printing Office, 1886–1924).

FSP Records of the Foreign Service Posts of the Department of State, State Department and Foreign Affairs Records, RG 84, National Archives, College Park, Md.

ILR   U.S. Department of Labor, Bureau of Immigration, *Immigration Laws and Rules* (Washington, D.C.: U.S. Government Printing Office, 1907–1924).

INS   Records of the Immigration and Naturalization Service, RG 85, National Archives, Washington, D.C.

USC-AZ   U.S. Commissioners Dockets and Minutes, 1891–1912, Arizona Territorial Court, Third Judicial District, Records of District Courts of the United States, RG 21, National Archives, Pacific Region, Laguna Niguel, Calif.

USSCRB   U.S. Supreme Court Records & Briefs on Microfiche (Bethesda, Md.: Congressional Information Service, 1984–present).

Introduction

In the late nineteenth and early twentieth centuries, U.S. officials created a national deportation policy. They were not alone in this endeavor. In the same period, Canada, Mexico, Venezuela, Australia, New Zealand, Brazil, Britain, and Germany, among others, also either revised existing immigrant removal policies or developed new ones.[1] Their efforts made deportation into an internationally recognized form of removal, which was unique in law, scope, motivation, and significance. The act of deporting individuals thereafter became one of the most far-reaching powers exercised by the United States government. Between 1892, when the U.S. government first started to establish its federal deportation policy, and 2015, the United States deported more than fifty million immigrants, almost 95 percent of them since 1970.[2]

This book examines the power of deportation, the national and international policies created to administer this power, and the changing meaning of deportability—the status of being deportable—during the first, formative decades of the deportation regime.[3]

Before 1882, the U.S. government had never formally deported anyone. That year, in the first of a series of laws, Congress created the power to deport Chinese workers. By 1888, policy makers had enhanced their power to deport all immigrants, and, over the next thirty years, the government expanded restrictions so that, by 1917, deportation provisions variously targeted Chinese workers, anarchists, suspected prostitutes, public charges, and contract laborers, to mention only a few of the categories. Immigration agents carrying out new federal policy deported several hundred or, at the most, a few thousand people each year. They deported fewer people in the first forty years of carrying out deportations than immigration authorities would in any single year after 1970.

In some ways, then, this book covers a time when immigration authorities administered deportation policy quite differently than they would a century later. Nevertheless, the grounds for deportation, the enforcement strategies, the negotiations behind deportations, and the defenses immigrants employed in deportation proceedings all reveal a great deal about the history of the period. Moreover, these years are critical to understanding the explosion of deportations since the 1970s because, between 1882 and 1924, Congress, the Supreme Court, and the Bureau of Immigration pieced together the policy and legal regime in which all deportations from the United States have occurred ever since.

In the years before the rise of the U.S. deportation regime, governments had long removed people from their communities. In North America, various authorities expelled individuals and entire groups of people. After Mexican independence in 1823, for instance, the new Mexican government expelled Spanish-born residents. Seventy years earlier, British colonial authorities expelled a group of French settlers—the Acadians—from Nova Scotia and sent them to Louisiana.[4] The earliest colonists in Virginia and Massachusetts Bay expelled religious outsiders and criminals. Indeed, expulsion from the colonies that would become the United States is as old as European settlement.

During the colonial period, removals often occurred on a case-by-case basis, driven mostly by locally defined economic and religious motivations. European and Euro-American communities "warned out" or expelled individuals they thought were unable to support themselves with little to no regard for the nationalities of the poor. Colonists could also be forced out of settlements for practicing the wrong religion. In the seventeenth and early eighteenth centuries, membership in the local community was what mattered for receiving assistance from the community or for simply being allowed to stay once poor or deemed disruptive to mores. Some colonies tried sending expelled criminals or poor immigrants back to England, but that was generally too expensive and inefficient. Consequently, expulsion was not a widespread practice in the colonial period, but when it occurred, people were ousted from the community with little concern for where they went.[5] Though it was very different from the federal deportation power developed in the late nineteenth and early twentieth centuries, there is a long history of sporadically expelling men and women deemed undesirable or foreign.

Through much of the nineteenth century, the federal government possessed but did not use a limited formal power to remove immigrants; instead some states operated immigrant removal policies. In the Alien

Friends and Alien Enemies Acts of 1798, Congress had given the president a restricted power, based on executive order with judicial enforcement, to expel foreigners from the United States. Some Republicans, including Thomas Jefferson, maintained that this expulsion policy was patently unconstitutional; they thought it represented an attempt by the opposing political party, the Federalists, to remove its political enemies from the country.[6] The constitutionality of the 1798 acts was never tested, and most of the Alien Friends Act expired two years after its passage.[7] For the first half of the nineteenth century, there was neither the popular will nor, after the election of the Republicans and the dissolution of the Federalists, the political will to legitimize the federal removal of immigrants. While the federal government did not formally remove people, some states had removal policies. And, from time to time, states carried out immigrant removals with the collaboration of federal authorities.[8]

Nevertheless, the U.S. government did forcibly remove people through exceptional power and violence in this period. With Indian removal, it exercised a violent, state-sanctioned power to remove whole nations of Native Americans. Though brutally effective, this type of power to remove people was an exception to the rule of law.[9]

In addition to the "warning outs," the occasional state-centered expulsions of the early nineteenth century, and the extralegal Indian removal policies of the 1830s, there were still other ways governments removed people prior to the U.S. deportation regime. At the request of foreign governments who wanted a person's return for judicial proceedings, governments extradited immigrants, while officials also removed people through banishment.[10]

In the second half of the nineteenth century, millions of immigrants moved around the world in unprecedented numbers. The United States became the largest immigrant-receiving nation, and between 1880 and 1924, over twenty-four million moved to the United States.[11] People on U.S. soil, from immigrants to citizens, lawmakers to bureaucrats, confronted enormous changes wrought by the numbers of immigrants, the new streams of immigration, and massive industrialization and urbanization. Early in this large wave of migration, officials from states like New York and California began to pass restrictive immigration laws, and it was at this point that two key developments occurred. First, in the 1870s, the U.S. Supreme Court ruled these state laws unconstitutional. Second, in the wake of the Court's rulings, the federal government stepped in and began a new phase in regulating immigration, what would become one of its major functions—gatekeeping.[12] It is at this crucial juncture that this book opens.

In addition to chronicling the rise of the U.S. deportation regime at the turn of the twentieth century, a second aim of this book is to understand U.S. officials' interactions with an international legal framework in building this policy. Some scholars studying deportation have long understood that national deportation policies function as a part of a larger international system, what anthropologists Nicholas De Genova and Nathalie Peutz have labeled the "deportation regime."[13] In this complex international framework, a nation-state cannot carry out a formal, legal deportation outside of the international community of states. Much of the work on this larger international regime, however, concentrates on the post–World War II era, when populations of the deported around the world grew to the millions.[14] *Deportation: The Origins of U.S. Policy* takes the international perspective back to the formative period of deportation policy in the United States.[15]

To examine the international regime that facilitated U.S. deportations, this book examines the deportations of immigrants from the United States *and* the receiving of deported U.S. citizens from abroad. Finding evidence of the latter proved more difficult than the former, in part because the United States deported more people than other countries deported U.S. citizens. Yet the small numbers of cases of U.S. citizens returning to the United States are important for understanding the international legal regime that facilitated deportations. When countries like Canada, Germany, or Mexico wanted to deport a U.S. citizen, they approached U.S. State Department officials. Some—but certainly not all—of these correspondences have thus been preserved in State Department records or in the archives of the country removing the U.S. citizen. Some of the same files contain diplomatic correspondence initiated by U.S. officials as they tried to arrange the deportations of people from the United States.

Diplomatic records help render the shape of the international legal regime facilitating immigrant removals in the late nineteenth and early twentieth centuries, but they provide little insight into the reasons *why* there were no deportations of U.S. citizens from some countries, such as China. In this case, international law treatises help explain the ways the international legal regime prevented nations or polities in the Middle East and Asia, including China, from deporting people from Western nations and empires. Together, diplomatic sources and international law treatises reveal parameters and even restrictions the international legal regime set on a nation's ability to deport immigrants.

Another principal aim of the book is to document the ways that people facing deportations defended themselves, which profoundly affected law within the United States.[16] Immigrants in deportation proceedings in the late nineteenth century and early twentieth became quick students of law. They did so while also navigating challenges common in immigration—learning new customs and languages, overcoming trauma caused by civil unrest or economic hardship, and building communities, homes, and careers. Immigrants defending against a deportation understood that the deportation policy they faced was shaped as much by the nature of enforcement as by the text of the law.[17] Policy enforcement was fluid: immigration officials responded to constituents lobbying for deportations and the ever-changing strategies of immigrants defending against deportations. Federal immigration agents also collaborated with and were influenced by state and local law enforcement officials, federal judges, and agents of the Bureau of Investigation (predecessor of today's FBI). As immigrants navigated deportation policy, they often forced immigration agents to reconcile immigration law with other kinds of law—including marriage, criminal, and naturalization—as well as the reach of the U.S. Constitution.[18]

To explain this pivotal era in history, the first half of the book examines the national and international logic that shaped early U.S. deportation policy, while the second half studies specific provisions of U.S. deportation policy that enhanced the power of deportation and extended deportability on U.S. soil.

In 1893, the U.S. Supreme Court decided *Fong Yue Ting,* a case that has remained the legal precedent for every deportation from the United States since. For the Chinese immigrants who ended up before the Court in *Fong Yue Ting,* one of their central questions to the Court asked if the federal government could deport immigrants at all. The Supreme Court ruled that it could. The power to deport belonged to the federal government, under what has become known as its plenary power, as a trait of sovereignty. As immigration officials began to enforce deportation provisions, they filled out the logic of just what the Supreme Court ruled in *Fong Yue Ting,* that deportation was a power protective of national security. Their efforts made deportation proceedings operate differently than criminal proceedings, which had important implications for the reach of the U.S. Constitution over immigrants, especially over the meaning of the Fourth, Fifth, and Sixth Amendments.

When immigrants challenged their deportations, some of their efforts drove important legal distinctions between three categories of residents in the United States: immigrants without legal residence, immigrants with legal residence, and U.S. citizens. The legal distinctions between these three categories of residents on U.S. soil reshaped civil rights and civil liberties, as well as social and economic rights, and conceptions of race and racial power. Sometimes, though, it was not clear where one legal status ended and another began. By the 1920s, the lines between the immigrants with lawful status, those "outside the law," and U.S. citizens, which were previously somewhat fluid, had hardened significantly, with profound national and international consequences that are unfolding still.[19]

Chapter 1

Creating U.S. Deportation Policy

In the late nineteenth century, the U.S. Congress created two sets of deportation policies. Congress began building the first in 1882 when it passed the Chinese Exclusion Act. This deportation law applied specifically, and exclusively, to Chinese laborers. Congress started the second in 1888, which applied to the millions arriving from everywhere but China, nearly 90 percent of whom in the late nineteenth century and early twentieth century came from Europe.

A key national logic shaping these early deportation policies was clearly articulated in the 1893 Supreme Court decision of *Fong Yue Ting v. United States*. The case originated the year before, when Congress passed a new law, now known as the Geary Act, designed to broaden the government's power to deport Chinese immigrants.[1] Three men—Fong Yue Ting, Wong Quan, and Lee Joe—challenged the law's deportation provision.[2] When the Supreme Court heard *Fong Yue Ting*, one particular question the litigants posed to the Court stood out: did the U.S. government possess the power to deport at all? In 1893, while immigration authorities and Congress certainly thought it did, it was not entirely clear to all Americans that federal authorities should have that power. The question had not ever been posed to the Supreme Court. In *Fong Yue Ting*, the Court upheld the government's power to deport people from U.S. soil as part of a nation-state's power of self-protection and found that it did not represent a punishment for a crime.

Yet, at the turn of the twentieth century, just what it meant that deportations served to protect the nation rather than as a form of punishment was sometimes unclear and hotly contested. In 1917, immigration policy makers folded the two deportation policies—the one aimed at Chinese immigrants and the other at everyone else—into one. By then, officials, lawmakers, judges, and immigrants had worked out the logic of deportation as protection: it mattered in terms of burden of proof and due process rights of people in deportation proceedings, and it made deportation proceedings very different from criminal trials.

The Government's Power to Deport in *Fong Yue Ting*

In the wake of the Chinese Exclusion Act of 1882 and the law known as the Geary Act of 1892, the Chinese immigrant community protested. One of the cases at the heart of their challenge was *Fong Yue Ting*, in which they challenged the way Chinese exclusion created a racial class in law—one in seeming violation of both the Fourteenth Amendment and an international treaty. The Chinese immigrant community also posed several challenges to the government's power to deport and the procedures designed to carry it out. They questioned if the federal government could lawfully deport a person at all. If the Supreme Court found that it could, they argued, then deportation should be classified as a punishment. Classification as a punishment would mean people in deportation proceedings would have constitutional protections under the Fourth, Fifth, and Sixth Amendments open to people in criminal proceedings. The outcome of *Fong Yue Ting* set an important national logic to U.S. deportation policy ever since.

Fong Yue Ting, Wong Quan, and Lee Joe, the men who became the litigants in *Fong Yue Ting*, had immigrated to the United States when the U.S. government had been relatively open to immigration from China. The immigration stream dates to the 1840s, with the California gold rush. The U.S. government signed the Burlingame Treaty with the Chinese government in 1868 to facilitate further migration. Between 1870 and 1880, just under 140,000 Chinese immigrants entered the United States. This represented roughly 4 percent of all immigrants to the United States during these years.[3]

Almost as soon as Chinese immigration began, however, many white Americans, especially workers from California, Oregon, and Washington, the western states where most of the Chinese immigrant population lived, began to call for governmental restriction of Chinese immigration. The anti-Chinese movement painted Chinese immigration as dangerous, as something that threatened not only livable wages and white racial superiority but the very essence of American democracy.[4] H. N. Clement, a California lawyer, captured sentiment for policy that excluded Chinese immigrants when he wrote that the United States had "a right to do *everything* that can secure it from threatening danger and to *keep at a distance* whatever is capable of causing its ruin. . . . We have a great right to say to the half-civilized subject from Asia, '*You shall not come at all.*' "[5] Democrats and Republicans at the national level adopted anti-Chinese stances, especially in the 1880 presidential election, when both parties considered the Pacific Coast vote essential for victory. As historian Andrew Gyory notes, in the campaign's final days, "party leaders catapulted Chinese immigration to the top of the national agenda, effectively reducing the contest to which party could 'out-Chinese' the other."[6]

Two years later, in 1882, Congress passed the first of the laws of Chinese exclusion, which created a separate racial class in federal law. It would be the first federal law that U.S. authorities used to formally deport anyone.[7] Under the 1882 law, Chinese laborers could not lawfully immigrate and federal authorities could deport those who immigrated unlawfully.[8] Congress repeated the immigration restriction and deportation provision in subsequent legislation that decade: the Chinese Exclusion Acts of 1884 and 1888.[9] These laws were both racial and classed, in that they targeted people of Chinese heritage who were also workers.[10]

In 1892, in another revision to Chinese exclusion, Congress passed the Geary Act and with it widened the deportability of Chinese laborers. Under one of the law's terms, all laborers of Chinese descent in the country were required to apply for and then carry a certificate of residence that proved their legal right to be in the country. This registration requirement was new and made even those lawfully in the country before the law deportable. To register for the certificate, the applicant listed his or her name, age, local residence, and occupation and submitted a photograph. The only exception was if the laborer could prove that he or she had been unable to obtain a certificate by reason of accident, sickness, or other extenuating circumstance.[11] If the laborer did not have a certificate, U.S. officials were to assume the person was in the United States in violation of exclusion laws and therefore subject to deportation. No law had ever required this of any immigrant on U.S. soil; it was a new "documents regime" that applied only to Chinese immigrant workers.[12]

The Chinese immigrant community quickly organized against the Geary Act. Led by the Chinese Six Companies, which was "the umbrella organization for the large kinship and mutual benefit organizations established in the United States to serve Chinese immigrants," individual Chinese immigrants refused to apply for the certificates of residence.[13] Then, when the government began ordering the deportation of Chinese workers who did not register for certificates, the Chinese Six Companies mounted a legal challenge to the new law and the government's power to deport. Their lawyers selected three test cases: Fong Yue Ting and Wong Quan, who had each lived in the United States for at least thirteen years, and Lee Joe, who had lived in the United States for eighteen.[14] The Supreme Court combined their cases into one, *Fong Yue Ting*, and heard it within a year.[15]

Once in front of the Supreme Court, lawyers for Fong Yue Ting, Wong Quan, and Lee Joe challenged both the way Chinese exclusion laws had created an explicit racial class and the government's ability to deport at all. The lawyers argued that Chinese exclusion violated the equal protection clause of the Fourteenth Amendment since it was aimed only at Chinese immigrants. Chinese immigrants, they pointed out, were certainly not being treated the same as Irishmen or Frenchmen.[16] Moreover, they claimed the law violated the Tenth Amendment to the Constitution, under which "powers not delegated to the United States by the Constitution, nor prohibited by it to the states, are reserved to the states, respectively, or to the people." Since the colonial period, some states had exercised the power to remove immigrants. When the federal government assumed this power in Chinese exclusion, the lawyers maintained, it was creating the power to deport, without enumeration in the Constitution.[17] The attorneys for the appellants, therefore, attacked the Geary Act by arguing that Congress could not create an explicit racial class, and, even if lawmakers could, they could not do it through deportation.

The lawyers then made the case that, if the Supreme Court upheld the federal government's power to deport and the racism of the law, then the deportation proceedings faced by Fong Yue Ting, Wong Quan, and Lee Joe were unconstitutional. Immigration authorities had arrested Fong Yue Ting, Wong Quan, and Lee Joe under civil proceedings, under civil law. Their lawyers argued that deportation represented a punishment. The proceedings to administer a deportation, therefore, needed to be consistent with the constitutional rights afforded to criminal defendants in the Fourth, Fifth, and Sixth Amendments. The proceedings set up under Chinese exclusion, they argued, did not protect against unreasonable searches as outlined in the Fourth Amendment. Nor did the administrative hearings of deportation provide Fifth Amendment due process or the Sixth Amendment right to a jury trial. The lawyers knew, as many others would find out not long after the Court decided the case, that there was a great deal at stake in the legal designation of whether or not deportations represented a punishment.

A large part of the case for the Chinese immigrant community also looked to challenge the ways that the new federal power of deportation violated rights of long-term residents. Lawyers for Fong Yue Ting, Wong Quan, and Lee Joe argued that since 1882, there were two separate classes of Chinese workers in the United States: unlawful residents and lawful, long-term residents.[18] The unlawful residents, the lawyers argued, had come to the United States in violation of the law of Chinese exclusion in operation since 1882. This class, the lawyers acknowledged, were "lawless intruders . . . having no right to be here."[19] The other class, though, the one that Fong Yue Ting fell into, was lawful permanent residency. The lawyers claimed that this class of immigrants constituted a large proportion of the Chinese laborers in the United States in 1893. "Tens of thousands of Chinese laborers," they argued, had entered the United States before the Chinese Exclusion Act "and remained here ever since."[20]

The Six Companies lawyers insisted that long-term Chinese residents had what amounted to permanent residence and that deporting them violated international law. The lawful right to remain for long-term residents, as the lawyers understood it, originated in two sources. First, it was rooted in a category of international law known as the status of denizen; second, it derived from the fact that the U.S. government had invited these workers to come to the United States under an international treaty. The immigrants were clearly not citizens. The lawyers claimed that Chinese laborers who had moved to the United States prior to 1882 fell into the category of "denizens," or what would soon become known as lawfully admitted immigrants. The lawyers also claimed that U.S. law granted long-term residents lawful status; these immigrants had lawful residence because, under the Burlingame Treaty of 1868 signed by China and the United States, thousands of Chinese laborers had set up legal residence in the United States by invitation.[21] The immigrants had, in effect, "been told that if they would come here they would be treated just the same as we treat an Englishman, an Irishman, or a Frenchman. They have been invited here, and their position is much stronger than that of an alien, in regard to whom there is no guarantee from the Government, and who has come not in response to any invitation, but has simply drifted here because there is no prohibition to keep him out."[22] The lawyers insisted it was unlawful to expel such immigrants, except as a punishment for a crime or during a war.

In a five-to-three decision, the Supreme Court ruled against Fong Yue Ting, Wong Quan, and Lee Joe and unambiguously endorsed the government's power to deport. To address the Tenth Amendment challenge, the Court linked the authority of the federal government to deport people to the power of exclusion, which the Court had earlier cleared. In *Chae Chan Ping v. United States* (1889) and *Nishimura Ekiu v. United States* (1892), the U.S. Supreme Court ruled that the federal government possessed the power to exclude immigrants.[23] In these cases, the Court described the ability to exclude immigrants as originating from the sovereign's authority to prevent foreign aggression. The Court looked to international law to justify the power of exclusion, citing scholars such as Emmerich de Vattel, Robert Phillimore, and Francis Wharton. As the Court put it, "It is an accepted maxim of international law that every sovereign nation has the power, as inherent in sovereignty, and essential to self-preservation, to forbid the entrance of foreigners within its dominions, or to admit them only in such cases and upon such conditions as it may see fit to prescribe."[24] Here, as legal scholar Sarah Cleveland has pointed out, the Supreme Court "utilized international law as a source of authority for U.S. government action, but did not recognize it as a source of constraint."[25] The justices then extended this logic of sovereignty to establish the government's additional authority to deport immigrants, finding that deportation was simply an extension of the government's power to exclude. "The power to exclude aliens," the Court wrote, "and the power to expel them rest upon one foundation, are derived from one source, are supported by the same reasons, and are in truth but parts of one and the same power."[26]

The Court declined to define or limit what constituted a foreign threat or an instance of aggression and, in doing so, resolved the Fourteenth Amendment challenge and upheld the racism behind Chinese exclusion. It did not matter what form a perceived aggression took, the Court wrote, "whether from the foreign nation acting in its national character, or from vast hordes of its people crowding in upon us."[27] If the federal government determined that some event or instance represented a threat to national security, it possessed the power and authority to protect its national independence. By this logic, if the government found Chinese immigrants a threat, it had the right to exclude and deport them. The government could create a distinct racial class in immigration law, and that did not violate the Fourteenth Amendment.

When the Supreme Court delivered its decision, it seemed to uphold the power to place long-term residents and new immigrants on the same legal footing. Yet, the Court included a statement in its decision that seemed to acknowledge the existence of the legal category of domiciled or legally admitted aliens. "By the law of nations," the Court admitted, "doubtless, aliens residing in a country, with the intention of making it a permanent place of abode, acquire, in one sense, a domicil there . . . while they are permitted by the nation to retain such a residence and domicil, [they] are subject to its laws, and may invoke its protection against other nations." But the Court quickly added that long-term Chinese immigrants "continue to be aliens, having taken no steps towards becoming citizens, and incapable of becoming such under the naturalization laws; and therefore remain subject to the power of Congress to expel them, or to order them to be removed and deported."[28] Thus, as the Court understood it, both groups of immigrants could be deported because long-term residence did not protect a person from deportation. On these grounds, Fong Yue Ting and Wong Quan could be deported for not registering for a certificate of residence.

Part of the plaintiffs' argument in Fong Yue Ting turned on the claim that if the government did possess the power of deportation, then it represented a punishment, but here, too, the Court disagreed. Deportation under the Geary Act, the Court determined, "is in no proper sense a trial and sentence for a crime or offense. It is simply the ascertainment, by appropriate and lawful means, of the fact whether the conditions exist upon which Congress has enacted that an alien of this class may remain within the country."[29] Because deportation was not a punishment, the Court reasoned, a deportee was not "deprived of life, liberty, or property without due process of law; and the provisions of the Constitution, securing the right of trial by jury, and prohibiting unreasonable searches and seizures, and cruel and unusual punishments, have no application."[30]

The Supreme Court further clarified the distinction between punishment and deportation by finding that removing or expelling a citizen represented a punishment, but that the removal of a noncitizen did not. As the Court majority asserted, "the order of deportation is not a punishment for crime. It is not a banishment, in the sense in which that word is often applied to the expulsion of a citizen from his country by way of punishment."[31] Instead, as the justices understood it, deportation "is but a method of enforcing the return to his own country of an alien who does not comply with the conditions upon the performance of which the government of the nation, acting within its constitutional authority and through the proper departments, has determined that his continuing to reside here shall depend."[32]

Not all the justices agreed with the Court majority, and in the dissenting opinions of Melville Fuller, David Brewer, and Stephen Field were different schools of thought on the range of legal questions posed in *Fong Yue Ting*. When the Court majority upheld the authority of the political branches of the federal government to deport by linking it to national protection, justices invoked a category of power in U.S. law known as the plenary power. Under the plenary power, as legal scholars Thomas Alexander Aleinikoff, David A. Martin, and Hiroshi Motomura write, "the judicial branch . . . defer[s] to executive and legislative branch decision making."[33] The plenary power doctrine limited the right of courts to review the powers of the federal legislative and executive branches. Justices Fuller, Brewer, and Field worried that what the majority proposed in its framing and interpretation of the plenary power was so radical that it cut at some of the most basic constitutional protections. In *Fong Yue Ting*, the dissenting justices feared that expansion of the plenary power would give rise to a despotic power.[34]

The dissenting justices questioned the majority's insistence that deportation and exclusion represented the same unlimited power created by sovereignty and, instead, found this logic to violate the Constitution. The key for Field was that the government's authority to exclude aliens did not give it the authority to deal with a person already on U.S. soil. "[W]hile the general government is invested," Field wrote, "in respect of foreign countries and their subjects or citizens, with the powers necessary to the maintenance of its absolute independence and security throughout its entire territory, it cannot, in virtue of any delegated power, or power implied therefrom, or of a supposed inherent sovereignty, arbitrarily deal with persons lawfully within the peace of its dominion."[35] As Brewer saw it, in building the power to deport based on the rights inhered by sovereignty, the government was effectively wiping away robust constitutional rights on the grounds that it was protecting the country. Deportation, Brewer said, "can be exercised only in subordination to the limitations and restrictions imposed by the Constitution."[36] Brewer's dissent further questioned the government's lack of constitutional limits. "It is said," Brewer wrote, "that the power here asserted [of deportation] is inherent in sovereignty." But this doctrine is, he warned, "one both indefinite and dangerous. Where are the limits to such powers to be found, and by whom are they to be pronounced?" Should those limits be set by Congress or the Court or international law? "The governments of other nations have elastic powers," but, Brewer declared, "ours are fixed and bounded by a written Constitution."[37]

The dissenting justices also insisted that if the government did have the power to deport, then it constituted a punishment. Brewer wrote that under the Geary Act a person who did not secure a certificate of residence might be deported, and this consequence for not acting was a punishment. Deportation, Brewer asserted, "involves first an arrest, a deprival of liberty; and second, a removal from home, from family, from business, from property."[38] "Everyone knows," he continued, "that to be forcibly taken away from home, and family, and friends, and business, and property, and sent across the ocean to a distant land, is punishment; and that oftentimes most severe and cruel."[39] As Field saw it, the deportation of long-term residents like Fong Yue Ting represented a "punishment . . . beyond all reason in its severity. It is out of all proportion to the alleged offense. It is cruel and unusual. As to its cruelty, nothing can exceed a forcible deportation from a country of one's residence, and the breaking up of all relations of friendship, family, and business there contracted."[40] Field here seemed to oppose the collapsing of the legal categories of long-term and short-term immigrants. Long-term residents, like citizens, should not be deported without the constitutional protections relating to punishments. Brewer and Field focused on the experience of a potential deportee and argued that since deportation felt like a punishment, it should be processed as one. The dissenting justices did not see the clear line between protection and punishment drawn by the Court's majority.

Justice Field argued against what he understood as the weight of the decision—that it established a separate tier of law that treated immigrants differently from citizens. To make his point, he raised two questions: "If a foreigner who resides in the country by its consent commits a public offense, is he subject to be cut down, maltreated, imprisoned, or put to death by violence, without accusation made, trial had, and judgment of an established tribunal following the regular forms of judicial procedure? If any rule in the administration of justice is to be omitted or discarded in his case, what rule is it to be?" Field warned that if the government constructed a second tier of law, it would be easy to put aside the rights and liberties valued in the American system of government. "If one rule may lawfully be laid aside in this case, another rule may also be laid aside, and all rules may be discarded," he wrote. "In such instances, a rule of evidence may be set aside in one case, a rule of pleading in another; the testimony of eye-witnesses may be rejected, and hearsay adopted; or no evidence at all may be received, but simply an inspection of the accused."[41]

The dissenting opinions brought into relief just what the Supreme Court upheld in *Fong Yue Ting*. The minority thought deportation should be classified as punishment; they worried about the expansions in the plenary power and the seeming violations of constitutional protections. The majority opinion understood the legal questions posed in the case quite differently. They upheld deportation, defining it as something as protective of national sovereignty, rooted in the government's power of immigrant exclusion. The Court's decision also stated that deportations were guided by the U.S. Constitution, and that the proceedings set up under the laws of Chinese exclusion were constitutional.

After *Fong Yue Ting*, administrative officials set out to enforce the meaning of deportability that the Supreme Court articulated. One of the first challenges federal officials in the post–*Fong Yue Ting* world had to face was the prospect of deporting perhaps the 110,000 people who had refused to register for certificates of residence. The government did not have the budget for deportations on this scale. Nor did law clearly define who was in charge of deporting this number of people. Throughout the West, a chaotic mix of local and state officials as well as private citizens began arresting people.[42] Six months after the *Fong Yue Ting* decision, on November 3, 1893, Congress solved some of the immediate enforcement challenges when it passed legislation known as the McCreary Amendment. The McCreary Amendment extended the time limit that Chinese laborers in the United States could sign up for certificates of residence. Chinese immigrants, by and large, registered.[43]

Deportation Proceedings Under Chinese Exclusion

A much longer term challenge facing those tasked with enforcing deportations under Chinese exclusion arose from the fundamental question: what did it really mean in the post–*Fong Yue Ting* world that deportation was not a punishment? Finding the answer was incredibly challenging and took decades. It was worked out on the ground in communities where people of Chinese descent lived, by a collaboration of federal and state officials, through the kinds of enforcement actions—arrest, hearing, and appeal—that made up deportation proceedings of Chinese exclusion.

The first stage of deportation proceedings as set up under Chinese exclusion took place in front of a federal administrative official known as a U.S. commissioner. U.S. commissioners were not unique to the immigration bureaucracy; they were administrative officers appointed to reduce the workload of the courts. The appellants had questioned the constitutionality of the administrative hearing in *Fong Yue Ting* in some of the finer points of their argument. Holding administrative hearings, the lawyers argued, was not consistent with Fifth Amendment due process rights. The Supreme Court had disagreed. The judicial branch was capable of hearing deportation cases, but, according to the Court, it was not the only branch that could do so. It was not unprecedented, the Court noted, for officials in other branches of the government to make decisions about laws, and that doing so did not represent a violation of due process.[44]

If a commissioner found an immigrant deportable, the immigrant could petition for a writ of habeas corpus and appeal the ruling.[45] The initial appeal needed to take place within ten days of the original deportation order. If done so, the case first went to the federal district court.[46] If an immigrant still wanted to challenge his or her deportation after a hearing at the district court, the case could then be appealed to the circuit court of appeals and finally to the U.S. Supreme Court. In all of these levels of appeals, judicial officers—federal judges—decided the cases.

People facing this civil proceeding did not have many of the constitutional protections open to people in criminal proceedings. The 1902 district court hearing of *United States v. Lee Huen* revealed the limits of the Fifth Amendment. "If defendants fail to give testimony in their own behalf," the judge said, "and explain doubtful matters peculiarly within their own knowledge, in these deportation cases, that fact may be commented on, and used to their disadvantage, possibly, for such fact may be considered by the court or commissioner, with all the evidence and circumstances of the case, and justify him in taking testimony they might have explained or denied, strongly against them."[47] Nor could the accused claim the right to trial by jury.

Furthermore, under civil law, the standard of judgment was the preponderance of credible evidence, whereas in criminal cases judgment had to be beyond all reasonable doubt.[48] This effectively placed the burden of proof on the defendant rather than on the government; in theory, federal officials needed to do very little to win a deportation hearing. One case, *United States v. Hung Chang*, outlined just how little evidence the government needed to make its case. "No greater degree of proof," the judge wrote, "is required on the part of the United States. It is not required to do more than satisfy the commissioner or judge, by affirmative proof, that the one under arrest is a person of Chinese descent. This does not mean to satisfy beyond any possibility of doubt, but only to a reasonable degree of certainty, such as a rational mind would demand in any serious matter of personal concern."[49] If a Chinese defendant did not produce a preponderance of credible evidence that he or she was not deportable, the decision went in favor of the government.

In 1892, Congress had outlined two ways for Chinese defendants to meet their burden of proof. The easiest way was to present the certificate. In cases where a Chinese laborer had lost or never possessed a certificate of residence, Congress created a second process to prove legal residence: the testimony of at least one white witness.[50] Obtaining a white witness statement posed a serious problem for some Chinese immigrants. Tsui Kwo Yin, a member of the Chinese legation in the United States, described the challenges: a Chinese person must "find a white man who knew him on or before 1882. The laborer who is now in Washington City or Texas most likely lived in California in 1882. He must go to California and see if he can find a white man who knew him ten years ago and return with the evidence to the place where he now lives." This was not a surprise to lawmakers framing the requirement; as Tsui Kwo Yin noted, "One of the Senators from Texas said that Chinese in his state would have to travel 500 miles to find a collector to give the certificate, and he would have to take a white witness with him."[51]

In *Fong Yue Ting*, on behalf of Lee Joe, the Six Companies lawyers had challenged the white witness requirement, but the U.S. Supreme Court upheld it. The justices' reasoning amounted to "not allowing such a fact [lawful residence] to be proved solely by the testimony of aliens in a like situation, or of the same race." Justice Horace Gray, writing the decision, noted that this practice had "existed for seventy-seven years in the naturalization laws, by which aliens applying for naturalization must prove their

residence within the limits and under the jurisdiction of the United States
. . . by the oath or affirmation of citizens of the United States."[52] Gray's
wording seems to indicate that what was at the heart of the case was testimony from noncitizens; this was not what the white witness requirement
addressed, because it equated whiteness with honesty and citizenship. The
laws of Chinese exclusion did not call for a citizen to testify. They called
for a white person to testify. Not all citizens were white and not all whites
were citizens. And, it was not sufficient for a U.S. citizen of color to testify.[53]
Justice Field dissented, writing, "Here the government undertakes to exact
of the party arrested the testimony of a witness of a particular color, though
conclusive and incontestable testimony from others may be adduced. The
law might as well have said that unless the laborer should also present a
particular person as a witness who could not be produced, from sickness,
absence, or other cause . . . he should be held to be unlawfully within the
United States."[54]

Over time, the lower courts further expanded on the legal justification for
the white witness requirement.[55] The 1902 decision in *United States v. Lee
Huen* in New York captures the ways courts tended to regard Chinese testimony: Judge George W. Ray of the U.S. District Court for the Northern
District of New York declared that "the testimony of Chinese witnesses . . .
may be regarded as more or less weak; and, when contradicted or really
impeached in any of the modes suggested and recognized by our law, the
commissioner is justified in regarding such testimony, standing alone, as
insufficient to convince the judicial mind."[56] Judge Ray stated that "it is common knowledge that enslaved peoples develop an inordinate propensity for
lying, and this is characteristic of most oriental nations. This comes largely
from their being subject to the caprice and exactions of their masters or
superiors, and, having no sense of moral responsibility to them, they come
to regard lying to them as no sin, and an habitual disregard of the truth is
thus engendered."[57] Accordingly, a white witness and Chinese witness might
say the same thing, but the white person's words held more legal weight.[58]

While the appellants in *Fong Yue Ting* had failed in their appeal to the
Supreme Court to shift the burden of proof in deportation cases from the
defendant to the government or to overturn the one white witness requirement, over the next decade individual Chinese defendants used the appeals
process to limit the effect of both. By 1901, Chinese defendants in districts
like San Francisco were defeating deportation orders in as many as 90 percent of all cases. There were many defense strategies defendants used that

explain these numbers. One of the most important, however, was that defendants appealed initial deportation orders decided by the U.S. commissioners to federal courts. Once there, federal judges tended to use the standards of evidence and rest the burden of proof as the courts did in criminal proceedings, rather than civil ones.[59] This made it easier for Chinese immigrants to argue their cases successfully. People of Chinese descent had great success overturning their deportation orders, because, through their appeals, the courts made the civil proceedings of Chinese exclusion more like criminal ones.

To the officials administering Chinese exclusion, the appeal rates in favor of Chinese defendants represented a policy failure. In 1901, Terence V. Powderly, the U.S. commissioner general of immigration, tried to do something about it. Steps taken by Powderly and his successor Frank P. Sargent would lead to more deportations, but they would not be as effective as later policy revisions. In the meantime, the round of revisions started with Powderly reifying the racial animus undergirding Chinese exclusion.

To Powderly, agents were not effectively using racial and cultural knowledge for Chinese exclusions when administering law. "The natural difficulties [in deporting under Chinese exclusion]," he wrote in a report to Congress, arose "from the apparent similarity, to those unfamiliar with the distinctive physical characteristics of the Mongolian, of all Chinese, from their totally different standards of morality, from their mental acuteness and ingenuity, and, worse than all, from their apparent ability at any time to command the use of considerable sums of money."[60] Here he espoused much of the same logic behind Chinese exclusion in the first place as well as behind the white witness requirement. Powderly hoped that officials better versed in the anti-Chinese racial attitudes of the era could more effectively prosecute Chinese immigrants.

Powderly also hoped to make policy more effective by the further centralization and specialization of immigration authorities. The early legislation of Chinese exclusion did not make clear who was authorized to swear out the complaints that triggered deportations. The Geary Act, for instance, stated that Chinese laborers could be arrested upon a complaint filed "by any party on behalf of the United States."[61] Labor council operators and some private citizens accordingly swore out warrants against Chinese immigrants.[62] Congress clarified jurisdiction in 1893: local and private citizens could not swear out warrants of arrest.[63] Yet, this clarification did not address the issue of divided enforcement within the federal bureaucracy.

Congress assigned responsibility for swearing out complaints and arresting Chinese workers to officials within the U.S. Customs Service known as "Chinese inspectors" and U.S. attorneys.[64] Powderly believed that this was "productive of confusion and relatively ineffective administration of the laws."[65] Powderly wanted Customs out of enforcement, because "[c]ollectors of customs are appointed primarily for the enforcement of customs laws. Their duties under the Chinese laws are additional thereto, and in many instances are regarded by them as merely subordinate to the former, if not occasionally rather in conflict with their interests as collectors of the ports."[66] Instead, he wanted a more centralized force dedicated to immigration enforcement.

Congress responded to Powderly's call for centralization by assigning most of the Chinese exclusion enforcement to the Bureau of Immigration in 1903, which had by then been developed to administer the immigration laws that applied to non-Chinese immigrants.[67] Immigration officers replaced customs officers at the ports. The voluminous records of Chinese exclusion, generated in large part by the issuance of certificates of entry and residence, were also transferred from the Internal Revenue Service to a central immigration office in Washington, D.C.[68]

A key part of the Bureau of Immigration's efforts to increase the efficacy of its enforcement of Chinese exclusion focused on increasing exclusion rates at major ports of entry. Under the new directives, the number of people admitted as Section 6 immigrants dropped over 60 percent at ports along the West Coast. ("Section 6" was popular shorthand for the portion of the Chinese Exclusion Act that defined as exempt teachers, students, merchants, and travelers, who could be admitted with the presentation of a certificate from the Chinese government.) To increase exclusion rates, officials turned the restrictionist law—one that allowed exempt classes—into one that operated more as a racial exclusion.[69]

As the number of Chinese immigrants excluded at the western borders of the United States increased, Chinese immigrants started to enter the United States through other entry points. More immigrants moved to enter the United States through Canada or Mexico, where there were very few border inspectors. U.S. officials responded by creating new inspection points for Chinese inspectors in efforts to close off these new migration routes through the nation's contiguous borders. This step pushed immigration routes farther east as Chinese immigrants tried to cross into the United States from Canada, beyond immigration inspection points in the West.[70]

Even before the changes, deportations under Chinese exclusion had cost the government more than it wanted to spend. The government paid for the initial proceedings through a system of facilitative payments. At each step in their hearings, U.S. commissioners charged fees for their services.[71] Between 1901 and 1906, for example, U.S. commissioners charged seventy-five cents for issuing a warrant of arrest; twenty-five cents for every sub-poena issued to a witness; five cents for each subpoena for an additional witness; ten cents for administering an oath; and forty cents for providing copies of the warrant of arrest. During the actual hearing, the commissioner charged thirty cents for the first witness and five cents for each additional witness. In addition, each commissioner charged five dollars per day for his role in charging and "reducing the testimony to writing when required to by law or order of the court."[72] In 1896, for hearing the case of *United States v. Charlie Oak*, the U.S. commissioner for Arizona's Third Judicial District charged a total of $7.80. In 2015 dollars, this came to around $220. In the case of *United States v. Cheong Foung*, heard in 1900, the same com-missioner charged $7.60.[73] In 1909, the facilitative fees in the *United States v. Sui Sing* case totaled $8.30.[74] Then there were the expenses of the appeals, which were even higher because they took place in the federal courts.

After 1903, as more Chinese immigrants immigrated farther east, the cost of deportations from eastern regions of the country increased. A deportation from northern New York cost more than a deportation from San Francisco. In 1901, the government spent on average about $52 per deportee under Chinese exclusion. That year, the government deported a total of 328 Chinese aliens at a total cost of $46,940.22.[75] In 1903, the Bureau of Immigration deported a total of 704 Chinese immigrants, includ-ing 307 from the eastern region along its northern border, 228 from the western Canadian boundary region, and 138 from the Mexican boundary region. These deportations cost $80,375.45, about $65,000 of which went to deporting people from communities along the U.S.-Canada border—increasingly from communities in the East. This represented about 25 per-cent of the entire operating budget for all of Chinese exclusion.[76] In 1904, the government spent $75,536.10 deporting Chinese immigrants, at an average cost of $112.24 each.[77]

In the first decade of the twentieth century, therefore, under Chinese exclusion much about deportation proceedings had been worked out. As a protection rather than a punishment, they fell under civil rather than crimi-nal law. The distinction was an important one in terms of burden of proof, standards of evidence, and the rights of defendants, all of which favored the government over defendants. Policy makers had also included in the deportation proceedings of Chinese exclusion explicitly racialized legal practices. Lee Joe, one of the litigants in *Fong Yue Ting*, had faced one of these. He was ordered deported because he had not secured a white witness to prove his legal residence.

Officials administering Chinese exclusion, however, felt the deportation policy was not working. The deportations cost more than they wanted to spend. And, in spite of the civil status, and in spite of the racialized procedures, Chinese defendants were defeating deportation orders in some districts in as many as 90 percent of the cases.[78] By the turn of the century, immigration officers were puzzling out ways to better realize the racial goal of the policy—to deport more Chinese immigrants—by restoring the civil nature of proceedings. Their early efforts centralized enforcement. In 1909, immigration authorities tried a new strategy, which relied on the general deportation policy that applied to all non-Chinese immigrants.

Deportation Proceedings Under General Immigration Policy

Congress and immigration officials built a policy to deport other immigrants that ran parallel to Chinese exclusion. To do so, they developed a list of qualitative deportable categories that applied to immigrants from everywhere else.[79] The deportation proceedings established to administer these categories differed from the deportation proceedings under Chinese exclusion. Most notably, immigrants processed under general immigration law had very limited access to the federal courts in their appeals. Yet, unlike Chinese exclusion, deportation policy under general immigration law did not have such specific provisions as the white witness requirement, nor was it as broad, and it contained protections for immigrants not allowed under the laws of Chinese exclusion.

An important starting point in the history of deportations under general immigration policy came in 1885, in a law known as the Foran Act, which did not actually contain a deportation provision.[80] Much of the support for this law came out of the ways white working-class Americans understood free labor, rights of contract, and immigration. As more Americans began working for wages after the Civil War, union organizers increasingly criticized the notion of "freedom of contract," the idea that a worker was not

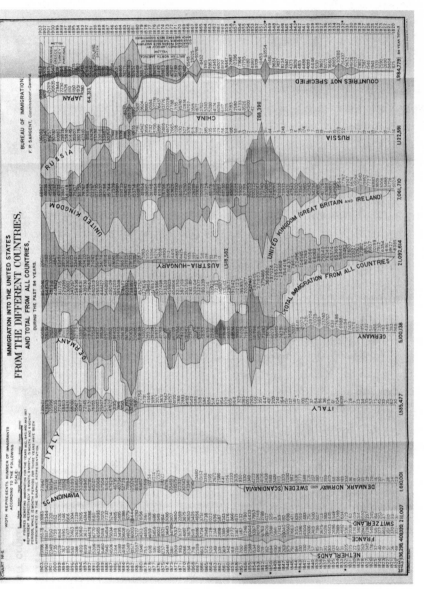

Figure 1. Bureau of Immigration's depiction of immigration patterns contained in the commissioner general's annual report of 1904. "Immigration into the United States from the Different Countries and Total from All Countries, During the Past 84 Years," *AR-CGI* (1904).

only an equal participant in making a contract with an employer, but that the ability to contract at all made him free. White unions argued that employers had so much more power than individual workers that the bargaining process was subject to considerable coercion; coercive contracts, in turn, made white American workers "unfree."[81] U.S. labor leaders saw union representation in negotiations as a way to make contracts fairer, and they saw immigrant labor contracts as a threat to their ability to bargain with employers. To them, foreign laborers of any ethnicity who signed contracts abroad were unfree—and the contracts foreign workers signed with American employers were more coercive than contracts signed in the United States. Competition with unfree labor, labor organizers claimed, would inevitably enslave white working Americans, making the United States a nation of unfree men unfit to participate in a democracy.

Labor organizers had included some of these ideas about contract and free labor in their campaign for the passage of Chinese exclusion, and in 1884 they were using them to lobby for a law that applied to contract workers. In 1884, for example, Terence Powderly, head of the Knights of Labor and soon to be head of the Bureau of Immigration, spoke out against a group of Hungarian contract workers. "They work for little or nothing," Powderly said, "[they] live on a fare which a Chinaman would not touch, and [they] will submit to any and every indignity which may be imposed upon them. . . . I believe this country was intended for a race of freemen and, believing that, I will always oppose the introduction of such men as are not capable of enjoying, defending and perpetuating the blessings of good government."[82] Here, those fighting to limit immigration of contract laborers used the rhetoric of national protection to justify the development of another immigrant exclusion.

Congress was unwilling to pass legislation to support bread-and-butter union issues such as the closed shop and collective bargaining, but it did support organized labor's position on foreign workers.[83] In 1885 it passed the Foran Act, which forbade all foreign workers under contract from immigrating to the United States.[84] Under its terms, a foreigner could not, while still abroad, sign a contract to work for an employer in the United States.[85]

An amendment transformed the Foran Act into the basis on which immigrants from all racial, ethnic, and national categories became deportable. Immediately after the passage of the act, U.S. customs officers charged with administering the law began to report that they found it almost impossible to identify and exclude contract laborers at the borders. The act contained so few provisions for enforcement that Congress quickly passed several amendments to rectify its perceived shortcomings.[86] The original law prohibited only the entrance of contract workers; agents had no power to remove contract laborers who evaded exclusion at the borders. Congress added a deportation provision in 1888.

Congress expanded the government's power to deport immigrants beyond contract laborers in 1891. Back in 1882, the same year it passed the law authorizing deportations under Chinese exclusion, Congress passed another immigration law that applied to all other immigrants. This law created excludable classes, including criminals and paupers—people who could not lawfully enter the United States. This law, however, did not link the excludable categories with a deportation provision. If criminals or paupers made it into the United States, immigration authorities had no mechanism to deport them. In 1891, Congress passed an immigration law that linked each category with a deportation provision.[87] From then on, all the existing categories of excludable immigrants, ranging from "idiots," the "insane," "paupers," "polygamists," "persons liable to become a public charge," people convicted of a felony or other crime or misdemeanor involving "moral turpitude," to sufferers "from a loathsome or dangerous" contagious disease, were all deportable.[88] This law enforced exclusions only—it dealt with people who entered the country who should have been excluded in the first place.

It is not explicit in the records why, but policy makers made deportation proceedings of general immigration law different from those under Chinese exclusion. Under general immigration law, the Board of Special Inquiry, the three-member panel of executive officers, held a deportation hearing. This was solely an administrative hearing. If the board found an immigrant lawfully resident in the United States, it canceled the warrant of arrest. If the board found the immigrant in violation of immigration laws, the agent assigned to the case applied to the commissioner general of immigration for a warrant of deportation.[89] Here, the government had expanded the plenary power—courts did not have the power to review these deportation decisions. These proceedings were less expensive, they did not operate on facilitative payments, and immigrants had fewer rights to appeal to the federal courts. Immigrants could appeal a case to the federal courts only if they asked a new legal question, such as the constitutionality of a law.

In 1903, Kaoru Yamataya, a sixteen-year-old from Japan, appealed her deportation under general immigration policy to the U.S. Supreme Court in *Yamataya v. Fisher* (also known as the *Japanese Immigrant Case*).[90] Yamataya had landed at Seattle on July 11, 1901. Four days later, immigration authorities arrested her on the grounds that she had entered the country surreptitiously and was likely to become a public charge—a deportable category under general immigration law—though she had come to stay with her uncle. Ten days after Yamataya's arrest, immigration officers convened a Board of Special Inquiry to hear her case. The three immigration agents, none of whom was a judicial officer, held the hearing in English, which Yamataya could not understand. The board found Yamataya deportable.[91] Yamataya appealed her deportation decision through the lower federal courts and then on to the Supreme Court. When in front of the Supreme Court, Yamataya posed several questions that cumulatively asked: were the deportation proceedings of general immigration policy legal?

Yamataya's case to the Supreme Court, argued by lawyer Harold Preston, included two key arguments about the nature of due process under general immigration deportations. First, Preston argued that, since the Immigration Act of 1891 did not explicitly provide for due process, the act was unconstitutional.[92] Second, Preston contended that even if the Court found that general immigration policy was consistent with Fifth Amendment due process rights in civil cases, immigration agents had denied them to Yamataya. The evidence used against Yamataya, as Preston described it, was "garbled, incomplete, and in many respects misleading and untrue."[93] Furthermore, Yamataya's hearing had been conducted in English, and the investigation was carried out without her having access to legal counsel or the chance to show she was not likely to become a public charge.[94]

The Supreme Court dismissed Yamataya's appeal and upheld the basic scope of the government's deportation policy under general immigration law. Addressing her lawyer's arguments about due process, the Court upheld the general immigration law in spite of its lack of explicit provisions for due process consistent with the Fifth Amendment. Justice John Marshall Harlan, writing for the Court, held that an act of Congress "must be taken to be constitutional unless the contrary plainly and palpably appears."[95]

The Court also dismissed part of Yamataya's argument that challenged the appeals process under general immigration policy. The Immigration Act of 1891 stated that immigrants could appeal the Board of Special Inquiry's decision to the U.S. secretary of labor, whose decision was final and not reviewable in the courts.[96] Preston argued that in deportations under general immigration law, the courts should have the authority to review the labor secretary's decision. The Court disagreed, ruling that, because deportations fell within the plenary power of the federal executive and legislature, investigations and actions of the executive officers in the deportation process were not "subject to judicial review."[97]

At the same time the Court upheld the appeals process under general immigration law, however, the Court created in *Yamataya* a backdoor appeals process to the federal courts—called a procedural challenge.[98] The Court ruled that while immigrants could not challenge the outcome of deportation hearings, they could challenge the legitimacy of the procedures. The Court added that administrative officers could not "disregard the fundamental principles that inhere in due process of law as understood at the time of the adoption of the Constitution."[99] If officers "disregarded" due process, immigrants could make a procedural challenge to the courts.

Just what the legitimacy of procedures looked like was the next question. One of the procedures that ordinarily made immigration decisions consistent with Fifth Amendment due process was the holding of a hearing. When describing it, Justice Harlan wrote, "no person shall be deprived of his liberty without opportunity, at some time, to be heard, before such officers, in respect of the matters upon which that liberty depends—not necessarily an opportunity upon a regular, set occasion, and according to the forms of judicial procedure, but one that will secure the prompt, vigorous action contemplated by Congress, and at the same time be appropriate to the nature of the case upon which such officers are required to act."[100] In Yamataya's case, the Court found that her executive hearing in front of immigration agents met the standard of due process. "[T]he decisions of executive or administrative officers, acting within powers expressly conferred by Congress," the Court asserted, "are due process of law."[101]

One point the Court made in the *Yamataya* decision about procedural challenges was that a hearing in a language that the immigrant could not understand did not represent a procedural challenge. Part of Yamataya's due process argument turned on the fact that her hearing had been conducted in English. Yet, the Court had no problem with the fact that Yamataya did not understand the proceedings against her. "If the appellant's want of knowledge of the English language," Justice Harlan wrote, "put her at some disadvantage in the investigation conducted by that officer, that was her misfortune, and constitutes no reason . . . for the intervention of the court by habeas corpus."[102] In other words, a hearing that an immigrant could not understand was consistent with Fifth Amendment due process standards.[103]

This appeals process under general immigration policy in action, even with the addition of the ability to make procedural challenges created in *Yamataya*, seldom worked in an immigrant's favor and so had very little impact on the overall rate of deportations, which remained quite high. In 1913, for example, the New York district reported that it had held over 1,100 deportation hearings under general immigration law and ordered deportations in about 90 percent of the cases.[104]

Despite the low numbers of successful appeals, in these early decades of operating its power to deport under general immigration policy, the government only deported a few hundred to a few thousand people a year—during periods when as many as one million people annually immigrated to the United States. That there were not many deportable people in the United States was one of the most important reasons for the low deportation numbers. Except for people from China, almost everyone could immigrate lawfully.[105] Another, related reason for the low deportation numbers was the way that time limits "legalized" those who entered the country in violation of immigration law.[106] Congress built a one-year time limit into its deportation provisions in 1891, though it revised that limit in 1903, 1907, and 1917, eventually extending it to one to five years.[107] Except for people from China, if an immigrant moved to the United States in violation of an immigrant exclusion, law protected him or her from deportability after a few years of residency in the United States.

By 1904, then, the proceedings under general immigration law were defined in large part by the appeal process. Under general immigration law a deportation appeal went to the secretary of commerce and labor and not to the federal courts (unless the immigrant had a procedural challenge or a constitutional challenge).[108] The difference between a procedural and substantive claim was important to taking a case to the federal courts. A procedural challenge under general immigration law was limited to asking if the immigrant had had a hearing or not. Insufficient evidence was not a claim the courts generally accepted. Matters of fact and the issue of whether the decision itself was justifiable could not be questioned.[109]

Folding Chinese Exclusion into General Immigration Policy

After decades of administering two parallel deportation policies, in their efforts to carry out more deportations of people of Chinese descent, immigration officers turned to a strategy of arresting Chinese immigrants under general immigration policy. As the Bureau of Immigration's *Annual Report* recorded in 1912, the "Chinese who might enter the United States in violation of law should be dealt with precisely as were the members of other races charged with the same offense." The report continued, "all Chinese charged with surreptitious entry should have their right to be and remain in the United States determined by the Department warrant of arrest procedure, rather than by the long drawn out and expensive judicial hearing process."[110] The new enforcement strategy, immigration agents hoped, would put a stop to the ways Chinese immigrants had been using the federal courts so effectively to overturn many deportations. Part of the government's strategy first depended on finding a way around the explicit racial category established in the Chinese exclusion laws.

In 1909, immigration officials took their first steps to what would, just a few years later, lead them to fold Chinese exclusion into general immigration policy when they arrested four Chinese immigrants under general immigration law rather than the laws of Chinese exclusion.[111] A man named Wong You was one of the four. Officials charged Wong on the grounds that he had entered the United States without inspection—a provision of general immigration law—crossing the U.S.-Canada border near Malone, New York. Officials then processed Wong under deportation proceedings of general immigration policy. The Board of Special Inquiry found against him and ordered Wong's deportation. Technically, he was charged with violating the Immigration Act of 1907, for entering the United States surreptitiously.[112]

Wong You hired a lawyer and appealed his case and asked the federal courts the new legal question about the jurisdiction of Chinese exclusion and general immigration law. His case hinged on the fact that Congress designed the Immigration Act of 1891 to regulate "immigration, other than those concerning Chinese Laborers."[113] In 1893, in a revision to the general immigration law, Congress reasserted this division by adding the phrase "that this act shall not apply to Chinese Persons."[114] Wong's lawyers argued that since he was Chinese, he could only be deported under the procedures of Chinese exclusion. Wong You's legal strategy, therefore, attempted to use the ways that immigration law constructed a racial class. In doing so, Wong and his lawyers hoped to protect Chinese immigrants' appeals to the federal courts.

Wong's lawyers attacked the new enforcement strategy in the lower courts. At the first stage of the appeal in the federal courts, Wong lost. George W. Ray, the judge in the federal court for the Northern District of New York, sustained the government's case. Wong and his lawyers then appealed the case to the circuit court of appeals, which reversed the lower court's decision, holding that Chinese laborers could be processed only under the Chinese exclusion laws.[115]

Immigration officials, whose efforts were made more determined by what they understood as a growing Chinese immigration crisis across their borders, appealed Wong's victory to the Supreme Court. "The importance of securing a decision favorable [in *Wong You*] to the Government," the then–commissioner general of the Bureau of Immigration Daniel Keefe wrote, "is well illustrated by the statement in the report of the United States commissioner of immigration for Canada." Just the year before *Wong You* reached the Supreme Court, therefore, immigration authorities worried that Chinese immigration through Canada as well as Mexico would "constantly increase in the future" unless they took steps to overhaul deportations of Chinese immigrants.[116] Closing access to the courts and processing Chinese immigrants under general immigration policy were important steps they took.

In 1912, three years after Wong You's arrest, his case, *United States v. Wong You*, reached the nation's highest court. On one side of the courtroom, Wong You's lawyers argued that Chinese immigrants could not be arrested under general immigration laws. If successful, Wong You's lawyers would keep all Chinese deportation cases out of general immigration deportation proceedings where it was much harder to win an appeal. On the other side of the courtroom stood counsel for immigration authorities. They wanted this Supreme Court victory, because, if successful, they could continue what they started in Wong You's arrest—limiting judicial review to Chinese immigrants.

The Supreme Court ruled in favor of the government. Justice Oliver Wendell Holmes, writing for the Court, found that, while Chinese immigrants "were tacitly excepted from the general provisions of the immigration act," the law was "broad enough to include them." Holmes wrote, "It seems to us unwarranted to except the Chinese from this liability [just]

because there is an earlier more cumbrous proceeding which this partially
overlaps. The existence of the earlier laws only indicates the special solici-
tude of the Government to limit the entrance of Chinese. It is the very
reverse of a reason for denying to the Government a better remedy against
them alone of all the world. . . . The present act does not contain the clause
found in the previous immigration act of March 3, 1893, . . . that it shall
not apply to Chinese persons."[117]

After *Wong You*, the Bureau of Immigration began instructing its agents
to arrest and deport Chinese immigrants under general immigration laws
in every case possible; deportation numbers dramatically increased. The
supervising inspector for immigration in District 23, which enforced the
U.S.-Mexico border, noted a spike in the number of Chinese immigrants
actually deported. "Formerly," he wrote, "owing to the difficulty of presenting to the courts sufficiently convincing proof of illegal entry, it was impossible to secure deportation of such Chinese unless they were actually
apprehended in the act of crossing the boundary."[118] In 1914, immigration
agents along that border tried to deport 1,090 Chinese immigrants, serving
224 warrants under Chinese exclusion laws and 866 warrants under general
immigration laws. By the end of the year, immigration officers had successfully deported 899 of the 1,090 arrested. Seven of the 191 who had not been
deported were awaiting deportation and 116 cases were still pending.[119]

One immigration district noted that Chinese immigrants unsuccessfully
attempted to bring the judicial standards back into the proceedings. The
inspector from the New York district reported that "sometimes the conduct
of the hearing is simple, but often it is complicated, partly through the
efforts of counsel of the alien to treat it as a judicial trial, whereas, in fact,
it is merely an executive hearing, and to introduce matter which is irrele-
vant or inconclusive upon the only issue, which is whether the alien should
be deported."[120]

While processing as many Chinese immigrants under general immigration proceedings as possible, U.S. immigration authorities continued to use
the Chinese exclusion proceedings. This was because general immigration
law contained time limits: immigrants could be deported only within one
to five years of their entry into the United States, depending on the deportation provision. The only exception was the antiprostitution provision.
Determined not to open the protection of time limits to Chinese immigrants, officials for a time operated both deportation policies when arresting Chinese immigrants. Immigration officers used general immigration

laws in cases where they could prove that a Chinese immigrant had entered the United States within the time limit.[121] In 1914, the department for the Mexican district explained that it went forward in a number of cases under Chinese exclusion laws because it had been "impossible to establish entry within three years."[122] In those deportations explicitly under Chinese exclusion, judicial review still remained open.

Other immigration districts reported their strategic use of both general immigration proceedings and those under Chinese exclusion to effect higher rates of Chinese deportations. In 1913, the New York district reported that it had held over 1,100 deportation hearings under general immigration law and ordered deportations in about 90 percent of the cases.[123] In 1914, the San Francisco district reported handling 414 such cases, a 300 percent increase over the year before.[124] The Chicago district had dramatic increases in 1914 as well.[125] While the number of Chinese deported under general immigration laws rose, the number deported under Chinese exclusion laws fell. By 1916, Chicago officials used the general immigration laws almost exclusively to deport Chinese. They arrested 233 Chinese under general immigration laws and only 23 under Chinese exclusion laws.[126] In 1918, the El Paso office reported that only 8 Chinese had been arrested under exclusion laws, while 132 Chinese cases were handled under general immigration laws.[127] In 1914, the U.S. government deported a total of 131 Chinese under Chinese exclusion laws. In 1915, it deported 119; in 1916, 104; and in 1917, only 69.[128]

In 1917, the government completed the process that Bureau of Immigration officials had begun with Wong You's arrest via changes to the Immigration Act. Section 19 of the Immigration Act of 1917 provided that "any alien who shall have entered or who shall be found in the United States in violation of this Act, or in violation of any other law of the United States . . . shall, upon the warrant of the Secretary of Labor, be taken into custody and deported."[129] Here, administrators put a stop to the remaining ways Chinese exclusion overlapped with the criminal justice system. They had taken Chinese exclusion largely out of the judicial system, making it almost entirely a separate administrative law. Hereafter, all immigrants would be processed under what immigration officials called general warrant proceedings of general immigration policy; there would be no more access to the judiciary in the appeals process, except for new legal questions and for procedural challenges.

The Supreme Court endorsed the federal government's power to deport in *Fong Yue Ting* in 1893, designating deportation as a power protective of the nation, rather than as a punishment for individuals. This set in motion an evolving national logic to deportation policy. With this designation, the Court made clear deportation proceedings were to be different from criminal trials, which limited the constitutional protections (particularly those of the Fourth, Fifth, and Sixth Amendments) available to people in deportation proceedings.

The appeals process under Chinese exclusion for many years, however, shared some procedures with criminal proceedings. The deportation policy that applied to all other nationalities did not, and that fact made it easier for immigration authorities to deport people under general immigration policy. By 1917, Congress folded the deportation proceedings of Chinese exclusion into general immigration policy, which was more efficient and led to higher deportation rates. In the process, the government streamlined its policy, making all deportation proceedings mostly administrative procedures and placing the burden of proof largely on the immigrant, who had few recourses of appeal.

At the same time that U.S. judges, politicians, and administrators were developing a national deportation policy, an international logic of deportation was emerging. The international context, which was set both in the sending and the receiving of deportees, set parameters on the U.S. government's power to deport.

Chapter 2

The International Regime

In addition to the developing national deportation policy, an evolving international legal regime structured immigrant removals. One illustrative case of this structuring power took place in 1884, when German immigration authorities sought to deport a U.S. citizen named Constant A. Golly. Golly was born in Germany, but in 1875, at age seventeen, he immigrated to the United States. Five years later, he naturalized as an American citizen and gave up his German citizenship. In 1884, Golly visited Germany. According to Golly, he returned to Germany in 1884 to look after his ailing, widowed mother, and, while he did, he believed his U.S. citizenship exempted him from the military service required of German men. The Germans, however, understood it differently.[1] Not long after his arrival, Golly received a notice from local authorities stating that he owed German military service. If he did not serve, the government would deport him. Golly chose not to enlist, but he wanted to remain with his mother. He contacted an American consular officer, hoping that the U.S. legation could help prevent his removal.[2] And, initially, U.S. officials tried. The steps they used at the start of Golly's case represented a large part of the international legal regime and it amounted to an international appeal, a diplomatic process that could stop a deportation.

At the end of the nineteenth century, the international legal regime was largely built out of the jurisdiction nations retained over their emigrants while they traveled abroad. There were two key variants of this jurisdiction. The international appeal represented one. The other was more imperialist and it imposed restrictions on the ability of many nations and empires located in Asia and the Middle East to carry out deportations. Both jurisdictions were forms of extraterritoriality. U.S. officials would use both to protect American citizens from removal. A nation or empire's place within the interstate community affected the reach and degree of both forms of extraterritoriality. When the U.S. federal government got into the business of deporting people from the United States, because of its place within the comity (or community) of nations, they found their policy structured by the international appeal.

By the early years of the twentieth century, national-level policy makers deemed the destination of an immigrant removal more important than it had ever been, and officials on the receiving end increasingly had to approve a deportation. Immigrant removals, once largely unilateral, were now increasingly bilateral. This convergence in national policies led immigration officials and diplomats to negotiate agreements and protocols. In these, along with many countries, U.S. officials made important additions to the international legal regime. As they did, officials changed the logic of the international regime, making it function less as a resource for emigrants abroad and more for nation-states to police sovereign soil. In the process, the international legal regime became even more elemental to carrying out deportations.

The International Appeals Process and the Ties of Male Citizens

Constant Golly's deportation was one of at least 447 deportations of U.S. citizens ordered in Germany and Austria-Hungary between 1868 and 1903. All of these cases involved young men, most of whom were in Europe to visit family or attend school. Some were there for business.[3] Men like Golly sometimes requested that U.S. diplomats intervene to halt their removal so that they could continue living abroad as U.S. citizens. Unlike a domestic appeals process, like the ones in operation in the United States examined in Chapter 1, the international appeal was a soft process that involved reciprocal diplomatic power, legal rhetoric, appeals to treaties, and sometimes even threats. Chinese officials tried to use the international appeal to protect some Chinese immigrants in the United States from deportation because all nations with sovereignty could use the international appeal. But, as it turned out, they could not all use it equally.

Using the international appeal in Germany and Austria-Hungary during the late nineteenth century turned out mostly to involve U.S. diplomats' protection of the citizenship of Americans abroad. They did so, for example, in the face of German citizenship laws that were seemingly making U.S. citizens into Germans. The German and Austro-Hungarian governments, of course, understood it quite differently.[4] At the heart of such interventions was one question: were they Americans or not? This question was intimately tied to another: did these men, all of whom claimed U.S. citizenship, owe military service to either Austria-Hungary or Germany?[5] Answering these questions was complicated because it was sometimes unclear where one citizenship status ended and another began.[6] As German or Austro-Hungarian and U.S. officials puzzled out the cases, their efforts contributed to what sociologist David Cook Martin has referred to as "a scramble for citizens." In this age of mass migration, government officials worked to preserve ties with their emigrants abroad, sometimes doing so in competition or conflict with officials from countries of immigration.[7] As the cases involving deportations from Germany and Austria-Hungary help illustrate, use of the international appeal protected immigrants from deportation and fostered positive ties between emigrants and their country of origin. It did so by serving as a resource that some emigrants accessed while outside their country of citizenship.[8]

The ability of U.S. officials to intervene in German or Austro-Hungarian cases like Golly's was rooted in international law of the nineteenth century that mandated channels for emigrant-sending states to look out for their emigrants. "All civilized states," Edwin M. Borchard, a professor of law at Yale University, stated in 1915, "must yield some share of their absolute liberty of action and that their rights must be reconciled with the reciprocal rights of other states." He continued, "Among these mutual concessions, the one of present interest is the fact that the territorial sovereignty or jurisdiction of a state has to be reconciled with the right of other states to protect their nationals abroad, an outgrowth of principle and practice, rather than the subject of formal written admission."[9] This meant that if the Germans wanted to remove an immigrant, then the emigrant-sending state could have something to say in the process. This amounted to an international appeal.

The 447 military cases in which U.S. officials used the international appeal originated in the second half of the nineteenth century, when diplomats from Germany, Austria-Hungary, and the United States faced the fact that some men were using "flexible citizenship" to avoid military service.[10] One U.S. consular officer, Bartlett Tripp, wrote in 1894: "It is an undeniable fact that hundreds of young Austro-Hungarian citizens approaching the age of military service emigrate to America, and, remaining there just long enough to acquire citizenship, return again to their native country to permanently reside, resuming their former citizenship and allegiance to the Government in everything but its military laws."[11] He continued, "Many of these returned *pseudo*-Americans are loud in their defiance of the military power, and openly and shamelessly boast of their smartness in being able to enjoy all of the privileges of a government without being obliged to share its burdens or responsibilities." Their actions, Tripp alleged, did great harm. "The example of these 'Americans' before the young men of the country, to say nothing of their teachings and boastful assertions of immunity," Tripp noted, "is pernicious, and against public order and ready obedience on the part of the citizens to the necessarily harsh enforcement of the military laws of this Government."[12]

U.S. officials publicly supported some of the deportations that German and Austro-Hungarian authorities pursued as a means of dealing with the flexible use of citizenship. A country had the right "to bar its doors against obnoxious citizens of other nations for reasons which to itself may seem sufficient," Tripp acknowledged, "without cause of complaint on the part of the nation whose citizen is thus debarred."[13] Indeed, the U.S. government already "assumed the right in the case of China."[14] In the case of Constant Golly, which opened this chapter, the consular agents handling the case soon dropped his defense. They found that Golly was using his U.S. citizenship to avoid military service, while intending to live permanently in Germany. U.S. authorities did not object when the Germans deported him.[15]

U.S. officials, however, felt that in general the Germans and Austro-Hungarians were too aggressive with their expulsions, and they set out to stop some through international appeal. The first step in protecting some of the U.S. citizens, especially naturalized citizens, from deportation in the military cases was for U.S. officials to convince the German or Austro-Hungarian officials that they were innocent of deliberate evasion of military service, with age of migration a key factor. If a person immigrated to the United States before he was drafted, and especially if he had immigrated at a young age with his family, the U.S. consulate defended the naturalized American. An 1889 statement from one U.S. consular officer in defense of Hugo Klamer, a naturalized U.S. citizen born in Austria, captures this argument clearly. This official wrote, "[T]he assertion is hardly maintainable that a boy who emigrates at the age of fourteen years, who resides twelve years uninterruptedly in the United States and acquires American citizenship during his residence there, and then returns to his old home for the purpose of a visit, and is compelled by circumstances to prolong his visit, but declares under oath that he intends to return to the United States at an early day, has emigrated for the purpose of evading military service."[16] U.S. officials, therefore, argued to European officials that so long as a man emigrated before he was sent a draft notice, they considered the migration and naturalization valid.

U.S. officials managed in some cases to convince the sending country to cancel the immigrant removal using the argument about youth. Three examples make this point. Charles George left Germany for the United States when he was fifteen; Gerhard Wientjes, born in Prussia, emigrated at thirteen with his parents; and Rudolph Lieffert, also born in Prussia, emigrated at the age of two.[17] In all of these cases, after the Americans sent a note defending against their expulsion on the grounds of age, the German or Austro-Hungarian officials agreed to drop the cases.

German officials took a different tack in some of the other military cases involving men who emigrated well before draft age, arguing that they had the right to expel men for evasion of military service on the grounds that they were German citizens by treaty and German naturalization law. In making this argument, the Germans turned to two treaties, one from 1828 and another from 1868.[18] Most important was the treaty of 1868, which set the protocols under which an immigrant could renounce his or her naturalization. According to the German interpretation of the 1868 treaty, if a German-born, naturalized U.S. citizen returned to Germany, he or she would lose American citizenship if he or she showed no intent to return to the United States. In the case of men of military age, the Germans held that the passive action of staying in one of the German states for more than two years indicated intent not to return to the United States.[19] These newly made Germans then owed military service. If they did not serve, then German officials would expel them.

The majority of the military cases involved naturalized Americans, but a minority dealt with U.S.-born men who had German-born fathers. Through their use of the treaties, the Germans tried to hold U.S.-born men accountable for military service, too. A number of U.S.-born sons traveled with their families to their fathers' country of birth in the last half of the nineteenth century. If such a family emigrated from the United States to Germany, some of the U.S.-born sons faced the choice to serve in the military or be removed. To make this argument, German officials noted that under German law, a father's citizenship determined the nationality of his minor child. As long as children remained under parental control, they "share[d] the nationality of the father."[20] Thus, when a German father who had lived in the United States without ever becoming a U.S. citizen returned to Germany with his minor son, German authorities understood the son to be German, not American. The same principle even applied to German fathers who naturalized as American citizens. The German government held that after two years of residence in Germany the father had renounced his U.S. citizenship and renaturalized as a German. By extension, the son, too, was German and therefore obligated to serve in the military.[21]

Where German and Austro-Hungarian authorities turned to their interpretations of treaties to require military service of U.S. citizens, U.S. authorities made three key arguments to protect naturalized Americans and people born with U.S. citizenship from expulsion.[22] First, in the case of naturalized Americans, they argued that the mere fact of residence for two years did not necessarily demonstrate "intent" never to return to the United States. Some naturalized Americans stayed in Germany longer than two years, but intended to return to the United States. The State Department argued that the two-year rule misinterpreted the 1868 treaty.[23] Second, the American authorities disagreed with Germany's interpretation of the treaties, holding that the treaty of 1868 "cannot of itself convert an American citizen into a German, nor a German into an American, against his will."[24] As one American consular official argued, "[e]ven the renunciation of one citizenship does not of itself create another . . . [the object of the treaty was not to convert citizens but] was rather to recognize the obligation of a new citizenship which had been lawfully acquired in the other country."[25] In these two arguments, then, U.S. officials contested the way that German or Austrian authorities were unmaking American citizenship through a passive, ascriptive process.

The third argument U.S. officials drew on involved gender and youth; to U.S. consular officers, Germany was inconsistently and unjustly applying the two-year rule. The U.S. Department of State believed that Germany tended to "reconvert" only men of military age. Not women, not older men. U.S. consular officers pointed out that many other Americans maintained their U.S. citizenship even after two years of residence in Germany.

Therefore, it appeared as if the issue mattered only if the person was male and of age to serve in the military.

By the 1890s, the German authorities had come around to the U.S. position on citizenship in the case of U.S.-born men. In a letter over one case, Count Paul von Hatzfeldt, the undersecretary of state in charge of Germany's Imperial Foreign Office, acknowledged concessions in response to repeated American requests: "His Majesty's Government has," Hatzfeldt wrote, "after repeated consideration, and after overcoming many scruples which suggested themselves, decided to still recognize the American nationality of the sons in question of former subjects of the Empire, even, also, when their fathers have lost the citizenship acquired in the United States." Hatzfeldt noted that agreeing to the American position went against the citizenship laws of the rest of Germany. It agreed to recognize the American citizenship of U.S.-born sons "in order . . . to pave the way for an amicable solution of the existing difficulties."[26]

As it turned out, this concession did not resolve all of the military cases. Germany articulated additional grounds that demanded military service of U.S.-born men, turning now to domestic (or national) law. Under German law, one official explained, "[f]ormer subjects of the Empire . . . are, in this case, not dispensed from military duty in Germany."[27] German officials maintained that even if U.S.-born sons of German citizens were U.S. citizens, while living in Germany, they enjoyed the protections and benefits provided by the state. Such a person was obligated to return the favor by naturalizing as a German and serving in the military. If he were unwilling to do so, German authorities could execute an order of expulsion. As a result, a U.S. consular officer explained, U.S. citizens of draft age were being "expelled from Germany on abrupt notice, at the pleasure of the authorities, under the alternative of becoming German subjects."[28]

In response, U.S. consular officials argued that treaties of commerce overrode the demands of military service dictated through national law. According to the 1828 treaty between Prussia and the United States, American officials pointed out, U.S. citizens abroad enjoyed the liberty "*to sojourn and reside in all parts whatsoever of said territories*, in order to attend to their affairs; and they shall enjoy to that effect the same security and protection as natives of the country wherein they reside."[29] Consular officials argued that this right was being undermined by the German authorities' treatment of young, naturalized or native-born American men. According to one U.S. consular officer, "the contention of the German Government, that such sons [U.S.-born citizens] may be expelled from Germany on abrupt notice, at the pleasure of the authorities, under the alternative of becoming German subjects is tantamount to claiming the right to expel any citizen of the United States." The German claim that "'international principles permit the refusal to such persons of sojourn in Germany,' in the interest of public order, . . . does not apply to any and every native born American citizen of military age who, for purposes of business, study, or pleasure, may take up a peace-able abode in Germany."[30] One U.S. consular officer further noted that the United States "learns with regret that the Imperial Government regards itself as justified by international principles in refusing the sojourn in Germany of these native born American citizens, although they are, as such, obedient to the laws and ordinances there prevailing. . . . This refusal of the right of peaceful sojourn, therefore, seems to the American Government to be in contravention of the spirit and even the letter of other treaties."[31] U.S. diplomats, therefore, protested the ways a foreign state's domestic law was overriding an international treaty.

In their appeals, the U.S. consular officers used diplomatic interventions similar to ones Chinese diplomats made on behalf of Chinese immigrants in the United States. Chinese officials had appealed the ways that U.S. immigration officials were using national law to undermine an international treaty. After a raid in Denver in 1897, for example, Wu Ting-Fang of the Chinese legation in Washington wrote to the U.S State Department, stating that raid was "contrary both to the spirit and letter of the Treaties solemnly entered into between the two countries." Hoping to persuade U.S. immigration officials to scale back the aggressive enforcement of Chinese exclusion laws, Wu added, "My fear is that, if such proceedings are allowed to be passed over, this Mr. Chamberlain [the immigration official who led the raid] or other Treasury officials will repeat them in other communities to the further injury and alarm of my countrymen."[32]

Members of the Chinese legation also used the international appeal to contest the ways U.S. officials violated the rights and liberties of Chinese immigrants. For instance, after an 1893 raid in San Francisco, Chinese official Yang Yu wrote to the U.S. secretary of state protesting that the Chinese residents were "treated as though they are guilty of the highest offenses known to the law, and held in custody while their property and effects are wasted or destroyed."[33] In a different appeal, Chinese consular agents stepped in to protect two men named Ping Yik and Poy Kwan. In 1899,

U.S. immigration authorities had arrested and ordered them deported. Both were Section 6 immigrants (those exempt from Chinese exclusion), having arrived in the United States two years earlier. They had been issued visas and admitted to the United States as merchants. The two appealed their deportations using the national-level appeal, and they also contacted Chinese consular officers to launch an international appeal. Ping Yik and Poy Kwan's national appeal was successful and the court released them.[34] Chinese diplomat Wu Ting-Fang followed up their release with a letter to the U.S. secretary of state, with the intent of shielding Ping Yik and Poy Kwan in the future from aggressive immigration enforcement that treated them as laborers. He wrote,

> It seems to me but just that these two men, after a fair trial which conclusively proves that they are entitled by law and treaty to remain in this country, should not be further molested in any way, and put to great inconvenience and expense in defense of their indisputable rights. I am informed that their arrest was part of a concerted scheme on the part of certain lawless persons to harass the Chinese in and about Buffalo. In view of these circumstances, I respectfully request that you will kindly communicate with the Honorable the Attorney General on the subject to the end that instructions shall be sent to the United States District Attorney at Buffalo, New York, to discontinue further proceedings against the said Ping Yik and Poy Kwan, and permit them to carry on their business in peace.[35]

There was an important strategy in an international appeal that U.S. officials used when trying to protect an American from deportation that Chinese diplomats could not: U.S. officials threatened to reciprocate. In defending Hugo Klamer from expulsion from Austria-Hungary, for example, the Americans likened him to Austrians in the United States who were, the U.S. legation's officials stated, allowed to sojourn, in some cases even to the detriment of U.S. interests. If the Austrian government continued to expel sojourning Americans, U.S. officials threatened, they would reciprocate in a manner that could severely hurt Austrian economic interests. One letter from the U.S. consulate to the Austrians stated,

> In the United States and especially in the port of New York reside hundreds of Austrian subjects who have, for a long series of

years, been engaged in the importation of Austrian merchandise and have never harbored the intention to acquire American citizenship. These Austrians have in course of time increased the export of Austrian manufactures to the United States to the sum of 25,000,000 florins per annum. They are very successful competitors of the American importer as well as manufacturer, and monopolize almost completely the trade in Vienna specialties. Most of these gentlemen return to their old home to enjoy their fortune after they have amassed it in the United States. These foreigners are of no particular benefit to the United States; on the contrary, they impair the business interests of the American importer and manufacturer.

In view of these facts the question arises in what manner the action of the American authorities would be judged here in Austria, in case they should suddenly expel these foreign importers from the country and thus injure the export trade of Austria and especially that of the city of Vienna. And yet such action would only be in the nature of a retaliatory measure if the proposed expulsion of Hugo Klamer is carried out.[36]

U.S. efforts to protect Klamer also included threats to demand similar military service of Austro-Hungarians in the United States. While U.S. officials agreed that nation-states had a right to enlist residents in the military, the United States, as a liberal-minded state, had not even required military service of foreigners during times of national crisis. Consular officer Edmund Jussen noted, "My Government has always made the most liberal concessions to foreigners." Even in the Civil War, "when a general conscription was ordered, the United States did not disturb the foreigners, although many of them, Austrians included, were transacting lucrative business . . . while the American stood in the field under arms and protected the persons remaining at home." Jussen then ominously added, "How long these liberal and extremely humane views will prevail if expulsion of American citizens like the one in question is decreed here can not be predicted."[37]

The agreements, concessions, and conflicts over different jurisdictions and discrepancies in laws and policies found in the military service cases of Germany and Austria-Hungary all illuminate the soft process of the international appeal. On the face of it, the international appeal established a kind of parity among nations within the interstate system, because all nations or empires with sovereignty could access it. Yet, as a quick contrast between Chinese officials' efforts in the United States and U.S. officials' actions in Europe makes clear, not all appeals were equal. A key determinant of strength was a far more extensive and imperialist variant of extraterritoriality, wherein immigrants fell under the laws of the country of their emigration rather than under the law of the land in which they traveled. This variant of extraterritoriality also represented another part of the international legal regime and it prevented some nations from carrying out deportations in the first place.

Extraterritoriality and Limits to the Power to Deport

China did not deport U.S. citizens through much of the nineteenth century and well into the twentieth, because the international legal regime that structured immigrant removals did more than mandate that emigrant-sending nations retain some jurisdiction over their emigrants abroad through the international appeal. It also required that national removal policies, when applied to Europeans and citizens of colonial-settler nations like the United States, be built on Western law. Countries and empires in Asia and the Middle East, like China, found themselves especially impacted by this requirement. This form of extraterritoriality was not explicitly created to protect people from deportations, but it did, and it was enforced or realized through a particular, imperial extraterritorial agreement.

Throughout the late eighteenth and nineteenth centuries, extraterritorial agreements put jurisdiction over an immigrant in the hands of the country of emigration rather than the country of immigration. Between 1787 and 1886, the United States signed extraterritorial treaties with China, Morocco, Algiers, Tunis, Tripoli, Muscat, Borneo, Persia, Japan, Madagascar, Samoa, Tonga, and the Ottoman Empire.[38] Britain, Russia, France, and Germany also practiced extraterritoriality. Extraterritorial jurisdiction represented essentially an inversion of immigration law, where, writes legal scholar Leti Volpp, a sovereign "is governing its insiders, outside its territory. With . . . [immigration law], the sovereign is governing its outsiders, inside its territory."[39] In countries under extraterritorial agreements, therefore, U.S. officials did not use the international appeals process to protect U.S. citizens from removal, because nations under this particular strain of extraterritoriality did not have the power to deport U.S. citizens.

The U.S. government's operations in China between 1844 and 1943 exemplify how extraterritoriality worked to prevent deportations of U.S. citizens.[40] In China, U.S. law traveled with a U.S. emigrant. For the first fifty years of U.S. extraterritoriality in China, jurisdiction of Americans there fell to U.S. consular officials. In 1906, the U.S. government established a U.S. District Court for China to preside over U.S. emigrants. This left Americans in China subject to a unique blend of U.S. jurisdiction, which legal scholar Teemu Ruskola says "consisted of a mélange of colonial common law as it existed prior to American independence, general congressional acts, the municipal code of the District of Columbia, and the code of the Territory of Alaska." As a California court explaining the extraterritoriality in China wrote, "American citizens residing for the purpose of trade in the ports of China are not regarded as subjects of that government, but that, for purposes of government and protection, they constitute a kind of colony, subject to the laws and authority of the United States."[41] U.S. officials prosecuted Americans in China, and, by extension, Chinese authorities did not have the power to deport U.S. citizens.[42]

Two cases help illustrate the ways U.S. citizens in China were subject to U.S. rather than Chinese law. Consular officials arrested U.S. citizen Robert Sexton in Shanghai in 1909.[43] Sexton helped run a gambling operation at a club called the Alhambra. U.S. officials prosecuted him for vagrancy under the criminal code of Alaska.[44] The Consular Court for the District of Shanghai found Sexton guilty; he appealed to the U.S. Court for China.[45] That court ruled in his favor and discharged Sexton on grounds that the evidence was "not sufficient to establish the crime of vagrancy in the defendant."[46] A year later, in 1910, U.S. consular officials arrested James Hadley at the Alhambra for operating a roulette table, in violation of Washington, D.C., criminal laws against vagrancy. Hadley was tried and found guilty in the U.S. Court for China. He was sentenced to prison for sixty days, which he served, in a U.S.-run carceral institution.[47] All U.S. citizens residing in China, like Sexton and Hadley, lived only under U.S. law, not Chinese law. If found guilty of a crime, they served their time in a U.S. jail.[48]

Legal scholars writing in the late nineteenth and early twentieth centuries such as L. Oppenheim and Edwin M. Borchard capture the ways a discourse of civilization was used to assert this variant of extraterritoriality.[49] "Owing to the deficient civilization of these countries and fundamental differences in law and social habits, the countries of European civilization have stipulated for certain exceptions for their citizens from the operation of local law," Borchard wrote in *Diplomatic Protection of Citizens Abroad* (1915).[50] He went on to say that if a state's "laws are arbitrarily unreasonable and out of harmony with the standard of civilized states, or if the administration of the laws transgresses the prescriptions of civilized justice . . . the personal sovereignty of the home state reasserts itself and emerges in the form of diplomatic protection."[51] "In the Orient and in semi-civilized states," Borchard wrote, extraterritoriality "often involves a complete surrender of local jurisdiction in favor of the foreign state, and in states conforming more closely to the highest type of civilized government, it consists in partial derogations from territorial jurisdiction in special classes of cases."[52] Historian Eileen Scully dates the rise of this discourse of civilization to the late eighteenth century, when "European governments [and European settler countries like the United States] successively imported [rights] into the capitulations [or extraterritorial agreements] concepts and doctrines taking hold in the Western world, such as diplomatic protection, due process, and non-Western inferiority."[53] This discourse of civilization asserted that the cultural superiority of the West justified the rights of Westerners to Western-style law, even if they traveled to nations where other types of law existed.

The nations or empires that found themselves denied jurisdiction over Western foreigners found it was also used as grounds to exclude them from full membership in the interstate community. By the late nineteenth century the power to remove immigrants corresponded to a nation's full membership in the "comity of nations." Western nations operated within a community (or comity) because they practiced Western-style law. These laws were markers of "civilization." Nations not operating with Western-style laws were, within the nomenclature of international law, outside the community because they were not "civilized." As Oppenheim, one of the leading jurists in international law, put it, China or the Ottoman Empire were under extraterritoriality because of "their deficient civilisation." They were, as a consequence, "only for some parts members of the Family of Nations."[54] This use of the discourse of civilization represented a change in the interstate system. Where "Western Christian states had coexisted with other regional systems, such as Arab-Islamic hegemony," writes historian Eileen Scully, "now [in the nineteenth century] the European standard of 'civilization' emerged as the yardstick of international relations."[55]

Some countries under extraterritoriality made progress in ending it in the late nineteenth century. Japan completely ended extraterritoriality by

1899. Ottoman officials were also trying to.[56] In 1856, Turkey had gained partial admittance into the concert of nations at the Treaty of Paris. On the partial membership of the Turks, Oppenheim wrote, "There is no doubt that Turkey, in spite of having been received into the Family of Nations, has nevertheless hitherto been in an anomalous position as a member of that family, owing to the fact that her civilisation has not yet reached the level of that of the Western States. It is for this reason that the so-called Capitulations are still in force and that other anomalies still prevail, but their disappearance is only a question of time."[57] Not satisfied by partial membership, Ottoman authorities moved to establish the jurisdiction over all foreigners, which would mark an important step in gaining more complete membership in the community of nations.[58]

In 1885, the trajectory of a pair of expulsions from the Ottoman Empire helps illustrate a connection between the two variants of extraterritoriality and the interstate community. That year, Ottoman officials moved to expel two U.S. citizens. The two men were brothers, Louis and Jacob Lubrowsky. They had been born in the Ottoman Empire, immigrated to the United States, where they naturalized as U.S. citizens. In 1885, the Lubrowsky brothers traveled to Palestine, then a part of the Ottoman Empire. As part of an anti-Semitic policy aimed at limiting the numbers of Jews in Palestine, the Ottoman government summarily ordered the Lubrowskys' expulsion not long after their arrival.[59] Upon receiving their expulsion orders, the Lubrowskys contacted U.S. consular officers, asking them to use the international appeals process to stop their removal.[60]

U.S. diplomats took up their case. U.S. officials questioned the legitimacy of the Lubrowsky expulsions, because to them the proceedings had not met the standards of rights required by the international regime. An American consular agent wrote that the Lubrowskys' "expulsion without due process of law and conviction of crime or misdemeanor would be illegal and in violation of international comity, treaties, and capitulations."[61] Furthermore, he argued, these two U.S. citizens were being unjustly harassed by Ottoman authorities because of their faith.[62] Using these arguments, U.S. diplomats hoped to convince Ottoman authorities to overturn the Lubrowskys' orders of expulsion.

Ottoman officials initially tried to prevent U.S. intervention in the Lubrowskys' cases, not by refusing to recognize the right of the international appeal, but rather by claiming the Lubrowskys were not U.S. citizens.

In the nineteenth-century Ottoman Empire, people needed state permission to emigrate, which the Lubrowskys had not received. To Turkish officials, then, the brothers' naturalization was null and void because they had emigrated in violation of Turkish law.[63] Thus, as neither man was a U.S. citizen, U.S. officials could not intervene on their behalf.[64] Yet even as they argued that the Lubrowskys were citizens of the Ottoman Empire, Ottoman authorities still wanted to expel them.

Conscious of the standing of the Ottoman Empire internationally, U.S. diplomats opposed the Ottomans' attempt to ignore the brothers' U.S. naturalization by questioning the "civilization" of their laws. Samuel S. Cox, the American minister to Turkey, wrote to the U.S. secretary of state, comparing Ottoman and U.S. laws: "The United States has emancipated itself from feudalism; it has announced on these very Levantine shores, with no ambiguous voice, its principle as to the indefeasible right of emigration and expatriation; it has fixed it in treaties with other civilized and progressive nations." Cox wrote that "civilized" states allowed persons to voluntarily emigrate and naturalize elsewhere. "The doctrine," he wrote, "is that no man can be bound in any service to a Government whose citizen or subject he has ceased to be by voluntary naturalization elsewhere. The old feudal doctrine was that no subject can go from the country where he was born or where he is without the consent of his lord and master, the Government."[65] In their arguments, U.S. officials attempted to force the Ottomans to recognize the Lubrowskys' emigration and subsequent U.S. naturalization. If they did not, Ottoman officials could perhaps risk some of their progress at gaining more complete membership in the comity of nations by being labeled "uncivilized."

At the end of 1885, the Turkish government suspended the Lubrowskys' expulsion order.[66] The documents do not explicitly explain the reasons, but the international appeal and efforts of the Ottoman authorities to establish a fuller membership in the community of nations played significant roles. To participate more equally in the comity of sovereign nations, the Ottoman sultanate had to recognize foreign states' right to diplomatically "protect" their foreign nationals through the diplomatic appeals process. This explains, in part, why U.S. officials were using it to protect the Lubrowskys from the growing anti-Semitism in the Ottoman Empire. Thus, the global legal regime had (at least) two levels: one of bilateral relations among "civilized" states and one that relegated China and the Ottoman Empire to a lower status. The maintenance of jurisdiction of emigrants abroad was central to both.

Changing the Logic of the International Legal Regime

By the time U.S. officials built the policy to deport people from the United States, many other nations and empires around the world either revised their immigrant removal policies or passed brand-new ones, too. In the wave of construction, people sometimes used the word "expulsion" interchangeably with "deportation." Both words meant that someone was being removed from some place, but there were important differences that fundamentally changed the logic of the international legal regime. The newer policies, labeled "deportation" in this book, made the question of *where* to send a person central. Answering the question about the destination of a deportation required officials from a sending nation to confront another question: would the country on the receiving end agree to the deportation? Without answers to both, authorities could not carry out a deportation. In the case-by-case negotiations behind individual deportations that answered these questions, along with treaties and agreements to facilitate deportations, immigration officials and diplomats added a layer to the international legal regime.

Through much of the nineteenth century, as several European countries help illustrate, nations operating immigrant removal policies did not necessarily tie the destination of removal to an immigrant's country of citizenship. In 1793, for example, the British government expelled the French politician and diplomat Charles Maurice de Talleyrand. He had sought refuge from the French Revolution, and when Britain expelled him, he did not go to France but to the United States.[67] Partly this choice of destination was humanitarian, a removal to France might have led to his death; it most certainly would have led to his prosecution. Yet, Tallyrand's destination was part of a larger whole. Countries with formal removal policies expelled immigrants, but not necessarily to their countries of origin. Oftentimes, the immigrant could actually choose which border to leave from and where to go next. Throughout the nineteenth century, Belgium, France, and the Netherlands allowed expellees "a choice of border."[68] Expulsions were, then, largely unilateral—those on the receiving side were not involved in the process.

German authorities were among the first in Europe to tie the destination of a removal to an immigrant's country of origin. They did this in both the sending and receiving of immigrant removals. First Prussian and then the newly constituted German Reich expelled immigrants in the direction of their country of origin. German authorities, therefore, restricted the ability of a deportee to choose the border from which he or she would leave the country.[69] The German state also closed its borders to the unauthorized expulsion of third-country immigrants along its western borders. It did so by increasing regulation at its borders and through a series of international treaties. In one treaty with Belgium, Germany agreed to receive German expellees from Belgium, but refused to allow Belgium to expel non-Germans into German territory without authorization. The treaty also contained provisions regulating the travel of third-party deportees; expellees who needed to travel through German territory on their return to their country of origin, like Russia, were allowed to do so only if they had enough money to pay for their transit.[70] Each treaty added to the international legal regime.

When Germany made the destination important to immigrant removals, it forced other countries to do the same. During the 1880s, Belgium continued to remove individuals to its borders based in large part on the immigrant's choice of destination, but it had become more difficult in light of recent German policies and treaties. If, for example, Belgium wanted to expel a German, it could not do so until the German state acknowledged that the alien was a German. Soon the Belgian state signed treaties with other states structuring its ability to remove immigrants from its territory. Belgium and the Netherlands signed a bilateral agreement in 1888 stating that Dutch authorities agreed to allow Belgian authorities to expel Scandinavians and Northern Germans through their territory. French and Belgian authorities reached a similar agreement in 1896. In 1897, a British-Belgian agreement stipulated that each country had to accept its own poor migrants or give free passage to those immigrants through their territories.[71] This regional system of treaties contributed to an emerging layer of the international legal regime facilitating deportations.

Officials in the United States designed a deportation policy rather than an expulsion policy. The deportation process required international negotiations that could be complicated by the particulars of individual cases. The experiences of Lily Taquensk and Flora Gendron provide examples of the ways women's marital status determined their citizenship and affected the destination of deportation. Under U.S. law, a husband's citizenship determined a wife's citizenship.[72] Lily Taquensk had originally immigrated to the United States from Russia in 1903. A year later she moved to Canada and married a Canadian citizen.[73] At some point between 1904 and 1908, she reentered the United States from Canada. It is not clear in the records why or if she came alone or with her husband. U.S. immigration officials arrested her on November 25, 1908, and ordered her deportation. As Canadian law, like U.S. law, made a woman's citizenship derivative of her husband's, they sent a request to Canadian immigration authorities for approval of the deportation. The case of Flora Gendron documents even more starkly the ways marriage determined a woman's citizenship and the destination of a deportation. Flora had been born on U.S. soil, making her a U.S. citizen. She moved to Canada, where she married a Canadian citizen.[74] At some time unspecified in the documents, she and her husband then moved to the United States and, in early 1915, to Mexico, where Gendron worked as a prostitute. After six months, the Gendrons planned to move to Cuba, where, according to immigration records, she intended to continue working as a prostitute. Immigration agents arrested Gendron in Florida as she made her way to Cuba. When determining where to deport her, U.S. officials noted her time in Mexico, but understood that Mexican authorities would not approve her deportation because she had no claims to legal residency in Mexico or Mexican citizenship. As in Taquensk's case, U.S. immigration agents approached the Canadian authorities about deporting Gendron to Canada, because her marriage had ascriptively made her a Canadian.

Countries on the receiving end of a deportation typically granted approval for U.S. deportations quickly, but, as both Lily Taquensk's and Flora Gendron's cases also document, the process could take weeks or even months. Canadian officials initially refused Gendron's deportation on grounds that her birth on U.S. soil made her a U.S. citizen. U.S. officials disagreed, arguing Gendron's marriage made her a Canadian citizen. Negotiations dragged on for five months, until late 1915, when the Canadians approved her deportation. All the while, Flora Gendron waited in departmental custody in the United States. When Canadian officials finally sent their approval to Washington, U.S. officials added her to a group of deportees, known as a deportation party, in Seattle and, after being transferred to the custody of several different agents, furnished her with a ticket to Toronto.[75] In Taquensk's case, five weeks passed before Canadian officials sent instructions for U.S. authorities to carry out the deportation. U.S. authorities deported her on January 2, 1909.[76] Neither case file spells out why the approval process took so long, but most likely officials needed the weeks and months to confirm the women's marriages with provincial and local bureaucracies that kept marriage records. Officials could have even have had to contact churches where the ceremonies took place. Whatever the case, Canadian officials eventually approved each deportation.

U.S. officials answered the destination question differently for people of Chinese heritage than for immigrants of other racial and ethnic heritages. Under one of the earliest laws of Chinese exclusion in the United States, the 1888 Scott Act, people of Chinese heritage living in other nations—like Canada or Mexico—fell under the jurisdiction of Chinese exclusion. The destination of a deportation in cases involving immigrants of Chinese heritage largely defaulted to China rather than the country of last residence. Congress repeated this in section 2 of the 1892 Geary Act, which stated,

> That any Chinese person or person of Chinese descent, when convicted and adjudged under any of said laws to be not lawfully entitled to be or remain in the United States, shall be removed from the United States to China, unless he or they shall make it appear to the justice, judge, or commissioner before whom he or they are tried that he or they are subjects or citizens of some other country, in which case he or they shall be removed from the United States to such country: Provided, That in any case where such other country of which such Chinese person shall claim to be a citizen or subject shall demand any tax as a condition of removal of such person to that country, he or she shall be removed to China.[77]

By 1911, U.S. immigration authorities attempted to change the default destination in some deportations of people of Chinese heritage. This change was driven by budgetary concerns (explained in the first chapter) and ways that immigration officials believed Chinese immigrants to be using deportation policy to their own ends. U.S. officials began to complain that some Chinese immigrants who were residents of Canada or Mexico seemed to be using Chinese exclusion as a way to secure passage to China on the U.S. dime; immigrant agents labeled them "free trippers." To stop free trippers, U.S. officials tried to deport Chinese immigrants to the country they migrated from last. As they did so, U.S. officials changed the destination of deportation. During 1910, for example, when 185 Chinese were arrested at Nogales, Arizona, under Chinese exclusion laws, all of them were sent to China. In 1911, immigration inspectors arrested only two Chinese immigrants in Nogales. The supervising inspector of the Mexican border understood the different apprehension totals as a result of the changing policy in determining the destination. He wrote that the "decrease in the number of arrests . . . is unquestionably due to the fact that in former years a considerable number of Chinese intentionally crossed into the United States for the purpose of being arrested and returned to their native land at the Government's expense." Along the U.S.-Mexico border, this meant that Chinese immigrants who had crossed into the United States were often deported to Mexico. The result, as the supervising inspector saw it, was "that this procedure has broken up a pernicious practice and resulted in the saving of thousands of dollars to the government."[78]

The need to secure the receiving country's approval complicated U.S. officials' efforts to carry out deportations of people of Asian heritage to Canada because, while Canada did not restrict Chinese workers as a race as the United States did, at least not until 1923, it did discriminate against Chinese immigrants by imposing a head tax. In 1911, U.S. immigration agents failed to get Canadian approval to deport a man named Yuen Pak Sune. In 1911, Yuen Pak Sune traveled from China to Vancouver, British Columbia, then took the train to Montreal, and crossed the border into the United States with a group of Chinese immigrants. Since Yuen Pak Sune was not staying in Canada, he did not pay the Canadian head tax. The first head tax was $50. The Canadian parliament raised it in 1900 to $100 and in 1903 to $500.[79] Upon Yuen's crossing the border into the United States, U.S. immigration officers arrested Yuen for unlawful entry and placed him in custody in Boston, where the immigration commissioner ordered his deportation to Canada. While this was not a case of a "free tripper," U.S. officials tried to cut down the costs of deportation by deporting him to Canada, rather than China. Canadian officials would approve deportations from the United States of people of Chinese heritage only if the deportee paid a head tax. Yuen, however, could not afford to pay the Canadian head tax and, consequently, Canadian officials refused to approve the deportation.[80] After the Canadians refused to permit Yuen's deportation there, U.S. officials rearrested Yuen and processed him under Chinese exclusion laws. This jurisdictional switch allowed officials to deport him to China, despite the greater expense.[81]

Another similar case involved Hen Lee. In 1916, U.S. immigration officials arrested Hen Lee and ordered his deportation to China. Hen, who had entered the United States from Canada, wanted to remain in North America. His lawyers argued that the particular provision of immigration law under which he had been ordered deported specifically stated that the deportee should be "removed to the country from whence he last came." The court found that Hen's appeal had merit and changed his deportation destination to Canada. But, Hen could not afford to pay the head tax and the Canadians would not let him in. Therefore, immigration officials re-arrested Hen under Chinese exclusion laws and deported him to China.[82]

Since U.S. officials were also on the receiving end of deportations, they had to provide approval to countries trying to deport a U.S. citizen. Canadian lawmakers passed their first deportation law in 1906 and the list of deportable immigrants included "any person landed in Canada who, within two years, has become a charge upon public funds, whether municipal, provincial or federal, or an inmate of or a charge upon any charitable institution." The Canadian government could also deport prostitutes and a certain class of Chinese immigrants.[83] In 1909, the Canadians wanted to deport a man named Nazair Chartier to the United States. Chartier was in a hospital for the mentally ill; in deporting him, Canadian officials wanted U.S. institutions to bear the cost of his hospitalization. A striking fact in this case was that Chartier was a Canadian citizen. The Canadians found him deportable because he had spent most of the previous ten years living in the United States. He had returned to Canada only the year before he fell ill. The Canadian government believed in this case that long-term residency trumped formal citizenship. U.S. officials refused to authorize the deportation and, in a theme examined in Chapter 6, prioritized Chartier's formal citizenship, not his long-term residency. Chartier remained in Canada.[84]

When the Canadian government moved to deport Asian immigrants who had come from the United States, officials encountered systemic problems such as those U.S. authorities had experienced in trying to deport people of Chinese heritage. Hirokichi Yasui is a case in point. Yasui, a Japan-born lawful resident of the United States, went to Canada in 1920 to conduct business in Vancouver, British Columbia. But when he tried to return to the United States at Blaine, Washington, border patrol agents refused his readmission. (By this time, the anti-Asian shape of U.S. policy had been expanded past Chinese migrants to all people of Asian heritage.)

As a result, Canada bore the cost of deporting him to Japan.[85] Canadian officials had dealt with similar cases before. For example, in 1912, the head of Canadian immigration sent out a memorandum to border agents, warning them to be careful about admitting immigrant railway workers from the United States, many of whom were Chinese. If these workers violated Canadian law, U.S. officials would not generally grant approval for their deportation to the United States, the country of their last lawful residence. Canada would then have to pay the greater expense of deporting the immigrant workers back to China.[86]

Deportations of U.S. citizens from Mexico to the United States sometimes involved other diplomatic communications than those used in deportations from the United States or deportations from Canada. In 1908, Mexican lawmakers revised the government's power of immigrant removal that dated back to its original constitution in 1824.[87] Article 7 of the 1908 law stated, "when a foreigner shall have entered after this law shall have gone into effect and in violation of its provisions the government may order that he be sent back to the country whence he came if he shall not have resided in the Republic for more than three years."[88] This Mexican law assigned jurisdiction to the minister of the interior and assigned the hearing of removal cases to three-member boards of immigration.[89] Soon after the Mexican Revolution, officials revised deportation policy again. In 1917, under Article 33 of the new Mexican constitution, a deportee need not be informed of the grounds for his or her deportation. This differed from U.S. or Canadian policies, where people knew the charges during the proceedings. As a U.S. consular official noted in 1922, however, it was "established policy" that "an American citizen ordered deported from Mexico be informed of the charges against him and be given an opportunity to defend himself against such charges, as well as ample time within which to arrange his affairs in case the deportation is carried out."[90] Mexican officials, therefore, may not have always told a deportee of the grounds for removal at the time of his or her arrest, but they informed deportees of the grounds after a request by the U.S. State Department.

When George Wilkins was deported from Mexico in 1925, he asked for an explanation for his deportation as well as help in overturning his removal—he wanted U.S. consular officials to exercise the international appeal. This international appeal looked slightly different from the appeal exercised in the German or Austro-Hungarian cases, or Chinese appeals in the United States, because it took place after the removal. H. F. Arthur

Schoenfeld, U.S. chargé d'affaires in Mexico took up the case and wrote to General Aarón Sáenz, Mexico's foreign affairs secretary. "I inform you that the action of the Mexican Government," Sáenz replied, "was based on the request of persons established in the district on the ground that this gentlemen held a position in connection with police matters and on reports rendered by the authorities of this District from which it appears that the above-mentioned foreigner engaged in gambling operations and . . . his character thoroughly immoral." The U.S. officials informed Wilkins of the grounds for his deportation, but in light of them, U.S. consular officials declined to pursue an international appeal.[91]

The majority of the deportations from Mexico to the United States seem to have involved prostitution, gambling, and drugs. In 1920, Mexican authorities deported several U.S. citizens employed in and running a house of prostitution in Nuevo Laredo. They included proprietor John W. Donahue, a former deputy sheriff of Bexar County, Texas, and Mrs. Gussie Carter, Miss Mabel Smith, and Miss Geraldine Riokabaugh.[92] In 1923, Thomas A. Green found himself deported from Tijuana to the United States. Green was a card dealer in a licensed gambling house in Tijuana that served largely American clients. He fought his deportation; he wanted to return to his job and stay near his family. A U.S. official contacted the Mexican authorities, which informed him that the grounds for Green's removal also included drugs.[93] That same year, U.S. citizen David O. Guaderrama was deported from Mexicali. Guaderrama operated a club called the Black Cat, and in addition to running a house of prostitution, was long suspected of smuggling drugs into the United States.[94] In all these cases, U.S. State Department officials intervened diplomatically to determine the grounds of a deportation, but they refused to exercise the international appeal.

A smaller subset of deportees from Mexico were U.S. citizens involved in public utilities, mining, petroleum, and textiles who ran afoul of the Mexican revolutionary government after 1917. In 1923, Harvey S. Leach fell into this category. At the time of his deportation, Leach managed the British-owned Tampico Electric Company and he had lived in Mexico for thirty-three years. Leach and some of his supporters asked the U.S. government to launch an international appeal. Among Leach's supporters was W. F. Buckley (father to conservative author and commentator William F. Buckley, Jr.), who had himself been deported on similar grounds. At the request of Leach and people like Buckley, U.S. State Department officials appealed Leach's deportation several times.[95] In response to the last appeal,

General Sáenz informed them "that in view of the strike situation at Tampico President Obregón could not at that time revoke his [Leach's] order of expulsion." The grounds for Leach's deportation, in other words, came from Leach's response to a labor strike and mistreatment of Mexican workers. In light his actions, the revolutionary government would not grant the appeal and overturn the deportation.[96]

U.S. officials created agreements and signed treaties to facilitate deportations with the contiguous countries of Canada and Mexico. In 1909, officials from both Canada and the United States wanted a reciprocal agreement to better navigate the sending and receiving of deportees between the two countries. Setting it up was not a simple process. Any agreement had to acknowledge the massive number of immigrants to both countries and the complexity of migration between them. At this time, the United States received more immigrants than any other country in the world. Between 1881 and 1920, just under 23.4 million immigrants landed in the United States.[97] Canada also saw significant immigration; nearly three million people, mostly from Europe but also from Asia, immigrated to Canada between 1897 and 1914.[98] At the same time, hundreds of thousands moved from Canada to the United States. In 1900, close to 1.2 million Canadian-born immigrants lived in the United States.[99] Thousands of immigrants from Europe and Asia landed in Canada and traveled to the United States, either immediately or after several years, accounting for one in five migrations to the United States from Canada.[100] Authorities from both Canada and the United States noted that, when it came to deportations, then, there were three types of immigrants: (1) U.S. citizens who immigrated to Canada or Canadian citizens who immigrated to the United States and naturalized; (2) European or Asian immigrants traveling through the United States or Canada on a continuous journey; and (3) people like Chartier, or in the words of the Canadian superintendent of immigration, "people who have resided some months or years in the other country, but have never been naturalized there."[101] A diverse set of factors, ranging from the numbers of migrants, nature of citizenship, meaning of race and ethnicity, and category of legal residency, faced Canadian and U.S. officials as they set out to streamline the sending and receiving of deportees.

To resolve the many deportation cases of the first and third categories of immigrants quickly, U.S. and Canadian officials consented to what became known as the "reciprocal agreement."[102] In 1909, this agreement created a zone of five or six miles along the border, and many aliens apprehended there within one year of immigration could be returned through a shortcut procedure: officials of either country could bring a deportable person to the border and transfer custody to the receiving side.[103] In 1914, U.S. officials attempted to deport to Canada a British subject of Asian heritage who had, by living in the country for a period of three years, acquired Canadian residency. U.S. officials attempted to use the reciprocal agreement. The Canadian immigration commissioner, W. D. Scott, however, prevented it, stating that the agreement did not include subjects of Asian origin.[104] Those cases had to be handled through the longer drawn-out process of individual negotiations.

U.S. and Mexican officials also promulgated formal agreements. In one section of a larger 1925 treaty, U.S. and Mexican officials facilitated the deportations between the United States and Mexico. In the drafting stages, the Office of the Solicitor of the U.S. State Department requested clarification of a proposed section of the treaty that addressed the deportation of people who resided in either country for several years but never naturalized. Richard W. Flournoy, Jr., of the Solicitor's Office, advised, "I think that the Department should be definitively informed as to the classes of persons to whom this paragraph is to be applied, I am inclined to think that it refers to aliens ineligible for citizenship." The term "ineligible for citizenship" was by then shorthand for Asian immigrants in the United States. When ratified in 1925, this treaty left out much of this language referring to Asian immigrants but set broad sending and receiving procedures.[105]

By the early twentieth century, then, the centrality of reception to carrying out a removal at all meant that the bilateral deportation, as opposed to the more unilateral expulsion, emerged as a dominant form of immigrant removal. When officials negotiated individual deportations, or when they promulgated treaties and bilateral agreements, their efforts expanded the international legal regime. They added a layer that structured the receiving of deportations.

In the years that U.S. authorities began deporting people, the international legal regime facilitating immigrant removals was in large part defined by the international appeal. Through it, diplomatic officers could negotiate, plead, and sometimes threaten a country to try to stop an immigrant removal; it could be used as a resource that people could access while outside their country of citizenship to protect rights and liberties. Before the systemic adoption of deportation policies, officials used this regime selectively. U.S. consular officers exercised it to preserve the status and rights of some U.S. citizens abroad. However, they could refuse to use it or drop it, as exemplified by Constant A. Golly's case. Chinese officials likewise used the appeal to protest U.S. immigration officers' violation of rights and liberties of some merchants.

The establishment of deportation policies changed the scale and operating logic of the international regime. With Canada and Mexico, U.S. immigration authorities acquired approval for some deportations through diplomatic arrangements, pieced together through reciprocal agreements and treaties. The international legal regime had become more than a tool that emigrant-sending countries used to protect emigrants; it now made countries responsible for receiving deportees and structured every deportation. When Chinese citizens found their ability to travel between Canada and the United States affected by this added layer, they could not rely on their government to protect their interests the way, for instance, U.S. emigrants could, because extraterritoriality weakened the Chinese government's international appeal.

As Chapter 3 examines, U.S. lawmakers, the courts, and immigration officials contended with questions about if and when deportability affected the civil liberties and civil rights of immigrants on U.S. soil. The answers would become part of the equation that U.S. officials used to determine where to send a deportee or whether to approve one.

Chapter 3

Deportation and Citizenship Status

In 1903, John Turner, a labor activist from Great Britain and self-proclaimed anarchist, was in the United States organizing workers. Fears over anarchism had been rising since the late nineteenth century, cresting after an anarchist assassinated President William McKinley.[1] Not long afterward, Congress passed a new immigration law that included an anti-anarchist provision, which for the first time made people deportable on political grounds. Turner was one of the first affected by that provision. After one of Turner's speeches in New York, Joseph Weldon, a Bureau of Immigration agent, arrested him for being an immigrant anarchist.[2] Thus began Turner's seven-month-long deportation ordeal. A Board of Special Inquiry made up of three immigration agents heard his case, one of whom was Weldon, who also testified as a witness.[3] Not surprisingly, the board ordered Turner deported. Turner challenged his deportation to the Supreme Court, where his lawyers claimed his deportation violated his civil liberties and civil rights, one of which was his freedom of speech, guaranteed under the First Amendment.

When people like Turner fought deportations on grounds that the law violated their civil liberties and civil rights, they asked questions about how the Constitution applied to immigrants. Lawmakers, the courts, immigration officials, and immigrants grappled with the ways that deportability affected the civil liberties and civil rights of people on U.S. soil.[4] In figuring out some of the answers, immigration authorities began to distinguish important legal differences among three categories of residents on U.S. soil—citizens, lawful immigrants, and immigrants in the country in violation of immigration law.

Protections against deportation—such as time limits—tempered some of these legal differences between immigrants and citizens. But those protections were not equally available to people processed under Chinese exclusion. Civil rights and civil liberties, therefore, applied differently to those under different immigrant statuses, which were further attenuated by the ways race operated in law and policy. As people puzzled out how deportability impacted the trajectory of civil liberties and rights, they also drove another significant legal change and set an important logic to policy—they made deportations increasingly a different legal process from immigrant exclusions.

Deportation and Immigrants Without Legal Residence

John Turner, his lawyers, labor leaders, and activists who rallied around him wanted to use his case for larger purposes. They hoped the case would help them strengthen the liberty of free speech, which many counted as a critical step to a larger, nationwide struggle to improve the rights of labor.[5] Instead, Turner's case turned out to limit civil liberties and civil rights. It would establish, for example, that immigrants who entered the country in violation of law did not have the same First Amendment rights as U.S. citizens or even immigrants who entered within the law.

John Turner was a man with powerful friends, who, after his arrest, came to his aid. They threw him rallies, spoke publicly in opposition to his deportation, and organized a prominent team of defense lawyers that included Edgar Lee Masters and Clarence Darrow. At a meeting in New York on December 3, 1903, attendees such as Henry George, Felix Adler, and Horace White, a member of the New York State Senate, adopted resolutions criticizing the anarchist provision of the Immigration Act of 1903 and Turner's treatment by the Bureau of Immigration. Columbia sociologist Franklin H. Giddings, the grandson of famed abolitionist William Lloyd Garrison, and Carl Schurz, a onetime editor of the *New York Evening Post*, attended the meeting.[6] A number of labor unions and their leaders, including Samuel Gompers, also rallied behind Turner. The Central Federated Union of New York and the Brooklyn Federation of Labor passed resolutions of support. The National Union of Shop Assistants protested, too.[7] Some of Turner's supporters, including Emma Goldman and other members of the recently established Free Speech League of New York, persuaded Darrow and Masters to take the case and paid their legal fees.[8]

For three months after Turner's 1903 arrest, the government detained him at Ellis Island. The Bureau of Immigration supplied Turner with thirty

MAIN ENTRANCE, IMMIGRANT STATION, ELLIS ISLAND, N. Y.

Figure 2. Ellis Island, location of immigrant processing and detention facilities. John Turner was held here until his deportation. "Main Entrance, Immigrant Station, Ellis Island, N.Y.," *AR-CGI* (1904).

cents a day for food, which the government required that he spend at the Ellis Island restaurant. He could buy "two cups of coffee, one bowl of soup and ten slices of bread a day." He relied on the generosity of friends and supporters to collect money so that he could buy more food and support his wife and three children back in England. Turner spent his days and nights in a nine-foot-by-seven-foot cell in one of the Ellis Island buildings, going outside for only short periods at a time. When the Supreme Court agreed to hear his case, Turner was granted bail.[9]

When Turner's case finally reached the Supreme Court, his lawyers challenged his deportation on many grounds. In one part of their argument, they asked the Court to reconsider the less robust due process rights of immigrants created over the past two decades. They argued, for example, that in *Fong Yue Ting*, the Court had, in effect, endorsed due process rights in deportation law that were weaker than due process rights under other law, especially criminal law.[10] They urged the Court to move back toward "[t]he better and larger definition of due process," which was "law in its regular course of administration, through courts of justice."[11] To underscore this point, they argued that being held in a cell for seven months represented a punishment, a denial of liberty, and as such, violated Turner's constitutional right to a public hearing and to life and liberty.[12] In addition, the lawyers argued that administrative officers were not trained for or capable of administering hearings, and because of this Turner's due process rights had been violated.[13] They also charged that an administrative hearing could hardly be fair or consistent with due process if one person served as both a witness for the government and a member of the body that decided the case, as Inspector Weldon had.[14]

The Darrow-Masters defense included a Tenth Amendment challenge, one similar to earlier challenges made in *Fong Yue Ting* and the *Japanese Immigrant Case*. Their brief argued that the U.S. government did not have power over immigrants because this power was not explicitly delegated to it in the Constitution.[15] Darrow and Masters further claimed that sections of the Immigration Act of 1903 were unconstitutional because the executive branch was doing the work of the judiciary and had overstepped the separation of powers. The brief noted that "the duties of the Commissioner General would appear to be more of a judicial than of an administrative character, or that they have at least stretched the administrative power so as to infringe upon the powers of the judiciary of the United States."[16]

In its decision, the Court refused to reconsider matters of due process, the appearance of punishment, or jurisdictional overreach. The justices restated that deportation was an inherent power of sovereign nations and reaffirmed their position that deportation by administrative process did not represent a violation of due process rights. As they saw it, Turner had received a trial and the mere fact that administrative officers heard his case did not violate due process. Chief Justice Melville Fuller wrote for the Court, "No limits can be put by the courts upon the power of Congress to protect, by summary methods, the country from the advent of aliens whose race or habits render them undesirable as citizens, or to expel such if they have already found their way into our land and unlawfully remain therein."[17]

What the Court did consider was the new anarchist provision, to which Darrow and Masters had raised two key challenges. First, on behalf of Turner, the lawyers argued for a narrowing of the provision's reach so that anarchists like Turner could lawfully immigrate to the United States. They tried to establish that there were two categories of anarchists, only one of which was deportable: one group hoped to establish "the rule of each individual by himself" through violence, while a second group peacefully advocated anarchy.[18] The Immigration Act of 1903 excluded "anarchists *or* those who advocate violence," and Darrow and Masters maintained that peaceful anarchists did not fall within the purview of the law because they did not advocate violence. The wording, they argued, was not anarchists *and* those who advocated violence. The provision should apply only to those who advocated violence against the government.[19] Darrow and Masters then insisted that, while Turner was a self-proclaimed anarchist, he did not advocate violence. They brought in affidavits from Turner's supporters, who testified to this effect. Louis F. Post, editor of the Chicago weekly *The Public*, who, nine years later, became assistant secretary of labor, spoke on Turner's behalf and signed an affidavit stating that Turner had expressed "the most peaceable theories and principles concerning government and labor conditions" and impressed Post by his "his conduct, appearance and language . . . as a gentleman of very high character."[20] In another affidavit, Samuel Gompers stated that he had met Turner in 1896 after one of Turner's speeches. Gompers said that Turner had not "intimat[ed] violence, disorder, force, revolution, or lawlessness of any sort."[21] Turner's lawyers also drew the Court's attention to the facts that the Board of Special Inquiry did not ask Turner about his anarchist views, that there was no indication that Turner had ever advocated the assassination of any government officials or that he believed in or advocated the forceful overthrow of the U.S. government or any other.[22] In this challenge, they wanted the Court to limit what Congress had defined as a national threat, allowing peaceful anarchists to lawfully immigrate.

Second, Darrow and Masters argued that the anarchist provision was unconstitutional because carrying it out violated the First Amendment.[23] As they saw it, under the First Amendment, the government could not restrain Turner's speech about anarchy.[24] Their argument took them through a discussion about the relationship between belief and speech. Darrow and Masters maintained that the First Amendment's guarantee of freedom of speech protected a person's beliefs, for there was no way to determine what a person believed unless he or she made a statement. They wrote, "There is no X-ray process for arriving at the convictions of the human mind, these convictions can only be ascertained by the utterance of the belief, to condemn the belief is really to condemn its utterance and can be nothing else." The brief went on to say, "We depart into the fantastic when we say that a man can speak what he pleases, but cannot believe what he pleases. . . . It results therefore that the proscription of belief is the proscription of speech."[25]

In ruling against both challenges to the anarchist provision, the Court did not believe that Congress had intended to distinguish between two categories of anarchists.[26] The federal government, it said, had the power to determine who and what represented a national threat. And in 1903, it had said that anarchists were such a threat—whether they advocated anarchy with or without violence. Anarchism, the Court ruled, was a condition on which the government could exclude and deport. The Court, therefore, reinforced its position in *Fong Yue Ting*: Congress had sweeping power to legislate what represented a threat.

Embedded in the logic used by the Court to uphold the anarchist provision was the answer to whether deportations that depended on an immigrant's speech in the United States violated his First Amendment rights. The Court ruled that the anarchist provision did not violate the First Amendment.[27] The justices rested their ruling on the link between exclusion and deportation. Under the Immigration Act of 1903, sections 3 and 38 explicitly excluded immigrant anarchists from entering the United States. Section 21 contained the deportation provision, which stated, "That in case the Secretary of the Treasury shall be satisfied that an alien has been found in the United States in violation of this Act he shall cause such alien, within the period of three years after landing or entry therein, to be taken into custody and returned to the country whence he came."[28] The anarchist deportation provision, therefore, did not authorize the government to deport immigrants who spoke about anarchism while in the United States, but it did exclude people who believed in anarchism from immigrating in the first place. As the Court saw it, the statute authorized the government to deport people like Turner who were already anarchists before they arrived in the United States. As an excludable alien, Turner possessed no right to be in the United States; therefore, he had no First Amendment rights.[29]

After the Supreme Court decision, American officials deported John Turner to England, where years later, in 1925, he would again meet up with Emma Goldman, one of the people who had helped secure his representation by Darrow and Masters. Goldman was deported herself, in 1919, under the anarchist provision of U.S. immigration law.[30] Many U.S. officials had wanted to deport Goldman for her radical beliefs decades earlier, but she had entered the United States within the law and by 1904 was a naturalized U.S. citizen.

The impact of deportations in demarcating differences in the liberties of immigrants in the United States in violation of law and citizens' rights explains why Turner was deported in 1904 and Goldman was not. The key Supreme Court cases that upheld the government's power to deport, from *Fong Yue Ting* to the *Japanese Immigrant Case*, clearly stated deportation was something that applied to immigrants, not citizens. The Court rearticulated in *Turner* that deportation was a protective process that applied only to immigrants. In 1903, Turner was not a citizen, but Goldman was. Her U.S. citizenship protected her until a larger anti-anarchist campaign during World War I. In *Turner*, then, the Court said essentially that it was a denial of liberty and due process for a U.S. citizen to be imprisoned without a criminal trial. Detainment in a cell while one awaited deportation, however, was different and perfectly legal.[31] In addition, after *Turner*, immigrants who entered the United States in violation of law did not have First Amendment rights when it came to their beliefs—if those beliefs established deportability. The Court stated in *Turner* that what an immigrant said while in the United States could be used to document whether the immigrant was deportable and was not a matter of free speech. In contrast, an immigrant with lawful residency, until 1917, could claim to be an anarchist without being arrested and sent out of the country.

The distinctions between liberties like speech for those who had entered the United States in violation of law and those who came to the United States within the law were not as fixed as they would become. One reason had to do with time limits for deportation. In 1904 a time limit of deportability ranged from one to three years. People of every ethnicity and nationality, except those of Chinese descent, who entered the United States without authorization obtained legalization once their time limit was up. Time in the United States, to borrow a term used a century later, "regularized" an immigrant's status.

Liberties of Lawfully Admitted Immigrants

In 1909, a man named Chan Leong Hee faced deportation. He had entered the United States lawfully six years earlier as a Section 6 immigrant, as a merchant. On his arrival, he started a grocery store in Los Angeles, but after two years the business failed. Chan then went to work selling fruits and vegetables at a Los Angeles market. In 1909, Bureau of Immigration agents arrested Chan for violating the Chinese exclusion laws, for being a Chinese laborer in the United States. Chan fought his deportation in the lower courts, questioning whether the government could deport immigrants for changing jobs, when their entrance to the country had been lawful.[32] In other words, his case involved the question of whether the government could deport lawfully admitted immigrants for what amounted to post-entry infractions on U.S. soil. The answer in Chan's case illustrated different liberties and rights of lawfully admitted immigrants from those outside the law.

In the late 1880s, Chinese immigrants with lawful residence fell into two groups: laborers who entered before the passage of the Chinese Exclusion Act in 1882 and those exempt from the law. The exempt category applied to teachers, students, merchants, and travelers. The latter group popularly became known as "Section 6 immigrants," after the portion of the Chinese Exclusion Act that defined them as exempt. Chan would lawfully enter as a Section 6 immigrant. Between 1894 and 1940, just over 1,800 Section 6 immigrants were admitted annually.[33]

At the turn of the century, according to the letter of the law, only immigrants who entered the country in violation of exclusions like John Turner could be deported. Deportation policy by 1904 officially served only as a second line of defense to exclusion. When U.S. immigration agents deported Turner, they did not have the power to deport people for actions taken on U.S. soil, for post-entry infractions. Immigration law stipulated that the causes of deportation had to exist prior to entry into the United States. Turner was deportable, because, as the Court noted, he believed in anarchism before his entry into the United States and his speaking about it proved he entered the country in violation of the exclusion provision. It was not a post-entry infraction. Only people who violated immigration exclusions and entered unlawfully in the first place were deportable. Deportations did not apply to people who lawfully entered the country.

As it turned out, since the 1890s under Chinese exclusion there had been some short-lived exceptions to the grounds of deportation predating entry into the United States. In the Geary Act, Congress temporarily created the power to deport people for actions taken on U.S. soil. For example, Fong Yue Ting found himself facing one of these exceptions and was deported for not registering for a certificate of residence. Federal immigration authorities also briefly expanded their ability to deport Chinese immigrants for post-entry infractions to include those who committed a crime on U.S. soil. The McCreary Amendment of 1893 stipulated that "no Chinese person heretofore convicted in any court of the States or Territories or of the United States of a felony shall be permitted to register under the provisions of this act."[34] Soon Chinese immigrants either registered or were deported from the United States.

Throughout the rest of the 1890s, immigration officials deported a small number of immigrants for what seemed to be their actions on U.S. soil, but immigration officials secured these deportations by redefining a lawful entry into an unlawful one. Ah Fawn, for example, had entered the United States as a Section 6 immigrant. Once in the country, he made his living by gambling. Immigration authorities ordered his deportation not on grounds that his gambling made him immoral or criminal—these actions did not make one deportable in 1893—but because Ah Fawn was not exempt from Chinese exclusion because his gambling made him a laborer. Ah Fawn challenged this legal maneuver in federal district court in 1893. His lawyers argued that the government could not deport him as a Chinese laborer under the terms of the Geary Act because he, quite simply, was not one.[35]

The District Court for the Southern District of California sided with the government and upheld the expansion of the term "laborer." "Undoubtedly," the court noted, "a gambler is not a 'laborer,' in the ordinary and popular meaning of that term."[36] However, the court reasoned, the treaty negotiations between United States and Chinese officials in 1880 and the Geary Act itself established a broad meaning of that term. The court also noted that in passing the Geary Act, Congress "did not use the words 'Chinese laborers' in any narrower sense than were the same words in the treaty under which it was legislating."[37] Consequently, the court ruled that the term "laborers" included "all immigration other than that for teaching, trade, travel, study, and curiosity."[38] By this logic, Chinese gamblers were laborers. Ah Fawn's once lawful entry had become an unlawful one, and he was deported.

Immigration authorities used similar tactics to deport Chinese women accused of prostitution. An 1875 immigration law known as the Page Act excluded prostitutes. Congress, however, had not included a deportation provision in that act. On April 26, 1901, immigration agents tried to deport a woman practicing prostitution by using Chinese exclusion. They arrested

Lee Ah Yin in a brothel, charging that she was a Chinese laborer unlawfully in the United States. Like Ah Fawn, Lee Ah Yin rejected the laborer designation. The court acknowledged that no evidence existed that "she ever did any manual labor." Still, the judge declared her deportable under Chinese exclusion because, as he explained in *Lee Ah Yin v. United States*, "a prostitute would be included in the term 'Chinese laborers.'" The Ninth Circuit Court upheld the broadening of the term to include prostitutes.[39] After 1902, therefore, any Chinese woman found practicing prostitution could be deported as a laborer.

Another group targeted for deportation after an entry initially labeled lawful were Section 6 immigrants who changed jobs like Chan Leong Hee. Before Chan immigrated to the United States, he was one of four partners in a rice, nut, oil, seed, and general merchandise store in the village of Lee Yin, in the Sun Woy district of China. His share of this partnership was worth about $1,500, enough to support himself, his wife, and their seven-year-old child. In 1903, at the age of twenty-seven, Chan immigrated to the United States. As he said, "at the time I was in China everybody talked that in the United States there was good business so I came over here." With a check worth two hundred U.S. dollars, Chan boarded the steamer *Nippon Maru* bound for San Francisco. His partnership, the two hundred dollars, and the fact that he had not worked as a laborer within the previous year made him eligible to enter the country as a merchant.

After two years, his business failed and Chan went to work at the Los Angeles public market. He worked there for three years, arriving at a little after two in the morning in the summer and at four in the winter. His workday ended between five and six in the evening. During these years, Chan was not self-employed; he did not own his own business; he worked as a laborer.

At the time of Chan's immigration, a lawfully admitted immigrant's employment was not legally tied to the employment for which he or she was admitted. Legal residents had the liberty to change jobs. By 1909, immigration officials were trying to change that. Rule 53 of the U.S. Immigration Bureau's 1905 "Regulations Relating to Exclusion of Chinese" stated: "Chinese persons who gain admission to the United States as members of the admissible classes and who after admission become laborers shall be arrested as being unlawfully in this country."[40] In composing this rule, the Bureau of Immigration authorized the deportation of immigrants who entered the United States as exempt Chinese if they later took up laboring. This provision fit in with the idea of "lawful admittance, unlawful staying." In Rule 53, then, immigration officials created policy that added lawfully admitted immigrants who changed jobs to the list of deportable people. On April 20, 1909, U.S. commissioner William M. Van Dyke heard Chan's case, found him unlawfully within the United States, and ordered his deportation to China.[41]

Chan, with $500 in the bank and a horse and wagon worth around $400, immediately appealed the decision to the district court, where District Judge Olin Wellborn puzzled out whether a Section 6 immigrant's legal status tied him or her to the employment under which he or she qualified for exemption at the time of immigration.[42] Judge Wellborn considered how courts had come down on the issue. Under a precedent set in *United States v. Ng Park Tan*, immigrants who engaged in manual labor immediately after landing in this country were deportable.[43] This amounted to fraudulent entry. Some judges had found that temporary work as a laborer, however, was not the same as fraudulent entry and did not forfeit an immigrant's right to remain in the United States. In *United States v. Yong Yew*, for example, a district court judge in Missouri wrote, "I do not wish to be understood as holding that a Chinese person, who has been a merchant in his own country, and enters the United States in good faith, intending to continue the business of merchandising here, and who in like good faith enters upon that business, but, through adversity or other sufficient cause, is unable to continue, and who enters other employment for a time, is liable to deportation."[44]

In the end, Judge Wellborn reversed the commissioner's decision and discharged Chan—going against the explicit instructions laid out in the Chinese exclusion regulations in Rule 53. Wellborn believed that Chan had, in good faith, immigrated as a merchant. "From all the evidence in the case," Judge Wellborn wrote, "I am satisfied, that the defendant entered the country as a Chinese merchant." Despite the fact he was currently a laborer, Chan clearly intended, as the judge understood it, "to resume the business of a merchant when he accumulates money sufficient to enable him to do so."[45] The balance of his bank account and testimony convinced the judge.

While people of Chinese descent lived in the shadow of the aggressive enforcement of immigration law, which often threatened to undermine their legal status, a difference existed between those who entered lawfully and those who did not. That is part of why Chan worked so hard early on in his residence in Los Angeles to maintain his status as a merchant. Continuing Section 6 status depended on it. Those like Chan who took up laboring and fought their deportation under Rule 53 helped ensure that their legal status remained different from that of immigrants who came outside the law.

In 1914, five years after Chan's case, the Bureau of Immigration noted in its *Annual Report* that immigration officials were not pursuing cases like his.[46] Six years later, in 1920, H. R. Sisson, special representative of the Bureau of Immigration on Chinese practice, wrote in his annual report, "It has been held repeatedly by the courts that Chinese 'exempts' permitted to land and later found employed as laborers are not subject to deportation unless the government establishes that their entry was fraudulent, or, in other words, that it was their intention at that time to become laborers."[47] That status of lawfully admitted immigrants, much to the frustration of immigration authorities, not only ensured liberties of people past the right to change jobs, it also, as Sisson noted in his report, meant that Section 6 immigrants had other liberties, including the right to bring their families.

Deportation Proceedings and the Rights and Liberties of U.S. Citizens

In 1906, immigration agents arrested an Illinois man named Moy Suey. They brought Moy Suey before a U.S. commissioner, who heard his case and ordered his deportation to China. Moy Suey appealed his deportation to the District Court for Illinois. Immigration agents wanted to deport Moy Suey because they believed he was actually an immigrant fraudulently claiming U.S. citizenship. To prove this, though, they brought nothing to the court—no evidence to disprove his citizenship at all. Going into the hearing, immigration authorities thought they would win their case. Explaining why the government believed it could win its case even without presenting evidence at all had much to do with two factors. First, many immigration officers believed that being of Chinese descent marked a person as an immigrant, despite the person's birthright citizenship. Second, many Chinese immigrants fraudulently claimed U.S. citizenship; it became a key strategy in evading exclusion.[48] To cut down on the ability of people of Chinese descent proving U.S. citizenship, immigration authorities built a process in which immigrants and U.S. citizens had the same basic rights when it came to distinguishing between them. A struggle over the rights of U.S. citizens played out over the next decade. The deportation cases in this struggle set other legal differences between immigrants and citizens and, in the process, differentiated deportations from immigrant exclusions.

When Moy Suey challenged his deportation, he testified that he was born in New York City, a U.S. citizen, and therefore, not deportable. To make his case, he had to prove his U.S. citizenship. While Congress passed laws stating that Chinese immigrants could not naturalize, people of Chinese heritage acquired birthright U.S. citizenship. They were U.S. citizens at birth under the principle of jus soli or by parental transmission under jus sanguinis. Proving U.S. citizenship in 1906 looked a lot different than it would a century later. In the early twentieth century, many Americans across all racial and ethnic categories were born at home without birth certificates.[49] Many never owned a U.S. passport. One common way to document citizenship was to rely on family members and community history for evidence of citizenship. This is just what Moy Suey did. His uncle and cousin testified that he was born in the United States. Moy Suey provided additional evidence by supplying detailed information on his family and his life in New York.[50]

In 1906, when officials argued their case against Moy Suey in the Circuit Court of Appeals for the Seventh Circuit, they did not present any evidence and believed they would win the case. This was because immigration authorities thought they had already firmly established their power to determine citizenship through an administrative process. When a person arrived at the U.S. border, immigration officials held sole jurisdiction over determining citizenship. If an immigration official did not believe a person's citizenship claim, he or she could not appeal the decision to U.S. courts; the person could only appeal to the Bureau of Immigration, and that decision was final. The burden of proof rested on the defendant to prove U.S. citizenship. Two cases established this—*Sing Tuck* and *Ju Toy*— which closed citizens' access to the courts in 1904 and 1905.[51] *Sing Tuck* and *Ju Toy* made clear that immigration agents had the power to rule on whether a person was a citizen—but these were exclusion cases.

Immigration authorities believed that their power to determine citizenship held for deportation cases, too.[52] Therefore, in the confident belief that the Circuit Court of Appeals for the Seventh Circuit would uphold *Sing Tuck* and *Ju Toy*, the government in *Moy Suey* "brought nothing," according to court records, "either to impeach the credibility of the witnesses or disprove the probability of their narrative." They did not challenge, in the court's words, "the fact that appellant attended the schools named, or the Sunday School; or of the fact that the street and number named was the residence of Chinese twenty-two years ago, when appellant was born; or of the fact that the uncle and cousin lived where appellant stated they lived, and were engaged in the business that appellant stated they were engaged in; or of any other fact upon which appellant built up his case of nativity."[53]

Moy Suey won his case and, in the process, limited immigration authorities' jurisdiction over people claiming U.S. citizenship in deportation cases in that judicial district. "[W]hen a person, physically and politically present in the United States at the time he is arrested for deportation, claims that he is an American born citizen, and resists deportation on the basis of his rights of citizenship," the court decided, "the case is an entirely different one."[54] The issue of citizenship was a "right that congress would be without constitutional power to curtail or give away. It is a right to be adjudicated in the courts, in the usual and ordinary way of adjudicating constitutional rights." The court continued, "No rule of evidence may fritter it away. When such right is in court asking for the protection of the law, no question of public policy can affect it." On this matter, the court clearly stated, "The citizen deported is banished, and banishment is a punishment that can follow only a judicial determination in due process of law."[55] In cases involving citizenship, therefore, the court distinguished deportation from exclusion. It maintained that a person residing in the country had access to the federal courts in ways that people at the border did not. If a U.S. citizen was not given a judicial hearing, he or she could be banished without due process—and that was unconstitutional because that represented a punishment.

Between 1906 and 1922, other lower courts split over the jurisdiction of immigration officials to determine citizenship in deportation cases. Many judges followed the spirit of *Moy Suey*. In those districts, persons of Chinese heritage who fought deportation orders on U.S. citizenship grounds found several factors working to their advantage. First, many people of Chinese heritage with U.S. citizenship had access to the courts. Furthermore, in citizenship cases, defendants were not held to the Geary Act's white witness requirement.[56] Yet another advantage was that the burden of proof rested with the government. Immigration agents had to disprove citizenship claims by more than simply relying on the person's Chinese heritage—as they had tried in Moy Suey's case. Once in court, if the government did not convincingly prove that the defendant was an immigrant, the judge released him or her.

Officials from the Bureau of Immigration complained that *Moy Suey* created a two-trial system that Chinese immigrants abused. Officials argued that Chinese immigrants circumvented deportation by using the gap between their hearing before a U.S. commissioner and their district court appeal to prepare new evidence of citizenship. "No matter . . . how weak or contradictory the evidence offered before the commissioner may have been," one official wrote, "the Chinese defendant goes before the court with the privilege of introducing anything he pleases, and usually after a long delay during which the opportunities for manufacturing evidence and coaching witnesses have been almost unlimited. So appreciative are the Chinese of this boon that frequently they deliberately fail to make out any case at all before the commissioner."[57] By effectively providing the defendant with two separate trials, the bureau argued, courts made it harder for the government to disprove citizenship claims. "Another undue advantage enjoyed by the Chinese," the bureau complained, "is the fact that the trial before a district court . . . is, as a matter of fact, no appeal at all, but a complete second opportunity to establish his case."[58]

To immigration agents, a defendant's access to the courts did more than just provide the tools to avoid deportation: it provided a way to fraudulently obtain U.S. citizenship. The Bureau of Immigration's 1914 *Annual Report* explained how some immigrants used citizenship claims to effectively obtain legal documents of citizenship. A revealing case involved an unnamed man in the Washington-Oregon district, whom immigration agents arrested for violating the Chinese exclusion laws. According to the Bureau of Immigration, the defendant initially presented identification papers showing him to be a lawful immigrant, but when inspectors discovered that these papers were false, he set up a defense of U.S. citizenship. The court believed the defendant's citizenship claim and dismissed the order of deportation. As the bureau noted, not only did this man evade deportation, the court had essentially declared him an American citizen.[59] In effect, he used the courts to find a way around the laws of Chinese exclusion. Chinese exclusion made it explicit that Chinese immigrants could not naturalize. In deportation hearings, though, a small number of Chinese immigrants found space in the courts to claim U.S. citizenship.

In the wake of *Moy Suey*, the Bureau of Immigration became selective in trying deportation cases that involved U.S citizenship claims because of the difficulties of disproving citizenship claims and the fact that the outcome could document citizenship. By 1908, the bureau pursued a policy of arresting people of Chinese heritage, primarily in border regions, where officials believed that they could more easily prove that the person was an immigrant and had entered the country unlawfully. As officials explained in 1911, "If Chinese are arrested in the proximity of the boundaries, generally there is either evidence or a strong suspicion that they have recently been smuggled in; if they are arrested in the interior, no such evidence or suspicion exists. It is only occasionally that a Chinaman arrested in one of the large interior cities having a considerable Chinese population can be deported." "The Government," they complained, "can do no more than show that the defendant is a Chinese laborer and has not a certificate, and must depend upon its ability to break down by cross-examination the testimony of witnesses carefully coached for the purpose of proving American birth."[60]

Nonetheless, officials on the borders still complained about the challenges of disproving citizenship in the cases they did pursue. The inspector at El Paso, for example, lamented that, "owing to the difficulty of presenting to the courts sufficiently convincing proof of illegal entry, it was impossible to secure deportation of such Chinese unless they were actually apprehended in the act of crossing the boundary—a physical impossibility except in relatively few instances."[61]

The struggle between immigration authorities and people of Chinese heritage over documenting citizenship played out in other enforcement strategies. When immigration authorities used a lack of English fluency as evidence to disprove citizenship, for example, some people of Chinese heritage began using this to their advantage. In 1916, the San Francisco department uncovered "unmistakable evidence of a scheme calculated to have Chinese adjudicated citizens by United States commissioners."[62] Under this scheme, an anonymous letter would be sent to the bureau informing immigration officials that a certain Chinese man had been recently smuggled into the country and where he could be found. The inspector would then identify and arrest the man, who "would profess very little or no knowledge

of the English language and . . . a vague claim of birth in the United States."
The bureau would set up a deportation hearing, but once brought before
the commissioner, the defendant would display English fluency and produce witnesses testifying to his citizenship.[63] After the department became
aware of this strategy, it ceased acting upon anonymous tips.

Not all immigration districts faced these challenges of disproving citizenship, however, because some lower courts ignored *Moy Suey* by stressing
the sameness of exclusion and deportation.[64] In *Yee Ging v. United States*
(1911), a Texas judge, Thomas Maxey, wrote, "[T]he burden of proving
citizenship rested upon the Chinaman." He noted that in the law, Congress
had written that the burden of proof in both exclusion and deportation
cases rested on the defendant. Judge Maxey noted that Congress had passed
no law changing this and the Supreme Court had not ruled to change it,
either. He wrote, "The statute makes no such distinction, nor is it to be
found, so far as the court is advised, in any case decided by the Supreme
Court."[65] Judge Maxey believed that the U.S. Supreme Court had settled
these matters in *Ju Toy*.[66]

The District Court for the Southern District of New York did not follow
Moy Suey, either. In *United States v. Too Toy* (1911), Judge Learned Hand
ruled that Congress had given the executive branch the power to determine
citizenship and the difficulties the government would encounter in proving
its case justified treating U.S. citizens equally to immigrants under Chinese
exclusion.[67] The court upheld that power in exclusion and deportation
cases, ruling that both were based on the same power of sovereignty. This
power to deport, Judge Hand wrote, exists "because it is a necessary incident to an unquestioned constitutional power, to the exercise of which it is
a reasonable adjective regulation." He continued, "A citizen, like anyone
else, must submit to that determination, if it be a reasonable adjunct to an
admitted national power. Therefore I affirm the holding of the commissioner that the defendant must affirmatively show that he was born within
the United States."[68]

The Bureau of Immigration's powers to determine citizenship in those
districts with supportive courts would not last, however. In 1922, when the
Supreme Court heard *Ng Fong Ho v. White*, its decision clearly took the
power to determine citizenship in deportation cases away from the Bureau
of Immigration. In 1922, two men, Gin Sang Get and Gin Sang Mo, challenged their deportations as part of the case, claiming U.S. citizenship
because their fathers were U.S. citizens.[69] (By 1922, statutes allowed for

citizenship to be transmitted through a father, in addition to obtaining citizenship from birth on U.S. soil.)[70] Both men had arrived at the port of San Francisco, where immigration agents admitted them as U.S. citizens. Bureau agents later arrested both men, and they were ordered to be deported. Gin Sang Get and Gin Sang Mo appealed their cases, arguing that citizenship could not be decided in an executive hearing held by immigration officials. Immigration officials argued that Gin Sang Get and Gin Sang Mo had no right to appeal the Bureau of Immigration's decision because Congress gave the bureau final say unless the deportees could prove they had been denied due process. The issue for the Court was to decide whether their claims of U.S. citizenship gave Gin Sang Get and Gin Sang Mo the right to a judicial trial.[71]

In *Ng Fong Ho v. White,* the Court found that as U.S. citizens, Gin Sang Get and Gin Sang Mo had a right to a judicial hearing. "Jurisdiction," explained Justice Louis Brandeis, "in the executive to order deportation exists only if the person arrested is an alien. The claim of citizenship is thus a denial of an essential jurisdictional fact."[72] The Court stated that deportation of a citizen represented banishment, which clearly violated a citizen's Fifth Amendment rights. "To deport one who so claims to be a citizen," Brandeis wrote, "obviously deprives him of liberty. . . . It may result also in loss of both property and life, or of all that makes life worth living. Against the danger of such deprivation without the sanction afforded by judicial proceedings, the Fifth Amendment affords protection in its guarantee of due process of law."[73]

Since *Ng Fong Ho* was a Supreme Court decision, the lower courts had to follow the precedent. Immigration agents in those judicial districts that had supported the power of immigration agents to collapse citizenship rights into the lesser immigrant ones could no longer do so. *Ng Fong Ho,* therefore, drew ever more distinctive boundaries between the rights of U.S. citizens and the rights of immigrants.

Ng Fong Ho did not, however, apply to exclusions. People at the borders trying to enter the United States did not gain access to the courts if immigration officials did not believe them. Once a person crossed into the United States, he or she could have access to the courts to determine citizenship. The Supreme Court's decision, therefore, endorsed broader rights to judicial hearings for people claiming U.S. citizenship on U.S. soil.

In 1924, a deportation case brought to light just how different deportation had become from exclusion.[74] Soo Hoo Yee was a U.S. citizen, born in

San Jose, California, in 1878. In 1918, Soo Hoo Yee traveled to China, where he lived for five years. When he returned to the United States, he entered the country illicitly because he feared that immigration authorities would exclude him. He sailed from China to Vancouver. From there, he took a train to Montreal. Early in the evening of June 14, an unnamed person drove him into Vermont. Soo Hoo Yee slept in the woods that night and in the morning, "walked to Cambridge Junction, where he took a train for St. Johnsbury, Vt."[75] Later that day, immigration agents arrested him for entering the country unlawfully and for violating the Chinese exclusion laws. They believed that his illicit entry went a long way to proving his deportability. On June 27, at his deportation hearing, he argued that as a U.S. citizen, immigration agents did not have a right to proceed. The immigration officials hearing his case ordered his deportation, but since his citizenship claim ensured him access to a judicial hearing, he appealed.

The court believed Soo Hoo Yee's U.S. citizenship claim and the justices even underscored the importance of his illicit entry because of the risks exclusion represented to his citizenship. The court wrote, "It is true that the manner of his return to the United States in June, 1923, was unwise and most indiscreet. It indicates a desire to escape the observation of the inspection officers with whom he thought he might have trouble." But, as the court saw it, "A person of his race well understood the difficulty he would encounter in establishing his right to enter the country under the circumstances."[76] The material point for the court in deciding in Soo Hoo Yee's favor was not his illicit entry; it was his U.S. citizenship. On that point, the judges found "no evidence in the record to contradict the testimony which he [Soo Hoo Yee] gave on that subject and which is substantiated by other witnesses."[77] Consequently, the court ruled in Soo Hoo Yee's favor.[78]

While the term "exclusion" was sometimes used interchangeably with "deportation," and while exclusions and deportations were rooted in the same power, they came to refer to two distinct legal procedures at the turn of the twentieth century. Exclusion meant the act of keeping an immigrant out of a country in the first place, while deportation meant removal from U.S. soil.

The cases of John Turner, Chan Leong Hee, and Ng Fong Ho, important to setting this logic of deportation policy, also contributed to the ways that deportations served to distinguish three legal categories of people on U.S. soil—citizens, lawfully admitted immigrants, and those who entered

CHINESE EXAMINATION STATION, MALONE, N. Y.

CHINESE EXAMINATION STATION, RICHFORD, VT.

Figure 3. Soo Hoo Yee was likely detained in Richford, Vermont,
after entering the United States from Canada. Wong You, discussed
in Chapter 1, would have perhaps been detained in the Malone
Station, New York. "Chinese Examination Station, Malone, N.Y.";
"Chinese Examination Station, Richford, VT.," *AR-CGI* (1904).

in violation of immigration law. Deportation cases demarcated liberties and
rights of U.S. citizens from those of immigrants in either of the two latter
categories. Yet, the distinctions were in some ways fluid. Furthermore, since
most deportation provisions did not formally control for actions taken on
U.S. soil, what an immigrant did after landing in the United States did not
make the immigrant deportable.

One more reason for fluidity between the categories had to do with race
and Chinese exclusion. The legal status of people of Chinese heritage—
either as U.S. citizens or lawful residents—was far more precarious than
that of any other immigrant group. U.S. officials administering immigration law at times tried to collapse all three categories of people of Chinese
descent into one, as those who entered in the United States in violation of
law. This strategy depended on immigration authorities' ability to treat U.S.
citizens of Chinese heritage and Chinese immigrants alike when it came to

their rights to due process and burden of proof. In some of the cases under Chinese exclusion, people of Chinese descent, immigration officers, and the courts struggled over what it meant, in practice, that a citizen could not be deported, and what it meant to claim citizenship at all.

An important turning point to this national logic of deportation would develop when the government successfully established the power to deport for post-entry infractions. It did so over fears of an international trade in women, as Chapter 4 will explain. Once the government firmly established this power, the rights of lawful immigrants would be further differentiated from those of a citizen. After that, immigration officers would revisit Chinese exclusion and revise policy to limit liberties that people like Chan Leong Hee had fought to ensure.

This book now turns from examining the national and international logic of deportations to the specific rationales for deportation from the United States: antiprostitution, political grounds, and economic grounds. Each of these significantly changed the scale and scope of the power to deport and U.S. deportation policy.

Chapter 4

From Protection to Punishment

In 1915, Ellen Costello found herself deported from the United States. Costello had worked in circuses across Europe and North America from the age of seventeen. She also performed burlesque in Canada and the United States for about a year. By the age of thirty-one, she had settled in New York City, where state police officers arrested her on prostitution charges. She was found guilty and sentenced to a brief term in New York City's notorious prison on Blackwell's Island. After Costello served her sentence, Bureau of Immigration officers took her into custody, held a deportation hearing, and sent her to Holland, her country of emigration.[1] Costello's case reflected a major development in the U.S. government's power to deport. In the antiprostitution provision that led to Costello's deportation, policy makers created the explicit governmental power to deport for actions taken while on U.S. soil—for post-entry infractions.

The impetus to develop the antiprostitution provision was a moral panic about prostitution and sex trafficking. Ellis D. Bruler, the commissioner of immigration in charge of the state of Washington, wrote in his annual report for 1913 that prostitution was "an ever-present evil which will require ceaseless attention in order to prevent the undermining of the social fabric." "There possibly is no other evil," he continued, "so far-reaching or so deadly in its ultimate results, and consequently there is no other evil which requires such constant vigilance."[2] Bruler was not alone in this analysis. Many others believed that immigrant prostitution was a grievous problem and that an international sex trade in women, the white-slave trade, was getting much worse by the day. Americans published almost a billion pages on prostitution and white slavery between 1900 and 1924.[3] Just what represented white slavery turned out to be difficult to concretely define; its meaning was broad and changed several times. The actual data on the rise of prostitution, however, hinted less at an epidemic than a politically and culturally driven moral panic.[4]

In their panic, Americans resorted to law: bolstering antiprostitution ordinances to help close down red-light districts—neighborhoods wherein prostitution, gambling, and drinking were concentrated—around the country. Not satisfied with local initiatives, reformers took their concern to the international stage. Representatives from the United States participated in several international conferences to suppress what they termed the "trade in young girls and women."[5] After a 1902 meeting, governments from around the world drafted a treaty to suppress prostitution. The treaty, which the U.S. Senate ratified in March 1905, required surveillance at all ports of entry, established formal procedures for the exchange of information, and set criminal sanctions to stop an international trade in young women.[6]

A major front of this larger campaign involved U.S. immigration policy. In the late nineteenth century, U.S. immigration policy had been concerned with prostitution, but it was limited and racialized. Congress had created the right to exclude prostitutes under the 1875 Page Act, but it made no provision for their deportation.[7] In intent and administration, the law specifically applied to women immigrating to the United States from China. Moreover, none of the other immigration laws passed between 1875 and 1902 contained an antiprostitution provision, though the federal government did deport a small number of Chinese women suspected of prostitution under Chinese exclusion.[8] As popular concern over white slavery grew, federal lawmakers and immigration officials turned their attention from Chinese women to the far larger immigration stream out of Europe. In 1903, Congress passed a new general immigration act that included an antiprostitution provision. Under this law, "prostitutes, and persons who procure or attempt to bring in prostitutes or women for the purpose of prostitution" could be deported if found within the United States within three years of their arrival.[9]

Between the passage of this law in 1903 and the outbreak of World War I, prostitution became the second largest deportable category, behind only those likely to become a public charge. Policy makers conceptualized a different purpose for this provision than all the others. They hoped that the antiprostitution provision could be used as a form of humanitarian intervention to care for women, who constituted between 30 and 40 percent of immigrants to the United States, as a kind of protected legal class.[10] A deportation under the antiprostitution provision, policy makers believed, could return women victimized by prostitution and white slavery to their communities of origin, where family, friends, women's organizations, and religious officials could care for and "reform" them. For this purpose, policy makers grafted unique procedures onto the existing arrest procedures, budgetary constraints, and detention protocols common to most turn-of-the-century deportations in an effort to realize their aspirations of making the provision operate as a kind of victims' rights program. Lawmakers' efforts to intervene in the sex trade also brought immigration enforcement into new kinds of crime control, including the power to deport immigrants for post-entry infractions, which remained important long after the panic over white slavery.

The Mechanics of General Immigration Deportations

In the year immediately after passage of the 1903 law, deportation cases involving prostitution still shared much in common with all deportations under general deportation policy. From the arrest, to the hearing, to possible detention, immigration authorities pieced together procedures for deporting people from the United States. It would be to these common proceedings, as will be examined below, that officials would add special procedures in their efforts to make the antiprostitution provision a victims' rights program.

In 1907, after immigration agents arrested a woman named Berthe Olivice, she paid a $5,000 bond and was released from federal custody until her deportation hearing. Three months later, she defended herself at a hearing before a Board of Special Inquiry in New York. Olivice initially claimed that she was a dressmaker from Paris and therefore not deportable as a prostitute. Immigration agents had, however, prepared a solid case against her, and after they presented their evidence, Olivice admitted that she had, in fact, been a prostitute both before and after her immigration. The board found Olivice guilty and ordered her deported to France.[11]

Maria Hernandez and Maria Carillo had both emigrated from the same town in Mexico and were working in a Texas brothel when immigration agents arrested them for prostitution. Hernandez and Carillo could not afford a lawyer, so they, like Berthe Olivice, represented themselves at their deportation hearing. After the hearing, the Bureau of Immigration deported Hernandez for violating the antiprostitution provision. They deported Carillo on two violations of immigration law: that she was a prostitute and that she had entered the United States without inspection.[12]

The first step in the deportation proceedings of Olivice, Hernandez, and Carillo under the existing deportation provisions began with immigration agents, who prepared a "preliminary hearing" at which they presented the evidence that would be used to justify a warrant of arrest. The evidence in preliminary hearings could include unsworn witness statements, anonymous tips, and incriminating remarks made by an alien.[13] In the case of Berthe Olivice, immigration agents searched the card index of ship manifests at Ellis Island to determine if Olivice had arrived in the United States within the previous three years; if so, she would be deportable. Agents were also prosecuting the man suspected as Olivice's procurer or pimp, Jan Amadee Couzin. Officials attempted to connect Olivice to Couzin in order to gather evidence on his "importation of her"—another violation of immigration law. The inspector at Ellis Island discovered that, while Olivice and Couzin did not arrive together, they both provided the ship's manifest list with the same fake New York City address. That evidence helped convict Olivice and Couzin as a prostitute and procurer.[14]

When Bureau of Immigration agents possessed evidence to indicate that an individual was in violation of immigration law, they applied to the commissioner general of immigration in Washington for a warrant of arrest. The commissioner general, at least as outlined in the regulations, would examine the application to determine that enough evidence existed to justify the warrant and, if so, issue it. Immigration inspectors complained that the mail was too slow to efficiently enforce the laws, especially against prostitutes and procurers. In response to these concerns, the bureau began to rely more and more on telegraphic warrants, which the commissioner general issued without examining any evidence, relying instead on the word of the agents. Once they had a warrant in hand, agents could arrest an accused immigrant, who would then be held for a deportation hearing.[15]

After an arrest, an immigrant who could afford to pay a bond would be released but was expected to return to the custody of immigration agents on the day of the hearing. Immigrants without financial means were held in departmental custody, sometimes for months, while they awaited a hearing. Some immigrants were detained in prisons, some in charitable institutions, and some in immigration offices.

For the government, pursuing deportation cases was expensive. The costs included those for trials, incarcerations, and transportation, as well as the salaries for agents, all of which came out of the fund for the administration of immigration law, which consisted of fees paid by immigrants when they entered the country.[16] Immigration inspectors incurred expenses, too, especially while investigating cases in other regions and even, occasionally, in other countries.[17] Immigration agents and inspectors generally paid their travel expenses out of their own pockets, for which they would subsequently submit reports for reimbursement.[18] In one case involving prostitutes and a "notorious procurer," the Bureau of Immigration paid private detectives in Canada to track down witnesses.[19] The Bureau of Immigration also paid interpreters for depositions.[20] It paid women and men who had their deportations delayed in order to secure their testimony at another hearing one dollar a day for each day they were incarcerated leading up to the trial.[21] Congress tried to reduce mounting costs by holding transportation companies responsible for paying the return passage for deported immigrants. Both the immigration acts and the written rules of deportation policy stated that shipping companies had to supply the costs of the return trip of the deportee. But if the evidence did not clearly indicate which company was responsible for bringing an immigrant into the United States, the government had to pay transportation costs.[22]

The government often weighed its budget against the possibility of proving deportability, and in this calculation not all deportees and witnesses were detained. In 1915, for example, Bureau of Immigration agents wanted to hold a woman, Helen Jeffries, to testify against her procurer. Bureau officials believed if she were released she would flee the country. The local district attorney, however, released Jeffries on her own recognizance, believing that he already had enough written statements to secure the conviction. After examining the case, the Bureau of Immigration agreed with the district attorney, and the department did not pay the costs of detaining Jeffries.[23] The reliance on bond was another practice that saved the bureau from having to pay witnesses detained by the government. A person whose deportation had been delayed in order to testify at the hearing of another immigrant could pay a bond and be released until the revised deportation date.[24]

As another cost-saving measure, religious and charitable organizations housed some of the immigrants who awaited their hearings or deportations at no cost. The Catholic Church, for instance, housed Marie Schetter following her arrest in 1908.[25] The Crittenton Mission, a home in New York for "lost and fallen girls," boarded Violet Runsdayl during her deportation trial.[26] With the outbreak of World War I in 1914, the U.S. government delayed all deportations to Europe until the cessation of hostilities, when it could guarantee the safety of the deportees. To defray the skyrocketing expenses of detaining immigrants at this time, the Bureau of Immigration instructed agents to house as many deportees as possible with charitable organizations until the end of the war.[27]

After a deportation order had been issued, immigrants were sometimes allowed to leave the country voluntarily and at other times were taken to the border by immigration agents, either individually or as a member of a deportation "party."[28] Helen Jeffries, for example, returned to Canada by herself.[29] In 1913, the Bureau of Immigration began instructing agents to coordinate deportation parties as another cost-saving measure. As the bureau described them, deportation parties generally began at one border and traveled to another, picking up deportees from various districts along the way. Parties headed west from New York, for example, stopped in Chicago. In 1920, Leo B. Russell, the immigration inspector in charge of deportation and transportation, observed, "Parties from the west coast generally leave San Francisco or Seattle. A specially constructed kitchen coach is furnished by the Southern Pacific Railroad, and meals are furnished at the rate of 75 cents each." The railroad provided guards and meals at a fixed rate, Russell noted, saving "annually a tremendous amount of money to the Government because of the fact that the rates for meals and guarding [were] so much cheaper than if the department had to pay those ordinarily charged by the railroad companies."[30] In 1920, the bureau organized nine cross-country deportation parties and another one to El Paso, Texas. Altogether that year, 1,479 aliens were transported to a border for deportation, 770 independently and 709 in deportation parties.[31] In 1923, the Bureau of Immigration estimated that the deportation party system saved the department about $20,000.[32]

The proceedings, expenses, rules of detention, and deportation parties all composed the turn-of-the-twentieth-century deportation regime within the United States. Policy makers, however, created the antiprostitution provision as a specific response to deal with the moral panic over white slavery and the sex trade. To do so, they would graft a unique set of procedures onto the general deportation proceedings.

The Antiprostitution Provision as a Victim's Rights Program

A key goal of the antiprostitution provision in the minds of policy makers and immigration agents was more than simply the deportation of women involved in the sex trade. Officials were driven by their concern over white slavery, what popular discourses described as a massive, global trade in women. As historians have documented, the definition of the white-slave trade changed several times, and, in the end, the term was difficult to concretely define.[33] In the early twentieth century, Americans triangulated a definition, resting it on Progressive Era notions about women's respectability, reputation, race, morality, and sexuality. Policy makers hoped to use deportation to intervene in white slavery. To do so, they added a set of procedures designed to make the antiprostitution provision operate in what would become known later in the century as a victims' rights program.

When Congress created the antiprostitution provision, there was some debate over the extent of immigrant prostitution and white slavery. Some believed it to be rampant. Edwin W. Sims, the U.S. attorney in Chicago, claimed, for example, that "the white slave traffic is a system operated by a syndicate . . . and that the selling price [of a young girl] is from $200 to $600."[34] Marcus Braun, a special undercover agent for the Bureau of Immigration, who investigated in Europe, Mexico, Canada, and the United States, estimated that there were 10,000 pimps and procurers and 50,000 foreign-born prostitutes in the United States.[35]

Those on the other side of the debate questioned both the veracity of these studies and the very existence of a large, global network of white slavers. Some argued that both the number of foreign-born prostitutes in the United States and the extent of the global white-slave trade were grossly overstated. Researchers like Braun based their reports on very little evidence and tended to overstate the numbers of prostitutes by conflating sexual promiscuity with prostitution.[36] One contemporary study of New York City arrest records between November 1908 and March 1909 found that neither white slavery nor foreign prostitution were statistically significant problems. During that year, 2,093 women were arrested for prostitution, only 19 percent of whom were foreign born.[37] In this study, immigrant women were actually underrepresented; in 1910, immigrants made up 41 percent of the total population in New York City.[38] The commissioner of immigration in New York was also at a loss to explain the public fervor over white slavery. "The total number of immoral women arrested and deported under authority of the Secretary of Commerce and Labor since I became Commissioner of Immigration is 33," he told a U.S. official in 1907, "the total number of aliens excluded at the time of arrival on the ground of immorality is 19; the total number of convictions under Section 3 of the Immigration Act of March 3, 1903 is 6."[39]

Congress and key members in the Bureau of Immigration came down on the side that perceived immigrant prostitution as a serious, large-scale problem. Congress expanded who could be deported under the antiprostitution provision in the Immigration Act of 1907. The new law broadened the logic of the 1903 immigration law's exclusion of any "woman or girl for the purposes of prostitution" to any "alien for the purpose of prostitution, or for any other immoral purpose." The 1907 law, as historian Mark Connelly writes, "made guilt by association grounds for arrest, prosecution, and possible deportation."[40]

One of the reasons for writing guilt by association into the revised law came from the fact that Congress operated on a very narrow definition of a woman's consent and an expansive one of a woman's victimhood. As scholar Pamela Haag points out, the Progressive reformers who influenced lawmakers did not consider "a woman's choice to act sexually immoral or practice prostitution . . . as a free, consensual choice." Reformers considered acts of sexual immorality, in effect, as "de facto nonconsensual and violent—not a 'genuine' enactment of a woman's sexual will." White slavery's victims, one government publication stated, were "those women who, if given a fair chance, would . . . have been good wives, mothers and useful citizens."[41] Understood in these terms, women practicing immoral sexuality were innocent victims of exploitation. Acts of sexuality, even commercial sexuality, became prima facie evidence of violence done to women.[42] Lawmakers, moved by this understanding of white slavery and the victimhood of women, wrote it into the 1907 law, hoping deportation proceedings would serve as an intervention to help make women into "wives, mothers and useful citizens."[43]

The 1907 law's centering of women's victimhood made the antiprostitution provision broad enough to conflate prostitution with white slavery. Immigration agents, for example, used the term "white slavery," sometimes referring to women perceived to have been coerced into prostitution or other sexual acts and sometimes to more traditional prostitution cases.[44] Take the case of the French immigrant woman arrested by the Los Angeles Police Department for running a brothel patronized by Japanese men.

Nowhere in her immigration files was there any testimony proving that this woman had been induced into prostitution; in fact, the evidence suggested that she had practiced prostitution in France before immigrating to the United States.[45] Yet the Bureau of Immigration treated this case as a white-slave case. A letter in the immigration file stated, "pursuant to the international agreement for the suppression of the white slave trade we are notifying Paris, France, and its central bureau for the suppression of the white slave trade in the ministry of the interior."[46] Historian David Langum found similar application in his study of the Progressive Era. "The term 'white slavery,'" Langum writes, "varied in meaning from coerced, imprisoned women to a psychological bondage to purely voluntary prostitution. Some . . . distinguished a free-will prostitute from a white slave. Others thought that prostitution and white slavery were the same thing."[47] The 1907 act wrote into law a provision that was broad enough so that in administration, immigration officials could launch deportation proceedings in prostitution cases, framed as white slavery cases.

Using a narrower definition of "whiteness" than that found in naturalization, but broader than some other definitions, officials' efforts prioritized helping women who were racially white. In some exceptional cases, immigration agents applied the white slavery label to women racially understood to be Asian or Mexican. In 1916, the inspector in charge of Chinese exclusion for New York and New Jersey, for example, reporting on "white-slave matters," stated, "That this traffic unquestionably exists among the Chinese in its most vicious form can not be gainsaid."[48] Most of the women processed under the antiprostitution provision when it was understood as a kind of social welfare program, however, were classified as white. Naturalization law defined whiteness as people of European and Mexican descent. In the Southwest, despite their de jure (legal) status in federal naturalization as white, people of Mexican heritage faced racism from a range of forces, including vigilante violence, state and local law, and dual wage systems. Eugenicists and those following the emerging field of scientific racism defined whiteness differently. Eugenicists described a hierarchy of ethnicities, in which some Europeans were less white than others. A virulent strain of popular racism behind a resurgence of the Ku Klux Klan defined whiteness narrowly, excluding Italians, Catholics, Jews, and Mexicans in addition to African Americans. Among the many definitions for white as a racial category, as the immigration records and the work of scholars on white slavery focusing on women have shown, the category of whiteness used in the enforcement of the efforts against white slavery was largely defined by European heritage.[49]

In 1914, the Bureau of Immigration added maternal and paternal procedures for administering the antiprostitution provision to bring it in line with the larger goal of having the provision work as a victims' rights program. The bureau hired Kate Waller Barrett, president of the National Council of Women and the National Florence Crittenton Mission, to make recommendations for improving the treatment of women in the custody of the Bureau of Immigration. In her "Proposed Plan for Treatment, Arrest, and Return to Their Native Countries of Women and Girls Excluded or Ordered Deported," Barrett proposed that "immoral" cases be handled differently from other deportations in the interests of "kindness." Women and girls, Barrett argued, should not be incarcerated in jails; they should instead be housed in "philanthropic and religious societies, preferably of the nationality or religious sect of the alien."[50] Here, Barrett insisted, detention practices should take into account that women arrested under the antiprostitution provision were vulnerable and victims. Detention could serve both as an opportunity to remove women from the sex trade and as an opportunity for religious authorities to help them. The Bureau of Immigration recommended adopting most of Barrett's proposals. The bureau's *Annual Report* proposed that "women and girls of immoral character" in departmental custody should be placed under the exclusive jurisdiction of female employees. If there were no female employees, then the commissioner in charge was to contact a local private organization to care for the female immigrant. Agents were also to stop detaining women and girls in prisons, unless authorized by the bureau.[51]

Barrett's plan also contained recommendations to ensure that women received additional care after their deportations. Barrett suggested that when a woman was investigated for deportation on antiprostitution grounds, the commissioner general of immigration contact a national committee of women in her home country. That organization would investigate the "conditions under which the woman or girl will be forced to live after her return," in part to ensure "her proper care and attention after her arrival there." After deportation, each woman would then be "brought under proper surveillance and influence when landed on the other side." This "care" would, Barrett hoped, prevent the further "degradation of the alien" and place deportees "in the way of opportunities for reformation."[52]

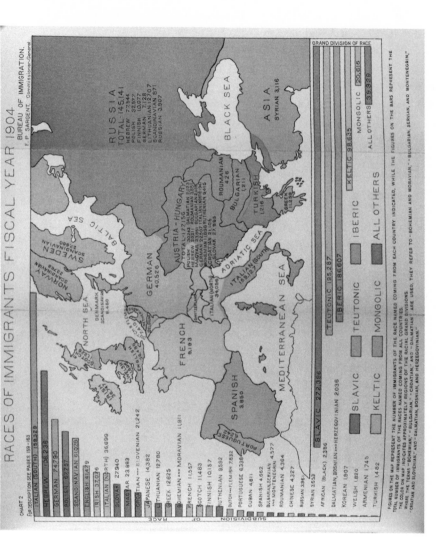

Figure 4. This map depicts racial categories of immigrants, many of which reflected a eugenicist understanding of Europeans. In the white slavery panic, people from Europe were also racially grouped as white. "Races of Immigrants Fiscal Year 1904," *AR-CGI* (1904).

In this respect, Barrett hoped that for those women deported, the process would help "reform" them by providing better care.

The Bureau of Immigration commissioned Barrett to travel to Europe to build a network of international acquaintances to help protect and care for women after their deportations.[53] The bureau encouraged Barrett to get the endorsement of the International Council of Women to help her approach European aid societies that might work with the U.S. government. The condensed report published in the bureau's *Annual Report* suggests that Barrett was relatively successful in doing so. She met with women's organizations across Europe to establish agreements concerning deported women and girls "guilty of certain immoral acts."[54] She composed a list of councils of women and contact names of women's societies "which have pledged their cooperation with the United States Government for the after care of deported women."[55] On the receiving end, policy makers like Barrett hoped that women ordered deported under the antiprostitution provision would be cared for maternally, too. The outbreak of World War I on the continent a few months later interrupted their efforts.

A few years before Barrett's plan, in 1908, a Canadian woman in New York named Josephine Bissonette faced deportation under the antiprostitution provision. The rhetoric behind the case, her family's involvement, immigration officials' commitment to carrying out her deportation, and her defenses against the charges were all relatively common in antiprostitution cases. But as the case proceeded, U.S. officials began to see that Bissonette's family was lying. The brother and mother were manipulating U.S. deportation policy in a fight over inheritance. Following her case in some detail illuminates how the antiprostitution provision operated.

The case began when Bissonette's brother and mother contacted a U.S. commissioner of immigration, asking him to begin deportation proceedings against Josephine, claiming that she conducted a house of prostitution.[56] They hoped, they said, that having Josephine returned to Canada could "better help her lead a moral life." The family seemed to be using U.S. deportation policy to "help" Josephine Bissonette. The family even went so far as to hire an attorney, a Mr. Gorman, who had also worked as a consular officer for the United States in Montreal, to facilitate Bissonette's deportation to Canada. Gorman arranged for testimony from a second brother and five other witnesses, all of whom testified to Bissonette's immorality. After hearing these allegations, officers from the Bureau of Immigration arrested Bissonette.[57] An immigration judge then ordered her deportation to Canada, where those on the receiving end could help in her "reformation." In this case, her family rather than an aid society seemed to be willing to step up to the task.

Josephine Bissonette contested her deportation immediately. With accumulated savings of about two thousand dollars, she hired a lawyer who built her case.[58] In her first hearing, Bissonette successfully countered accusations of immorality and running a brothel. She was still ordered deported, though, not on charges of prostitution, but on charges that she had entered the United States without inspection.[59] Immigration officials' attempt to deport Bissonette for entering without inspection rested on their ability to use another deportation provision as a proxy for the real grounds of deportation.[60] Immigration officials, as examined in Chapter 1, used other provisions when they handled Chinese immigrants under general immigration law. In Bissonette's case, after her first hearing, immigration inspectors admitted that there was not enough evidence to deport her on charges of prostitution, but rather than drop the case altogether, they turned to another provision to carry out the deportation. A few months before Bissonette's case began, Bissonette traveled to Canada to bury her sister. After doing so, she returned to New York in a first-class train car. Immigration officials routinely inspected third-class passengers but only rarely inspected first- and second-class passengers.[61] Bissonette arrived in New York without incident, but immigration officials would later use this uninspected entry as the proxy grounds for her deportation. Thus, immigration officials continued to try to deport Bissonette, technically through a different provision, in order to carry out the spirit of the antiprostitution provision.

Bissonette's lawyer refused to accept defeat. Utilizing his own family connections, he persuaded a New York City judge to write a letter to the commissioner general of immigration in Washington, D.C. The letter had its intended effect: Bissonette secured a rehearing of her case.[62] His next step in her defense was to disprove the hearsay evidence and testimony used at her first deportation hearing. He argued that Bissonette's brother and mother thought that they should receive a larger share of the inheritance from Bissonette's sister's estate and when Bissonette refused to send more money, the brother threatened that they would "drive her away from New York."[63]

Bissonette's lawyer countered the very strong discourses about consent and victimhood written into policy, which had been behind her deportation in the first place, by proving his client's respectability. A grocer who lived in the same building as Bissonette, a physician who had practiced in New

York City for forty-seven years and who had known her since 1876, her longtime lawyer, a real-estate manager for a large butcher company, an artist and author, and Bissonette's building superintendent all testified on her behalf. They testified that she had worked as a domestic servant for two families during her first seven years in New York City and then, for the next eighteen years, had cared for her married sister, who struggled with mental illness.[64] After her sister suffered a mental breakdown, the State of New York appointed Bissonette as a "committee of her person" to care for her. At the time of her appointment, Bissonette provided a $75,000 bond, furnished by surety companies, to hold her accountable for the proper care of her sister. Bissonette made frequent reports to the bonding company documenting that she was, in fact, acting according to law and in the best interest of her sister. The bonding company investigated the sister's affairs, several times, always concluding that Bissonette was a moral, law-abiding woman.[65] All of this testimony convinced the immigration officials hearing her case. They canceled Bissonette's warrant of deportation, which meant they overlooked her technical violation of entering the country without inspection. What made immigration agents willing to do so was, in addition to her ability to afford a good lawyer, the picture the defense painted of a respectable, twentieth-century working-class woman.[66]

The importance of respectability that ran through Bissonette's case helped a small subset of women actually involved in the sex trade "unmake" their deportability or obtain a stay in deportation.[67] In 1916, for example, immigration authorities in San Francisco arrested an immigrant named Berthe Husson under the antiprostitution provision. Husson was from France and, as a commissioner noted in the annual report, she was "of the peasant class, who, after being inveigled into marriage was brought to this country and immediately placed in a disreputable house" by her husband. The Board of Special Inquiry found her to have been involved in the sex trade but allowed her to remain in the country. The hearing's outcome did not upset immigration authorities. In fact, they praised it. The commissioner wrote, "The commendable attitude of the department in its efforts to uplift and improve the conditions of these unfortunate women is emphasized by the fact that, instead of deporting the woman, she was granted parole to a philanthropic association which secured suitable employment for her."[68]

For a woman to stay her deportation, she needed to present respectability and a compelling narrative of female victimhood. The case of Marie

Schetter is a revealing example. Schetter was a young, single immigrant who had worked as both a nurse and a domestic servant in Germany. According to her testimony, she met Marie Gau during the Atlantic passage to the United States.[69] Gau offered Schetter domestic employment in California and a free train ticket from New York, but, much to Schetter's dismay, the ticket took her to Seattle, where Gau and her husband apparently forced her into prostitution.[70] In 1908, immigration authorities arrested Schetter. According to the investigation by immigration agent W. W. Husband, Schetter was "from a good and respectable Prussian family and was a governess and then trained four years as a nurse and . . . he believed that because she was innocent and did not speak English, she was tricked into prostitution by Mrs. Gau."[71] He wrote that Schetter was a "naturally good girl and behaves lady like" and recommended against her deportation.[72] Therefore, despite the fact that Schetter could have been deported for practicing prostitution, her status as a victim that so convincingly fit the white slavery narrative allowed her to remain.[73]

A component critical to a successful stay of deportation was the willingness of male religious and charitable officials to assume a paternal role. After her arrest, Marie Schetter was housed at the Catholic diocese. While there, she became acquainted with Reverend Emil Kauten, chancellor of the Diocese of Seattle, and Reverend Hugh Gallagher, the president of Seattle College.[74] At her deportation hearing, both men testified that Schetter was a hardworking, moral immigrant who deserved a second chance. They told the panel that Schetter "already had several job offers and has given testimony against Gau and her husband/accomplice."[75] The priests then agreed to be morally and financially responsible for her and to see that she would not become deportable in the future. Similarly, in 1915 Anna Pfister, another woman ordered to be deported, gained the support of a representative of the Women's American Baptist Home Missionary Society, who agreed to take charge of Pfister and find her suitable employment.[76] Pfister, too, received a stay in her deportation.[77]

The federal government set out to serve as a paternal and maternal force in the name of caring for immigrant women with the antiprostitution provision. Officials hoped the power to arrest, detain, and deport immigrants would serve to protect women by returning them to their homes and families. In cases like Husson's, their efforts included staying a deportation. In a small way, stays of deportation represented an expansion of authority to control immigration behavior on U.S. soil through deportation policy. For women like Husson, residence in the United States was contingent on future "respectable" behavior. Laws passed in 1910 gave immigration authorities far wider legal jurisdiction over the actions of immigrants.

Post-Entry Infractions and Federal Police Power

From the start, in addition to their aspirations to have it serve as a victims' rights program, policy makers had conceived of the antiprostitution provision to prosecute those running the sex trade. Operating what amounted to a new punitive mandate in immigration policy depended on two interrelated developments—the creation of a federal police power and the broad power to deport for post-entry infractions.[78] With these developments, prostitutes and those associated with the sex trade would become the second-largest category of deported immigrants. Of the 1,577 people deported by the Bureau of Immigration in 1911, 422, or nearly 27 percent, were deported on prostitution-related grounds.[79] Between 1913 and 1918, about 400 people were deported annually on charges that they practiced prostitution, procured prostitutes, or received the proceeds of prostitution.[80] Reaching these numbers required the Bureau of Immigration and Congress to get around the Supreme Court, which in 1909 ruled the newly created police power—a linchpin in the new anticrime or punitive mandate—was unconstitutional.

The antiprostitution provision was not the first time immigration authorities took up crime control. Congress had included a criminal-status provision in deportation policy dating back to the 1875 Page Act, but it focused only on keeping immigrants with criminal backgrounds from landing on U.S. soil.[81] The Page Act did not contain a provision allowing for the deportation of immigrants if they managed to land on U.S. soil in violation of the law. Nor did it contain a deportation provision to deal with immigrants who committed crimes on U.S. soil. In 1882, Congress passed another immigration law that expanded the definition of an immigrant's criminal past to include "persons who have been convicted of a felony or other infamous crime or misdemeanor involving moral turpitude."[82] Nine years later, Congress matched the exclusion with a deportation provision.[83] After 1891, immigrants to the United States became deportable for crimes that they committed while outside the United States. In practice, the early criminal-status provision was almost never used. In 1896, the Bureau of

II.

Q. What is your full name?
A. Marie S———.
Q. How old are you?
A. Twenty-five years.
Q. Are you still a German subject?
A. Yes.
Q. Never been married?
A. No.
Q. What occupation did you have in Germany?
A. First I was four years a trained nurse in Germany, then I went to France and was a governess for one year, and after that I came home and assisted running the house.
Q. Where are your parents?
A. In ———, Prussia, and also my four brothers.
Q. When did you first leave Europe for the United States?
A. On the 29th of September this year; I left Bremerhoffen on the steamship *Kaiser Wilhelm II*, on the same day as Marie G———.
Q. Who is this Marie G———?
A. I do not know her except that I became acquainted with her on board the ship; I do not know her parents.
Q. Where were you going when you left Germany?
A. I wanted to go to Rochester, N. Y., in company with my friend, Katie H———, and was a friend of my mother's, and she frequently visited us, and I had the intention of coming to America; and on one of these occasions she told me if I wanted to come with her I could.
Q. Where did you go when you landed in New York?
A. We went to the Hotel ———, in Hoboken.
Q. Who went with you to the ——— Hotel?
A. Marie G———, Mr. Kalt S———, and his brother, and Miss Eliza W———, a girl that Marie G——— brought over with the intention of taking her along with her.
Q. Where did you see Eliza W——— last?
A. Eliza W———'s brother came to the hotel in Hoboken, took her downstairs, had a conversation with her, and probably induced her to go with him, though I was not present at the conversation, because she took her things away and went with her brother. Marie G——— had prepaid her ticket to Seattle, although she told me it was for California; the following day Marie G——— was quite indignant at Eliza's going away, took the ticket away from her, went to the office and had it transferred to my name.
Q. What is the name and address of the brother of Eliza?
A. I do not know; Marie G——— has it.
Q. How did you come to fall in with Marie G———?
A. On my way to Bremerhoffen in the train Marie G——— happened to be in the same compartment. Marie G——— asked whether I was going to America. She asked me all about myself and my family. Had I suspected the nature of her mission I would not have confided anything to her. She told me that she worked very hard around the camps in America as a cook, and also her sister and her husband. The nature of the work that she claimed to have done seemed to me almost impossible for a woman, but she was so emphatic that I believed her. She told all of us that she had to drive for hours sometimes to get water for the camp where she worked, although I doubted it, but I heard so much that I really did not pay any further attention to it after all. She told me that she was a respectable married woman and owned a house in Los Angeles, Cal., and said that she just made a visit to Germany and was going back to Los Angeles, Cal., to join her husband.
Q. What was the name of this husband that Marie G——— spoke of?
A. She gave her name as Marie G——— at the ticket office on the ship, and I naturally thought her husband's name was G———.
Q. On the ship did Marie G——— ask you to go with her to California?
A. No.
Q. Where did she first extend the invitation to you to accompany her?
A. When we arrived at Hoboken my friend from Rochester, N. Y., Katie H———, took sick, an operation was performed on her at Hoboken, and the doctor advised her to remain there some time before proceeding to her home in Rochester. I was alone, did not know the language, and didn't know what to do, and I am not sure whether Marie G——— asked me to accompany her;

Figure 5. Testimony of Marie Schetter, reprinted in the Dillingham Commission Reports, with the names of Schetter and Gau redacted. Dillingham Commission, "Partial Testimony in Two Seattle Cases," *Reports of the Immigration Commission: Importation and Harboring of Women for Immoral Purposes* (Washington, D.C.: Government Printing Office, 1911), 104.

but since Marie G—— had told me that she was a respectable married woman, owned a house, and was going to join her husband in Los Angeles, Cal., I thought it quite natural to ask her if she could not assist me in obtaining a position. She willingly consented. She knew I had no money, and as Eliza's brother took Eliza away, she changed that ticket and asked me to come with her to Los Angeles, Cal. I was of the opinion that we were going to Los Angeles, Cal., and did not think that we were going to Seattle, because Marie G—— had led me all the way to believe that we were going to California. I did not know we were going to Seattle until after we landed here. The same day that we arrived in Seattle she mentioned to me that she was short of money; that we would probably have to stay in Seattle until we had sufficient money to continue the voyage. Marie G—— received $100 in Hoboken and twice on our way West she received $50 each time.

Q. From whom did she get that money?

A. She told me the first $100 came from her sister, and that her sister was well off and married; the second time she told me that she had telegraphed for $50 to a good friend of hers, and how she obtained it the third time I do not know.

Q. When Marie G—— asked you to accompany her, what did you expect to do, what kind of work?

A. I understood either as a nurse, as a governess, or as a domestic.

Q. Did Marie G—— say that she would get you that kind of work?

A. Yes; she said that there was plenty of work and it would be easy here to get a position; she said, " I will be good to you; we will remain together good friends."

Q. When did you reach Seattle?

A. I do not know the exact date, but we were five or six days on the way. In Chicago we remained over night; Marie G—— knew I had no money, and already on the way out she began to treat me rather harshly. The ticket I traveled on was in Eliza W——'s name, and I repeatedly asked her to ask the conductor whether it would be all right, but she always answered me gruffly and said I could stay in Chicago, knowing very well I did not have a cent of my own.

Q. When you reached Seattle with Marie G—— where did you go?

A. We went to a hotel, the name of which I do not know. She told me we will only remain over night. I told her, " How is it we are not going to California? You own a house there." She said to me she had sold the house there in California, and had bought one in Seattle.

Q. How far from the railroad station was the hotel that you and Marie G—— stopped at?

A. Probably ten minutes' walk.

Q. Did you walk up hill or was it on the level?

A. We walked a little on a hill to the right; walked straight up from the station a couple of blocks, and then to the right.

Q. How many nights did you stay at this hotel?

A. Two nights.

Q. Was Marie G—— with you both nights?

A. Yes; I had a room for myself, and Marie with her alleged husband in the other.

Q. Who was this alleged husband?

A. She used to call him Claude; on the ship she did not wear her wedding ring, but when she came here she put it on. I presume she put that ring on in order to make believe that she was married.

Q. Then where did you go?

A. After two nights she told me, " Well, now we go to my house." Of course, I did not know the nature of the house. She told me that she left the house in an uncollected state of affairs and that she would have to fix it up; I followed her. The house was not far from the hotel; it was a wide shack; it made a very bad impression on me, but still I went in with her; I saw girls half dressed, and Marie turned on me right away, and said I should not bother about what I saw, and not look around so much.

Q. Where was that house?

A, I do not know; it is the same house where the officers got me.

Q. You went into that house when?

A. It was in October, two days after we arrived in Seattle, about the middle of the month.

Figure 6. Testimony of Marie Schetter, reprinted in the Dillingham Commission Reports, with the names of Schetter and Gau redacted. Dillingham Commission, "Partial Testimony in Two Seattle Cases," *Reports of the Immigration Commission: Importation and Harboring of Women for Immoral Purposes* (Washington, D.C.: Government Printing Office, 1911), 105.

Immigration did not deport a single immigrant under it.[84] Four years later, out of a total of 356 deportations, immigration authorities removed only four people under the criminal-status provision.[85]

Congress's steps with the antiprostitution provision into crime control originated in large part from a new police power. The 1903 Immigration Act included criminal sanctions. The law stated: "Whoever shall import or attempt to import any woman or girl into the United States for the purposes of prostitution, or shall hold or attempt to hold, any woman or girl for such purposes in pursuance of such illegal importation shall be deemed guilty of a felony." If found guilty of procuring in a criminal trial, a person could be imprisoned "not less than one or more than five years and pay a fine not exceeding five thousand dollars." In 1907, Congress added the sweeping phrase "whoever shall keep, maintain, control, support or harbor in any house or other place."[86] Throughout much of the nineteenth century, in addition to controlling crime, police provided services such as feeding and lodging the homeless, inspecting docks, and issuing licenses for serving liquor, among others. With the massive industrialization and urban growth of the late nineteenth and early twentieth centuries, fire departments and city bureaucracies professionalized and, in the process, pared down the broad list of police responsibilities. Meanwhile, state and local governments passed a wave of legislation, from new labor laws to new antiprostitution laws, which expanded the list of crimes. Police saw the breadth of their responsibilities narrow at the same time as the law they enforced expanded.[87] The antiprostitution provision brought the federal government into this expanding police power throughout the country.

Buttressed by the 1907 expansion in the antiprostitution provision, the Bureau of Immigration strengthened its enforcement policies. In March 1908, it established a task force for the sole purpose of "rooting out resident alien women practicing prostitution within three years of entry."[88] Instructions for streamlining of enforcement originally intended to increase deportations under other provisions in 1907 also ended up tightening enforcement of the antiprostitution provision. This occurred when bureau leadership sent out a department circular designed to improve its ability to deport criminals and political radicals by "cooperating" with local authorities and showing them how to conduct deportation investigations.[89] The response to this circular reveals the increased attention immigration offices across the United States were directed to give to the deportation of immigrant prostitutes and procurers.

While the circular ostensibly aimed at increasing the deportations of anarchists and criminals, reports from immigration districts emphasized the success cooperation brought in deporting prostitutes and procurers.[90] U.S. immigration agents in Montreal reported that along the U.S.-Canadian border, local police quickly agreed to cooperate more closely with immigration agents. Yet, since the circular had been issued, the Montreal District had arrested only one anarchist; it had, however, deported ten women for prostitution, along with one Elbert Bonk, the "keeper of a notorious house of ill fame," who had been deported "for the importation of two women for immoral purposes."[91] Another district reported that the governor of Puerto Rico "heartily cooperates with this office, placing the entire insular police department at the disposal of the commissioner of immigration." Still another showed that the immigration inspector in charge in Florida had met with the mayor and chief of police of Jacksonville and came away with their support and cooperation.[92]

Two years after its passage, the U.S. Supreme Court issued a ruling that limited the reach of the federal government's crime control mandate. In 1909, the case of *Keller v. United States* tested the constitutionality of the antiprostitution provision's criminal sanctions. The case originated when police arrested two men, Joseph Keller and Louis Ullman, for harboring an alien prostitute, a woman named Irene Bodi. Bodi had emigrated to the United States from Hungary in 1905 and lived in New York until she moved to Chicago in 1907, where she worked as a prostitute in a brothel owned by Keller and Ullman. The defendants had not assisted her immigration to the United States, but they were nonetheless found guilty in an Illinois criminal court for employing an immigrant sex worker within three years of her entry into the United States. They were found guilty of the federal crime of *indirectly* importing a woman for an immoral purpose.[93]

Keller and Ullman appealed their conviction to the Supreme Court, where their attorneys challenged the sweeping logic in the antiprostitution provision and, of even more importance, made the case that the power to regulate vice and morality on U.S. soil rested with state and local authorities, not the federal government.[94] Keller and Ullman met Irene Bodi after she entered the United States, when she was already working in a "house of prostitution."[95] The defense questioned the government's ability to punish people who employed foreign-born prostitutes, but had nothing to do with their original immigration. Their attorneys also made the case that the power to regulate vice and morality on U.S. soil rested with state and local authorities, not the federal government. As lawyers for Keller and Ullman saw it, federal immigration laws had only to do with "entering this country." Once a person was admitted, however, the operation of immigration law "terminated."[96] The power to punish those involved with the sex trade on U.S. soil, whether U.S. citizens or immigrants, therefore, rested only with state governments. It did not rest with the federal government, the lawyers for Ullman and Keller agued, because it had never been enumerated as a federal power under the Tenth Amendment. If states wanted to prosecute the criminal sanctions of the federal antiprostitution provision, then they had to pass and enforce laws empowering state officials to do so. The federal government could not.[97]

Lawyers for the federal government defended the criminal sanctions, linking them to the ability to carry out the humanitarian intent of the antiprostitution provision. They told the Court that since it was an "easy matter to cover up an arrangement with a female that she come to the United States for an immoral purpose," immigration authorities needed the criminal sanctions. Without them, government lawyers argued, the ability to prevent immigrant women's sexual enslavement would be destroyed. The criminal sanctions were essentially an extension of the right and responsibility of the government to restrain the evil of immigrant prostitution. Lawyers for the government also argued that since "[t]he admission of an alien female under this act may be regarded as only conditional, and for three years she is on probation; and, if within that time she be guilty of the acts therein mentioned, she forfeits her right to remain. And it is certainly within the power of Congress to provide a punishment for those who thus bring about her expulsion."[98]

The Supreme Court found against the government. Quickly addressing the defendants' first argument, the Court stated that indirect inducement was not a material point in the case and limited its reach. People could not be prosecuted for indirectly inducing a person. Most of the *Keller* decision answered the larger constitutional question of immigration officials' police power and whether the government could punish people for procuring at all. As the Court saw it, the police power of the antiprostitution provision represented a stunning, unconstitutional expansion of federal power. Writing for the majority, Justice David Josiah Brewer noted that the police power under the antiprostitution provision was not enumerated under the Tenth Amendment. The police power was not, for example, related to the federal authority to sign treaties with foreign nations—something enumerated by

Article II of the Constitution. Nor did the Court agree with the government that the expansion of police power was integral to the intent of the antiprostitution provision. Instead, if upheld, the Court believed that the antiprostitution provision would lead to "such a change in the internal conditions of this country as was never dreamed of by the framers of the Constitution." The criminal sanctions were, Brewer wrote, "broad enough to take cognizance of all dealings of citizens with aliens." As such, this police power would open the door "to the assumption by the National Government of an almost unlimited body of legislation." The larger constitutional question addressed more than just the power to punish. Instead, the question for Brewer was actually, "can it be within the power of Congress to control all the dealings of our citizens with resident aliens?"—to police the morality and norms of people's behavior under immigration law? The Court said no and struck down the police power of the antiprostitution provision.[99]

As a result, several procurers who had been sentenced to prison terms prior to the decision received pardons or found their sentences quashed. A federal grand jury in El Paso, Texas, had indicted Simon Chavez for "keeping, maintaining, controlling, supporting and harboring [a woman] in a house of prostitution in the United States for an immoral purpose." After the *Keller* decision, a U.S. district court quashed the indictment.[100] An assistant U.S. attorney general wanted to take the case to a higher court, but the commissioner general of immigration Daniel J. Keefe decided that it was "useless to carry the case any further, in view of the recent decision of the Supreme Court . . . rendering that part of Section 3, relating to the keeping, maintaining, etc., of alien prostitutes, unconstitutional."[101] In Atlanta, Georgia, another man, Jan Amadee Couzin—the man convicted in 1908 of harboring Berthe Olivice as an alien prostitute and sentenced to two years in prison—received a pardon in November 1909 because "the law under which he was sentenced was declared unconstitutional by the Supreme Court."[102]

In 1910, Congress made two legislative changes that quickly reconstituted the police power that the Supreme Court had struck down the year before.[103] In the White Slave Traffic Act, known as the Mann Act, passed in 1910, Congress reestablished the police power by linking it to explicit, enumerated powers of the federal government, such as the power to regulate interstate commerce.[104] Sections 2 and 3 of the law criminalized the transport of women across interstate or international lines.[105] Further, Congress tied the act's sixth section to a 1904 international treaty on white slavery and designated the U.S. commissioner general of immigration as responsible for carrying out the treaty obligations.[106] Enforcement of the criminal sanctions of the antiprostitution provision was a part of the federal government's treaty power. This forged a place for immigration-related federal crimes that stood alongside state and local law enforcement. When reestablishing the police power, policy makers explicitly tied it to the humanitarian objectives of antiprostitution policy. The committee writing the Mann Act announced that one of its intentions was to have the state "protect women and girls against *this criminal traffic.*"[107] The government would prohibit "any person from 'knowingly persuading, inducing, enticing, or coercing' any woman or girl from moving or being transported within the state or internationally to 'engage in the practice of prostitution . . . or any other immoral practice, whether with or without her consent.' "[108]

Congress broadened the reach of the anticrime mandate even further with changes to immigration law explicitly. In the Immigration Act of 1910 Congress strengthened officials' capacity to secure felony convictions. It made admissible the testimony of a spouse and it increased the fine for importing, holding, or harboring an alien prostitute to $10,000. Congress also added language that collapsed even more activity into the category covered by the antiprostitution provision:

> Any alien who shall be found an inmate of or connected with the management of a house of prostitution or practicing prostitution after such alien shall have entered the United States, or who shall receive, share in, or derive benefit from any part of the earnings of any prostitution; or who is employed by, in, or in connection with any house of prostitution or music or dance hall or other place of amusement or resort habitually frequented by prostitutes, or where prostitutes gather, or who in any way assists, protects, or promises to protect from arrest any prostitute, shall be deemed to be unlawfully in the United States and shall be deported.[109]

Of even greater importance with the 1910 immigration law, Congress would get immigration officials around two systemic problems that had hampered immigration's enforcement from the start. The first dealt with the time limit. In 1909, for example, a scandal broke involving suspected corruption related to the time-limit clause of the deportation law. An immigration agent at Ellis Island noticed that a suspiciously large number of immigrant women arrested for prostitution were evading deportation. He suspected that a transportation agent was selling verification-of-landing documents, which helped prostitutes avoid deportation by proving they had been in the country for more than three years. The department launched an investigation. An immigration inspector at Ellis Island compiled a list of women arrested and released because they claimed to have been in the country between three and fourteen years. She determined that all of the women on the list had actually arrived since 1907 and should have been deportable. The inspector suspected that either someone was selling these women false landing verifications or a member of the New York City Police Department was coaching women to tell their arresting officers that they had lived in the United States for more than three years. Further investigation uncovered that New York police were not involved; rather, a former employee of the Department of Immigration, Solomon Lubliene, who was then working for the courts, was selling the landing verifications.[110] By then, immigration officials had developed some irregular means for carrying out deportations. Immigration officers in the Bissonette case, discussed earlier in this chapter, used her uninspected entry, after her return to Canada to bury her sister, to restart the clock on the time limit and apply the antiprostitution provision. Even with their irregular means, as officials saw it and as the New York scandal acutely showed, the time limit was particularly vulnerable to exploitation and fraud.

Another problem lawmakers solved with the Immigration Act of 1910 was the way the antiprostitution provision previously linked intent with immigration. Back in 1903, the first antiprostitution provision provided only for deportations based on causes predating entry into the United States. The law made those involved in the sex trade ineligible for legal entry.[111] In his dissent in the *Keller* decision, Supreme Court Justice Oliver Wendell Holmes critiqued this logic. Holmes wrote that "there was an extraordinary range of forces—from the psychological to the economic—working on an immigrant woman during her initial years in the strange land, any or all of which could push her toward prostitution. Indeed, it bordered on the irrational to believe that if a woman became a prostitute within three years it was what she had planned to do all along."[112] Still, the text of immigration law before 1910 restricted immigration officials from considering what on U.S. soil caused prostitution. Only in cases where they could make the claim that a person had come with the intent to participate in the sex trade or was induced could immigration officials deport a person.

In the Immigration Act of 1910, Congress resolved both problems of enforcement by removing the time limit on the antiprostitution provision and creating the power to deport for post-entry infractions. Three types of deportations now fell under the category of "Deportation Compulsory Without Time Limit": "prostitutes and females coming for any immoral purpose"; "aliens who procure or attempt to bring in prostitutes or females for any immoral purpose"; and "aliens who are supported by or receive proceeds of prostitution."[113] The new expansions in 1910 meant that the federal government now could control for actions on U.S. soil with immigration law, without a time limit.

In 1910, the government tapped the Bureau of Investigation to help enforce the re-created federal police power and broader antiprostitution provision.[114] At its creation in 1908, the Bureau of Investigation had been responsible for policing the very small list of federal crimes, which included antitrust, postal act violations, and other miscellaneous crimes. The Bureau of Immigration's efforts to deport "white slavers" very quickly became central to the Bureau of Investigation's mission.[115] By 1912, white-slave investigations made up the majority of the bureau's work. The mandate to enforce the Mann Act drove an expansion of the bureau, as it opened field offices throughout the country. The numbers of agents grew within three years from sixty-one to over three hundred.[116] The Bureau of Investigation and Bureau of Immigration cooperated closely, resulting in an increase in antiprostitution investigations and deportations. In 1913, for instance, the Immigration District Office in Philadelphia reported that it had investigated eighty-five cases and deported a total of twenty-nine aliens. This was a 30 percent increase in investigations, more than a 100 percent increase in warrants of arrest, and almost a 300 percent increase in the deportation of prostitutes and procurers. "This increase," reported the Philadelphia office, "should be ascribed to the hearty cooperation of this office with the local office of the Bureau of Investigation of the Department of Justice, whose increased activity during the past fiscal year developed many of the cases."[117]

By 1910, then, policy makers had made actions on U.S. soil into deportable offenses, without time limits. No matter how long an immigrant had lived in the United States, immigrants involved in prostitution could be deported. The expanded jurisdiction and collaboration of the Bureau of Immigration with the Bureau of Investigation made deportation under the antiprostitution provision the second most commonly used deportable category over the next few years. Moreover, immigrants could face both a criminal punishment and then, if that punishment was for a prostitution-related offense, face deportation, too.

Discretionary Limits to the Antiprostitution Provision

Immigration officials used a great deal of enforcement discretion to navigate the sweeping nature of the antiprostitution provision with what they often found to exist in reality. Discretion, notes legal scholar Hiroshi Motomura, is the "gap between law on the books and law in action," which is filled by "countless government decisions" made in response "to political and economic pressures that fluctuate over time and across locales."[118] A form of procedural discretion that mattered a great deal to the antiprostitution provision derived from the belief of some officials that many women were not victims of white slavery.[119] This belief led immigration authorities to ignore marriage and naturalization law to deport a small number of women married to U.S. citizen husbands. A shift in the foci of the Bureau of Investigation and Bureau of Immigration—another form of discretion—reversed the upward trend of deportations under way since 1910. Both uses of enforcement discretion, by 1917, signaled a retreat from federal efforts to use the antiprostitution provision as an early victims' rights program.

In some cases, immigration agents used their discretion *not* to prosecute. In 1915, for instance, immigrant inspectors suspected two recent immigrants from Finland of being a prostitute and a procurer. Immigration agents noted that the woman had paid for her own passage, so it could not be argued that she had been imported for purposes of prostitution. Agents also believed that her partner was not a procurer or pimp because, as the investigators reported, "he has a good job and is a stonecutter, making $3.85 per day." Agents believed the two "met up in the U.S. and are having a relationship, but not anything immoral that violates immigration statute."[120] They canceled the warrants for arrest. As historian Martha Gardner explains it, sometimes "[c]lass distinctions and the appearance of moral respectability led judicial officials to reevaluate illicit sexual relationships as private wrongs rather than public offenses."[121]

Another type of enforcement discretion limited the reach of the paternalism and maternalism of the antiprostitution provision, but left in place the anticrime procedures. In 1920, for instance, of the women detained in the U.S-Canadian border region as they awaited deportation, about one-third were treated under Barrett's recommended maternal and paternal measures. Twenty-five women and girls were "cared for by philanthropical or similar institutions." The rest of the women detained that year were placed either in "public institutions" or jails.[122]

Reasons for restricting the paternal and maternal procedures ranged from a woman's actions to race.[123] In explaining the two detainment options along the Canadian-U.S. border, the commissioner of immigration along the Canadian border noted that some women "were so immoral" that the policy of housing them with charitable organizations was simply "inadequate."[124] Race also mattered to the limiting of maternalism and paternalism. Immigration agents' depictions of Asian women often differed from their perceptions of European women duped into prostitution. Immigration officials, as historian Martha Gardner finds, often treated young Asian women not as "victims of male sexual debauchery or economic destitution" but as "'wayward' girls who spurned the protection of the home and sought unwarranted independence from their families." "Wayward" girls, to this way of thinking, were complicit in the crime of prostitution. Similarly, officials often assumed women from Mexico were prostitutes rather than victims of white slavery.[125]

Officials' discretion in applying procedures that made the provision into a kind of victims' rights program brought them into conflict with the laws of marriage and naturalization. Early on in the use of the antiprostitution provision, immigration agents believed that some women willingly participating in prostitution were marrying their pimps or procurers to evade deportation. In 1907, for example, a woman named Mari Latapi faced deportation proceedings. She avoided deportation, though, by marrying a U.S. citizen—the man identified as her pimp.[126] In 1914, the inspector in charge of Indiana reported on this problem. "The marriage of arrested prostitutes to American citizens is becoming a common practice," he wrote. "It is apparent that if the courts sustain the proposition that marriage under these circumstances to an American citizen confers citizenship upon the alien prostitute," he continued, "the deportation of alien prostitutes will be seriously interfered with, as it is no difficult task to secure a disreputable citizen who will marry a prostitute."[127] The evidence suggests that there were not large numbers of women marrying U.S. citizens in order to avoid deportation, but the numbers did not discourage officials from trying to deal with the alleged problem.[128] Bureau of Immigration leadership asserted that "a woman of such grossly immoral character as to be a public prostitute" should not be able to claim citizenship and skirt deportation "by merely having a ceremony of marriage performed between herself and some depraved American citizen willing to marry her for the protection of her nefarious business or for a consideration paid by those engaged in the business."[129]

The Bureau of Immigration came up with two plans to deal with women who married U.S. citizens to avoid deportation. The commissioner general of immigration asked Congress to change naturalization law. In 1911, the *Annual Report* to Congress recommended, as it had for several years, that the statute be revised so "an alien woman who marries an American citizen, especially if such woman is a member of any of the immoral classes" be denied U.S. citizenship.[130] In the absence of a legislative change, officials from the Bureau of Immigration suggested reinterpreting the current laws of naturalization and marriage. Bureau officials made the argument that women married to American men bore the burden of demonstrating their eligibility for U.S. citizenship based on immigration law; that is, they had to prove that they were "moral."[131] This would then allow the bureau to find that women officials deemed "immoral" could be deported, since their marriages—and subsequent claims to citizenship—had been illegitimate.

The strategy of reinterpreting the law on the books was not likely to succeed widely because U.S. courts had already determined that a woman's eligibility for citizenship through marriage came from two sources: her marriage and her race.[132] Case law held that the Bureau of Immigration could deport women married to U.S. citizens who were racially ineligible for citizenship—namely, Asian women—but that those considered white and black were eligible for naturalization through marriage, claims of immorality notwithstanding. In the 1868 case of *Kelly v. Owen,* the U.S. Supreme Court had ruled that the Citizenship Act of 1855 conferred "the privileges of citizenship upon women married to citizens of the United States if they are of the class of persons for whose naturalization the previous acts of Congress provided [and] . . . the terms only limit the application of the law to free white women."[133] In another case, *Leonard v. Grant,* decided by the Circuit Court, District of Oregon, in 1890, the court held that the wife of a U.S. citizen "might be herself lawfully naturalized," even if she did not meet "the qualifications of residence, good character, etc., as in a case of admission to citizenship in a judicial proceeding." The judge decreed that it was the case "if she is of the class or race of persons who may be naturalized under existing laws."[134] By the turn of the century, naturalization law permitted people who were white (including Mexicans) and of African heritage to naturalize. For immigration officials who were trying to deport women categorized as racially white, legal precedent posed a serious problem.

Nevertheless, the Bureau of Immigration did try to deport some white women married to U.S. citizen husbands. Bureau records note that agents would cancel a warrant of deportation if the woman was aware of her rights as a married woman or if, on appeal, a circuit court judge found against the department. In 1916, Nancy Looskoke, who was married to a U.S. citizen, was ordered deported to Canada. Agents went ahead in this case because they knew that if she appealed the deportation order, it would likely end up in the court of Judge Arthur Tuttle of Detroit, who, they noted, had "already freely expressed his opinion that [prostitute] women can not acquire citizenship though marriage." Playing the odds, the immigration inspector recommended that the department "should order her deportation, and then when she challenges it, the judge will probably find for the government."[135]

In a similar 1909 case, both immigration agents and judges willfully disregarded the legitimacy of marriage to naturalize an immigrant woman. Immigration officer A. C. Ridgeway arrested Sicilia DeBeelde Heyndrekx, alias Alice Martin, on charges of practicing prostitution in violation of the Immigration Act of 1907. Heyndrekx was remanded to the custody of the Los Angeles County sheriff W. A. Hammel.[136] She immediately sued for a writ of habeas corpus, arguing that she was being unlawfully detained because she was not an alien subject to immigration law but rather a citizen by virtue of her 1905 marriage to an American citizen.[137] The Bureau of Immigration disagreed. Immigration inspector J. C. Nardini wrote to the district court judge that Heyndrekx "is not now and never was, nor was ever entitled to be or to become, a citizen of the United States of America. That she is now and was at all times herein mentioned an alien and a subject of Leopold, King of Belgium."[138] Nowhere in the government's case was there any discussion or acknowledgment of her marriage. The district court, like the bureau, did not address the issue of marriage and dismissed Heyndrekx's petition for habeas corpus.[139]

In 1917, Congress revised naturalization law as it affected white foreign-born women married to U.S. citizens.[140] Congress made it law that "the marriage to an American citizen of a female of the sexually immoral classes the exclusion or deportation of which is prescribed by this act shall not invest such female with United States citizenship if the marriage of such alien shall be solemnized after her arrest or after the commission of acts which make her liable to deportation."[141] Congress gave immigration authorities the legal power to disregard white women's derivative citizenship.

Driven by a different form of discretion, however, the number of those deported under the antiprostitution provision dropped from its high of nearly 27 percent of all deportations in 1911 to 5 percent or below in the years following 1917.[142] By the time Congress widened the deportability of women under the antiprostitution provision in 1917, it did not have the effect that immigration officials had hoped because, by then, the priorities of U.S. law enforcement had shifted. The Bureau of Investigation, whose efforts had been elemental in the provision's enforcement, turned away from foreign-born women to cases involving white native-born women.[143] A different panic—one about political radicals and the rise of Soviet Russia's agents—took up more and more of the Bureau of Immigration's enforcement energies.

Federal authorities started the antiprostitution provision partly as a victims' rights program, especially for women racially understood as white. Immigration authorities did help some women under this program. For example, with the aid of immigration officials, Berthe Husson got away from her husband, who had forced her into prostitution back in France. Policy makers' efforts to deal with the sex trade also included a new anticrime mandate, made up of criminal sanctions (despite initial opposition of the Supreme Court) and the power to deport for post-entry infractions. After 1910, then, not only could an immigrant processed under general immigration law be deported at any time after his or her entry, but he or she could also be deported for crimes committed on U.S. soil. These were post-entry infractions.

These expansions in the anticrime mandate outlasted the humanitarian intent of the antiprostitution provision. In 1914, the commissioner general of immigration praised the anticrime mandate and argued that "the law should be the same with regard to criminals and anarchists."[144] As we will see in Chapter 5, when the government panicked about the threat posed by radical workers, communists, and radicals, lawmakers did just that.

Chapter 5

The Limits of Deportation Power

At the end of World War I, workers in the United States started a wave of strikes and riots, which aggravated public fears of a larger anarchist and communist threat. In May and June 1919, these fears were heightened after a series of bombings that targeted prominent Americans, including Attorney General A. Mitchell Palmer, cabinet members Albert Burleson and William B. Wilson, Supreme Court Justice Oliver Wendell Holmes, and business leaders John D. Rockefeller and J. P. Morgan. In the first wave, thirty-six bombs were mailed from New York and were timed to detonate on May Day. Most were never delivered. Though accounts vary, the post office uncovered half of the bombs, and most of the others were intercepted before delivery. Still, one was delivered to the home of Thomas R. Hardwick, a senator from Georgia who served as the chair of the Commission on Immigration. As a maid opened the parcel, it exploded. The blast dismembered her and severely injured Mrs. Hardwick.[1] A second round followed on June 3. This time, bombs exploded in seven cities: Philadelphia, Paterson (New Jersey), Boston, Pittsburgh, Cleveland, New York, and Washington, D.C.[2] The U.S. government responded to the bombings and fear about radical leftist threats with deportations.

When the United States had been swept by panics about Chinese immigrants and prostitutes' threats to national security, immigration authorities had taken the opportunity to expand their deportation powers. During the first Red Scare, Bureau of Immigration authorities did the same. On November 7, 1919, the U.S. Bureau of Immigration and the Department of Justice launched the first of several coordinated immigration raids across the country, now known as the Red Raids or the Palmer Raids. Their intent was to arrest and deport "Russian Soviet agents" and politically radical immigrants from the former Russian Empire who, they believed, were largely responsible for both the bombings and the labor unrest. This and subsequent raids were different from federal operations under the panics about Chinese immigration or immigrant prostitution, however, because federal officials linked the bombings and the political radicals to a specific regime—the new Soviet government in Russia.

Repercussions from the development of the bilateral nature of immigrant removals would play out in these deportations. U.S. officials were in a thorny spot. On one hand, U.S. officials claimed the new Soviet government was behind a larger plot to bring down the U.S. government. On the other hand, since they wanted to carry out deportations, not expulsions or prisoner exchanges, they also required approval on the receiving end. Because the United States did not officially recognize the new Soviet government, U.S. officials could not get formal approval from the receiving state. The Bureau of Immigration, with the help of U.S. State Department officials, found ways to carry out hundreds of deportations through negotiations with third-party countries. Occurring just after World War I, this was a tenuous, ad hoc process, and it was complicated by famine and political unrest in Europe.

Within a year, Bureau of Immigration efforts ran into two additional problems. One source of opposition came from within the U.S. government. Some officials started challenging the arrests and hearings, arguing that they represented significant violations of due process rights and government overreach. Another source—the Soviet government—possessed the power to stop the Red Scare deportations altogether.

Expanding Deportation Power and Launching the *Buford*

On December 21, 1919, U.S. immigration agents put 249 Russian deportees on an old army transport ship named the *Buford*. Several congressmen, Anthony Caminetti, the U.S. commissioner general of immigration, William J. Flynn, the director of the Justice Department's Bureau of Investigation, and other federal agents, including a twenty-four-year-old J. Edgar Hoover, watched as the "Russian Ark" set sail out of New York Harbor.[3] The passengers on board the *Buford* represented the culmination of antiradical activism by federal authorities. Many of the arrested immigrants claimed their innocence and petitioned their embassy to make an international appeal to prevent their deportations. Russia's diplomatic status in

1919, however, complicated the international appeals process. The U.S. government refused to recognize the brand-new Russian Soviet Federated Socialist Republic (RSFSR) and, by extension, Ludwig Martens—the diplomat that the RSFSR had sent to the United States. Martens and his staff tried to act as the official legation and use the international appeal. But the U.S. government ignored Martens's efforts to help defend the deportees. Russia's diplomatic status presented another complication—if the U.S. government did not have diplomatic relations with a country, how could U.S. authorities carry out the deportations without the approval from officials on the receiving end? U.S. officials undertook the *Buford* deportations using expanded anarchist provisions and finding ways through the international legal regime. The Bureau of Immigration used panic over anarchism to expand—even abuse—its deportation power.

In 1917 and 1918, Congress passed legislation that expanded the government's ability to deport immigrants on political grounds.[4] In the Immigration Act of 1917, it expanded the causes for deporting political radicals and removed the time limit on their deportations.[5] Anthony Caminetti believed that the expansion of his department's ability to deport immigrants on political grounds was important, but he complained that the changes to the political radical provision did not go far enough. According to Caminetti, the law did not allow his department to deport aliens who "developed anarchistic beliefs after arrival." "[E]ven if they advocated or taught anarchy," he complained, they "could not be expelled from the country." The 1917 act limited deportations to aliens who came to the United States already believing in anarchism, immigrants like John Turner, as discussed in Chapter 3. Congress addressed Caminetti's complaint by including a clause in the Immigration Act of 1918 that made immigrants deportable if they believed in political radicalism at any time.[6] Congress also added a clause that gave the Bureau of Immigration the power to deport aliens who were members of radical organizations. Under this clause, bureau officials would not have to prove that immigrants individually believed in political radicalism—something often difficult to do. Instead, the bureau only had to prove an alien was a member of an organization that espoused radical beliefs or objectives—something much easier to do.[7] The government created a new post-entry infraction.

The most famous of the *Buford* deportees were anarchists Emma Goldman and Alexander Berkman, two people whom the government had wanted to deport for some time. The Bureau of Immigration had looked into deporting Goldman many years before. Although born in the Russian Empire (Kovno), she had gained American citizenship in 1887, when she married Jacob Kershner, a naturalized U.S. citizen. Goldman soon divorced Kershner, but that did not affect her U.S. citizenship. Berkman had lived in the United States since emigrating from the Russian Empire in 1888. He was famous for his thoughts on anarchy and infamous for his attempted assassination of Henry Clay Frick of the Carnegie Steel Company during the Homestead Strike of 1892. Berkman did not have U.S. citizenship, but he had been protected from deportation because he had outlasted the time limits that previous laws had placed on deportations.

In 1918, while Goldman and Berkman were in prison for speaking out against the draft, the Bureau of Immigration found a way to deport both of them.[8] The process of deporting Berkman was relatively straightforward, since in 1917, Congress had removed the time limit on deporting anarchists. Goldman's case was more complicated, but two factors dovetailed to enable her deportation. First, Goldman's ex-husband's citizenship had been revoked in 1908, twenty-five years after it had been issued.[9] Immigration and Justice Department agents, one of whom was J. Edgar Hoover, the head of the department's Radical Division, looked to denaturalize Goldman by extension. Second, the removal of the time limit meant that if agents could denaturalize Goldman, they could deport her.[10]

In 1919, Goldman and Berkman were released from jail and immediately arrested by Bureau of Immigration agents for being anarchists. Pending the outcome of their Board of Special Inquiry hearings, both were released on bail. Their lawyer, Harry Weinberger, had secured $15,000 from their friends and supporters to pay their bonds.[11]

Berkman had no legal grounds to fight his deportation. In a move that harked back to the older, more unilateral form of immigrant removal of expulsion, Berkman wanted to choose the direction of his departure from the United States. He inquired into the possibility of simply leaving the United States at his own expense, for France, Mexico, or Germany. His reluctance to return to Russia most likely had to do with the chaos and civil war raging there. Louis F. Post, the acting secretary of labor, refused this request.[12] Goldman did have legal grounds to challenge her deportation. Her lawyer questioned the legitimacy of her denaturalization, especially since she had not been part of the official proceedings that revoked her ex-husband's citizenship.[13] But Post upheld her deportation, deciding that her ex-husband's denaturalization automatically denaturalized her.[14] Goldman initially appealed to the U.S. Supreme Court, but she soon withdrew her appeal because she was in love with Berkman and wanted to stay with him.[15]

Most of the other deportees on board the *Buford*, 184 of them, were members of the Union of Russian Workers.[16] After the bombings in 1919, the Department of Justice and the Bureau of Immigration saw deportation as the key to national security. Neither contemporary investigators nor historians have found much evidence to indicate who was behind the bombings or to support the reputed conspiracy by politically radical immigrants from the Russian Empire. During the investigation into the abuses of the Palmer Raids in 1921, Senator Thomas J. Walsh stated, "Nothing, so far as the evidence here has described, has evinced anything in the nature of preparation for a military uprising. No guns, no munitions of war were accumulated; there was no drilling of soldiers or anything of that kind."[17] One of Palmer's biographers wrote, "Even the new Bolshevik regime in Russia was not yet in a position to offer leadership or funds to the disorganized American Communists," adding that radical organizations did not pose "a serious threat to national institutions. American anarchists were capable of isolated bomb atrocities, but a more ambitious organized attempt was far beyond them."[18]

Nevertheless, contemporaries grew fearful of both a third wave of bombings and a larger Bolshevik revolutionary conspiracy. New York police and Justice Department officers believed that the bombings were an IWW-Bolshevik plot; so, too, did Attorney General Palmer, President Woodrow Wilson, Vice President Thomas Marshall, and Secretary of State Robert Lansing.[19] These beliefs encouraged federal officials to collapse the category of Russian immigrants, many of whom were Jewish, with the category of radical and, thus, a threat to national security.[20]

In the fall of 1919, Mitchell Palmer, head of the Department of the Justice and William B. Wilson, head of the Department of Labor, agreed to collaborate in order to rid the country of Russian radicals. If radicals who planned to bring down the U.S. government and Russian immigrants were one and the same, deportation made sense. The Immigration Act of 1918 made mere membership in a radical organization enough to render a person deportable. In deportation hearings held before passage of the 1918 act, many immigrants had defeated their deportations because the Bureau of Immigration could not prove that individual immigrants disbelieved in government. Under the membership provision, the government no longer had to prove personal or individual beliefs. Congress, however, only provided extra appropriations for the Department of Justice, not for the Department of Labor or its Bureau of Immigration. Determined to work together, the agencies decided to share the congressional appropriation. On Wilson's orders, three Labor Department officials—Commissioner General of Immigration Caminetti, Solicitor General John W. Abercrombie, and A. W. Parker, chief legal adviser, met with Justice Department officials to prepare for the arrest and deportation of alien revolutionaries. Their first targets would be the Union of Russian Workers.[21] The organization's manifesto advocated political radicalism: "We must teach the working class to take the initiative . . . in order to bring about the necessary and inevitable strike to abolish government."[22]

On November 7, 1919, the Department of Justice and the Bureau of Immigration launched a coordinated raid on the Union of Russian Workers in twelve cities. Though Department of Justice agents carried warrants of arrest signed by Caminetti, many immigrants were arrested without warrants. In New York, for example, agents raided the union's "People's House." The Bureau of Investigation had obtained only twenty-seven arrest warrants, but federal officials arrested nearly two hundred men and women. Government officials also entered homes without search warrants. Some of the suspects turned out to be U.S. citizens, and some were not even members of the union. Some were taken into custody because they roomed with suspects or lived in rooms formerly rented by a suspect. In New York City alone, the agents arrested 650 people.[23] This raid, the first of the so-called Palmer Raids, therefore, violated numerous long-standing procedures and immigrant rights, but both justice and immigration officials believed that the Bolshevik threat justified exceptional measures.

Louis F. Post, the assistant secretary of the Department of Labor, saw this raid differently and criticized both the excessive use of force and the seemingly indiscriminate arrests. "Officials of the organization [the Union of Russian Workers], professional teachers peaceably leading their night-school pupils in legitimate studies, members of the organization and non-members, men and women, aliens and citizens," Post remembered, "were indiscriminately and in many instances brutally swept into custody."[24] Some members of the union, Post complained, were imprisoned for months in Hartford, Connecticut, without a deportation hearing. Post also noted that "many of the aliens arrested in the November raids and later released swore they were beaten and threatened while being questioned by

Department of Justice agents."[25] Post went so far as to wonder whether the Union of Russian Workers was actually a national threat. He believed it to be a loose confederation of about four thousand Russian immigrant members, made up of largely autonomous branches.[26] According to Post, "The organization served chiefly as a social club for the lonely and an educational institution of the ambitious." He noted that while one of the union's bylaws contained an antigovernment clause, members were not required to read the union principles and, as testimony at deportation proceedings would show, many were not even aware of this clause.[27] Post's criticism of the antiradical efforts would take on greater importance to U.S. policy six months later, after another round of raids.

Some of the immigrants arrested during the November 7 raid appealed to Ludwig Martens, the head of the Soviet legation in the United States, where a serious problem soon became apparent. The diplomatic status of Russia was in flux. In 1917, after the Bolsheviks overthrew the provisional government, the new government became known as the Russian Soviet Federated Socialist Republic (RSFSR). Over the next three years, the new Soviet regime waged a bitter civil war against uncoordinated opponents, known collectively as the Whites. Many countries around the world, including the United States, provided some support to the White Russians.[28] But the U.S. government continued to recognize Boris A. Bakhmeteff, who had been appointed ambassador to the United States by the provisional government back in April 1917.[29]

Nevertheless, Martens and his staff tried to use the international appeal to help the arrested men and women. Martens wrote to the U.S. secretary of state, complaining, "Contrary to the comity of nations, citizens of Soviet Russia in the United States have in effect been denied the protection of the law."[30] He argued that thousands of emigrants from the Russian Empire in the United States were "indiscriminately accused in the most sweeping terms by government officials, of criminal and subversive acts and intents against the Government of the United States, of which they are quite innocent." Martens pointed out that these people were in an especially vulnerable position because of the U.S. refusal to diplomatically recognize the RSFSR.[31] Martens also protested the overarching logic behind the Red Raids. He insisted that, while "the Communist Party [in Russia was] at the head of revolutionary movement of the working masses in all countries," the struggle and activism was "rooted in the actual conditions of all countries," including the United States.[32] Political radicalism in the United

States, he insisted, resulted from conditions there, not from the existence or actions of Soviet Russian agents.

Martens's international appeal included entreaties for reciprocal treatment and the sanctity of private property. Martens maintained that the new Soviet government was treating U.S. citizens in Russia with respect consistent with international law—even in the face of a possible U.S. military invasion. The new government had arrested some U.S. citizens, and Martens maintained that those Americans were getting far better treatment in Russia than Russians in the United States. Martens noted that the "[p]roperty of American citizens who have complied with the laws of the country has not been interfered with, and wherever any complications have arisen in this respect the Government of the Soviet Russia has been, and is, ready to adjust matters so as to safeguard the rights and the interests of American citizens." Even U.S. soldiers, who were actively fighting against them, Martens continued, were "treated in Soviet Russia with especial consideration, and were unconditionally released as soon as it was practicable to send them home."[33] In contrast, emigrants from the Russian Empire in the United States had had "[t]heir homes, and the places where they associate, . . . invaded by public officers . . . in a manner which caused much suffering and physical injury to these Russian citizens and . . . property belonging to them was wantonly destroyed."[34] U.S. authorities, Martens implied, should reciprocate.

Martens's international appeal put the U.S. government in a tricky spot. It refused to recognize Martens and the government he represented, and therefore did not need to respond to his objections. But U.S. authorities could deport people to Soviet Russia only with the permission of the RSFSR. The Americans might be able to deport some to the territory under control of the White Russians. Both U.S. officials and Martens, however, understood that the deportation of anarchists and other political radicals to such territory would lead to their treatment as criminals and spies, perhaps even to their execution.[35] Martens objected to the deportation of the arrested immigrants to areas under control of anti-Bolshevik forces on grounds of international law. Contrary to the law of nations, he wrote, "citizens of the Russian Socialist Federal Soviet Republic are being held in custody by United States immigration officers, and it is proposed to deport them to parts of Russia which are under control of enemies of the Soviet Republic." This "would mean certain death to those Russian citizens and would constitute a most flagrant breach of all principles of international law."[36]

In the end, the Bureau of Immigration would let neither Louis Post's critiques nor these tactical problems stand in its way. The solution was to deport people to Soviet territory without official arrangements with the RSFSR government. Public statements made by Martens provided the Bureau of Immigration with reason to believe that the deportees might be accepted into Russian territory.[37] Immigration authorities, therefore, hoped to carry out the deportations, with the tacit approval of authorities on the receiving end. F. W. Berkshire, supervising inspector in charge of the immigration service on the Mexican border, was tasked with organizing the first deportation party.[38] The Bureau of Immigration contacted the War Department, which provided the army transport, the *Buford*, and military personnel—a colonel, a lieutenant colonel, four lieutenants, and fifty-eight enlisted men.[39]

None of the Russian ports was under Bolshevik control, so U.S. authorities had to arrange transit through third-party countries to get the *Buford* deportees to Soviet territory. As noted in Chapter 2, several European countries signed bilateral agreements to facilitate the transit of third-country deportees, but none existed between the U.S. government and countries that bordered Soviet territory. The Bureau of Immigration contacted the State Department to make arrangements for the *Buford* deportees. The first country U.S. officials turned to was Latvia. The U.S. secretary of state wrote to the U.S. commissioner stationed at Riga, Latvia's capital, asking him if the government there would permit the landing of the deportees, and if the infrastructure existed to transport the deportees by train to the Soviet border.[40] Latvia was in the midst of an economic crisis and facing severe food shortages in the aftermath of World War I. In exchange for permitting the third-party transit, the Latvian government requested flour and canned goods, along with $1,000 in direct payments. The Latvians also requested U.S. help in securing the return of 3,500 Latvian soldiers held by the Soviets at Vladivostok.[41] John A. Gade, the U.S. commissioner in Riga, forwarded these terms to Washington for approval and, it seems, Gade told the Latvians that Washington would probably agree to them. Secretary of State Lansing, however, refused the Latvian terms; Lansing had hoped the third-party transit would be a simple and straightforward diplomatic process. "[T]o offer the local authorities compensation for what is asked as a courtesy [was inappropriate]," Lansing chided the commissioner. Lansing wrote that the "offer of flour and canned goods was in excess of your instructions." Lansing also refused to help the Latvians with their soldiers.[42]

Deportations could involve reciprocal treatment, but helping the Latvians with their citizens represented something different. It implied, perhaps, a kind of prisoner exchange.

U.S. authorities and Latvians soon agreed to terms, but they were not the simple diplomatic arrangement Lansing had hoped for and, instead, reflected the broader, capricious political context. In exchange for their approval of the third-party transit, U.S. immigration would provide "[f]ood of a value equivalent to [the] cost of the transporting Russians, estimated at $4000."[43] The Latvian government estimated that the total cost to Latvia would be about four pounds sterling per person and it sent word to Washington that it would like this paid immediately, "if possible by [the] same steamer, equivalent value in flour."[44] In one cable to Secretary of State Lansing, the U.S. commissioner at Riga noted that landing the deportees in Latvia represented a considerable favor because there were strong Bolshevik sympathies there. Because of this presence and "[o]wing to [unreliable] Latvian guards," the commissioner even urged the U.S. government to send "sufficient American guards to take charge of [the] train."[45]

On December 21, at two o'clock in the morning, the *Buford* sailed out of New York Harbor for Latvia. Many of the deportees left wives and children behind.[46] No relatives had been told when the ship would sail and many of the deportees had not said good-bye to their families and friends.[47] When the *Buford* sailed through the English Channel and North Sea, mines remained from World War I. As the *Buford* crew navigated them, a destroyer drew alongside to provide support in case the ship collided with one of the floating mines.[48]

While the *Buford* was at sea, the U.S. State Department commissioner stationed at Riga cabled Secretary of State Lansing, telling him it would be impossible to land the deportation party at Libau (Liepāja) in Latvia as planned. In the beginning of January, the U.S. State Department learned that there was no train engine available to transport the deportees to the Russian border from Latvia.[49] Of graver concern, the growing pro-Bolshevik opposition in Latvia had learned through the Latvian press that its government was aiding the Americans. In efforts to keep that opposition in check, the Latvian government asked U.S. authorities to land the deportation party elsewhere. By this time, the *Buford* had been at sea for more than two weeks and was nearing the coast of Latvia.

The State Department needed to quickly find another place to land the transport. On January 7, 1920, it cabled its commissioner at Helsingfors

(Helsinki), Finland, requesting the deportees' transfer through Hangö (Hanko).[50] The U.S. commissioner responded, noting in his cable to Washington that if it permitted the landing of the deportees, the Finnish government, like the Latvians, would make itself vulnerable to Bolshevik attacks.[51] On January 10, the commissioner cabled the secretary of state with a list of six conditions for Finnish cooperation: (1) that the U.S. government bear all transfer expenses and furnish food for the deportees for three days; (2) that the transfer be made in closed wagons under Finnish military surveillance; (3) that any intercourse between the deportees and the Finnish population would be forbidden; (4) that the deportees could not leave the *Buford* until all the details for their journey from Hangö had been arranged; (5) that arrangements for crossing the Finnish-Russian frontier be made with the Soviet officials through the Estonian authorities (Estonia was the only country on speaking terms with the Soviets); and, finally, (6) that the U.S. government provide an accurate list of the deportees. The Finnish government also requested permission to detain ten of the deportees until Soviet Russia fulfilled an agreement it had made through the Danish Red Cross on May 13, 1919, to liberate Finnish subjects.[52]

On January 10, 1920, the *Buford* was diverted from Libau to Hangö.[53] It was not, however, until January 13 that State Department officials in Washington responded to the Finnish conditions and received approval to land the deportees. Washington agreed to conditions one through four and six. Instead of making arrangements with the Soviets via the Estonians, "word should be sent to the Bolsheviki," the secretary of state wrote, "through the Estonians that on a certain day these people would be permitted to pass though the Finnish lines and that it is presumed that there will be no firing from the Bolshevik side but that on the contrary their crossing will be facilitated." Washington also refused to permit Finland to detain ten of the deportees. "The terms of the law under which these aliens are deported make it necessary to send them to the country of their origin," U.S. officials insisted. "There is no authority for delivering them into the hands of a third country except for the purpose of immediate transit to the country of their origin."[54] The Finns and U.S. authorities agreed to terms, which, as had been the case with the Latvians, balanced the tense geopolitical situation with the structures of deportations.

Changing the destination was not the only problem that had to be resolved while the *Buford* was at sea. In an effort to secure the ship's secret departure, Bureau of Immigration officials had completely overlooked the finances of the deportees. Many had dependent wives and children in the United States, some of whom "were in abject want." Husbands had left money in postal-savings or bank accounts, and others were owed unpaid wages, but immigration officials had made no arrangements to have powers of attorney transferred. Consequently, what money remained in the United States was beyond the reach of many of their families.[55] On January 10, 1920, the State Department cabled ahead to the U.S. commissioner at Hangö. "If certain of the deported aliens desire to execute Powers of Attorney," he wrote, "or other documents relating to the disposition of their property in this country, and this can be done conveniently, there is no objection provided the documents are executed before an American official."[56] Many of the deportees did just this, filing about one hundred documents relating to "postal-savings credits, credits on checking accounts at commercial banks, uncollected wages, personal debts and Liberty-bond holdings." The total funds administered amounted to $45,470.39.[57]

Emma Goldman's and Alexander Berkman's letters and memoirs describe the final days of their deportation. On January 16, 1920, at 4:25 p.m., the *Buford* docked in Finland; the passengers disembarked the next day.[58] The deportees boarded a Finnish train, where they were locked in unheated compartments. A soldier was posted at each door. Most of the food intended for the deportees had been stolen, so there was little to eat or drink. At about noon on January 19, the train stopped near the Finnish-Russian border. Finnish guards instructed the deportees to walk fifteen minutes to the boundary between Finland and Russia. While the details are not entirely clear, it appears that a cable had been sent to the Soviet Russian authorities, likely by one of the deportees. The cable had not yet been answered and some of the deportees were afraid that the party would be mistaken for invading Finns and shot. Their fears proved unwarranted because a three-person group of delegates from Petrograd met them, and had sleighs waiting to transport the *Buford* party and their luggage. As Berkman, Goldman, and the other *Buford* passengers walked across the border, a Soviet military band even played to welcome them.[59]

The U.S. government made the most of its expanded power to deport anarchists and members of the Union of Russian Workers who, despite their individual beliefs, were grouped as deportable on the basis of membership alone. U.S. authorities refused to recognize Ludwig Martens and his government, so the Russian deportees were without diplomatic protection. U.S. officials did not formally negotiate with the government on the receiving end. Yet, these *Buford* removals were not expulsions; they were not unilateral immigrant removals, as Berkman had hoped when he asked to leave the United States for Mexico. The emigrants from the Russian Empire were deported to Soviet Russia, and the Soviet authorities, while not providing formal approval, gave it unofficially. And diplomatic negotiations with Latvia and then Finland arranged the third-country transit. These deportations had not been easy, but the people at the head of the U.S. Bureau of Immigration and Bureau of Investigation hoped that the *Buford* deportation party would be the first of many. Their next attempts to deport immigrants to the RSFSR under the political radical provision, however, would encounter stronger national and international opposition.

National Limits on Political Radical Deportations

Shortly after the November 7 raid, the Bureau of Immigration and the Bureau of Investigation began preparing for additional ones. Federal officials targeted two more organizations under the membership clause of the Immigration Act of 1918: the Communist Party of America and the Communist Labor Party. Both organizations had antigovernment mandates in their charters and Russian immigrants made up much of the membership.[60] Federal agents carried out raids on both organizations on January 2, 1920, and in several subsequent mop-up raids. These raids continued the pattern of violations of rules, rights, and regulations. Opposition, however, soon gained traction. Some within the U.S. government saw the warrantless arrests and detentions, the collaboration between the Bureau of Investigation and Bureau of Immigration, and the unprecedented reach of the membership clause as gross violations of immigrants' civil rights and liberties. The courts, and especially the secretary of labor, began undoing much of the work carried out during a second round of raids. It soon became clear that thousands of these arrests were the result of enforcement overreach and abuse rather than a warranted reaction to a credible threat.

On January 2, 1920, government agents launched the largest of all the Palmer Raids, in thirty-three cities and towns, concentrated in the Northeast and the Midwest.[61] Twenty were in New England, fourteen in Massachusetts alone.[62] Thousands were arrested in Cleveland, New York City, and Detroit. Federal officials arrested more than three thousand people, and, according to Louis Post, three thousand more were taken into custody and questioned as suspects.[63] The Bureau of Immigration and the Department of Justice supplied much of the staffing for the raids, but extra help was hired to process the detainees. In Chicago, the "clerical force was increased for 90 days by two temporary stenographers and . . . by the services of some stenographers from the Department of Justice."[64] For the raids in New England, the immigrant inspector in charge had a staff of three hundred to five hundred men. Most of these were Department of Justice officers and policemen in various cities and towns.[65] Officers in Cleveland reported that the raids were

a very heavy burden [on immigration officials] and subjected them to the hardship of unusually long hours or absence from their official stations, or both, in the most severe winter weather experienced in this vicinity for many years; and when it is considered that most of the records were taken with the aid of stenographers who were either loaned by commercial organizations through arrangements made by the Department of Justice, coupled with the constant clamor and harangue of the aliens, their relatives, and attorneys with respect to bond matters, etc., and a considerable absence of inspectors owing to illness, a slight conception of our difficulties and embarrassments may be gained.[66]

Since the Palmer Raids focused on people from the former Russian Empire, agents arrested few political radicals who lived west of the Mississippi, even though groups may have been of concern to people like Hoover. Government agents did not target radical organizations in San Francisco, such as the Equality Society, which had been formed by Chinese anarchists in 1910.[67] In San Francisco, Department of Justice officials did raid the headquarters of the Communist Labor Party and arrested thirty-nine immigrants, of whom they would deport only five.[68] The Portland district investigated twenty-three members of the Communist Labor Party, none of whom were deported.[69] The inspector in charge of the district comprising Colorado, Wyoming, Utah, western Nebraska, western Kansas, and western Oklahoma stated that his office investigated thirty-six cases of suspected anarchists, syndicalists, Communist Labor Party members, the IWW, and kindred organizations. The district issued twenty-three warrants, thirteen of which were for members of the Communist Labor Party.[70] The inspector for the Alaska district noted that it was "remarkably free from the activities of radicals and anarchists."[71] In the district that covered much of Texas, the commissioner stated, "The entire district is singularly free from the activities of anarchists, communists, extreme radicals, etc. Even the I.W.W.'s have made no attempts to perfect organizations in this section of the country. A number of investigations were conducted during the past year regarding alleged extremists, but only one alien of that class was deported from the district."[72] The Washington district, which administered the western Canadian border, seemed busier than most of the western region. In 1920, it secured fifty-seven warrants of deportation. Of these twenty-eight were canceled, and the Washington office deported only nineteen radicals.[73]

The Bureau of Immigration and Bureau of Investigation focused even less on the South. The Bureau of Immigration's annual reports recorded little radical activity occurring there. In 1919, the immigration district in New Orleans, which administered Louisiana, Mississippi, Arkansas, and Tennessee, for example, reported that "[a]narchists are not prevalent in the Southern States, and their acts of violence appear to be confined to the more congested sections of the country."[74] The next year, the commissioner from New Orleans noted that, while there had been labor strikes in the region, none had involved "political radicals."[75]

The arrested immigrants were mostly men who held primarily working-class jobs. The study by the Commission on the Church and Social Service, *The Deportation Cases of 1919–1920,* which interviewed 168 of the arrested immigrants and examined the case files of 200 more, found that the immigrants "were steel and brass workers, carpenters, painters, printers, restaurant waiters, teamsters, mechanics, shoemakers and manual laborers." According to the Commission on the Church and Social Service, "a number had interests in various kinds of business. One man had interest in an ice and coal business; one owned stock in a mining concern and another in a motor truck company. One man owned an automobile, two persons owned a home, nearly paid for, while two others owned grocery businesses worth $2,000 and $7,000 respectively." The arrests, not surprisingly, had seriously hurt the finances of those in custody. One noted that he had lost $1,700; four others said they had lost all of their savings since being arrested.[76]

Some of those arrested for wanting to overthrow the government had ironically bought Liberty bonds during World War I or served in the U.S. Army. The Commission on the Church and Social Service study found that of the 368 arrested immigrants in the survey, a small number of the men had served in the U.S. Army. Four men arrested in Detroit had received honorable discharges from the army, one had served seventeen months in France. Three more men had waived their right to exemption when registering for the draft and one had not been allowed to volunteer for medical reasons. Among those surveyed, thirty-seven had purchased Liberty bonds and twenty-four had contributed to some other patriotic funds.[77] For those who had bought them, the Bureau of Immigration even encouraged the use of Liberty bonds for bail. As reported in the *Annual Report*, "The use of Liberty bonds as collateral for bail worked to the advantage of the service and the aliens; real estate bonds in the State of Illinois are worth little more than the paper they are written on, as the bondsman may transfer his property five minutes after he gives the bond and render the bond absolutely valueless."[78]

Many of the detainees had reasons for belonging to the two Communist parties that did not have anything to do with the violent overthrow of the U.S. government. The Communist Labor Party and the Communist Party of America had seceded from the Socialist Party in September 1919. Some people who had been members of the Socialist Party were automatically, without their knowledge or consent, transferred to the rolls of the Communist Party of America.[79] Many others joined for the educational services and social activities. For example, John Huacuk wanted help with reading and math, which the party provided. William Vorinin was a member so he could sing in the Socialist Party chorus. Joe Rive signed up for the music and singing, too. Rive also used the party's Russian connections to send money home to his mother and brothers. Some members did join for political reasons, but even within this group the motives were more complicated than the desire to overthrow the U.S. government and capitalist system. Sam Kot was a member because he wanted "to be met by the Soviet Government of Russia as a citizen" where his wife and children still lived. Maxim Bazeluk joined because he understood the party's efforts would overthrow the czar's regime, but not the United States.[80] Still, all of these people were deportable under the membership clause of immigration law.

Many of the arrested had been affected by a change in the rules of procedure and many immigrants had little access to legal counsel. In preparation for the new round of raids, Anthony Caminetti, the commissioner general of immigration, and J. Edgar Hoover, the head of the Justice Department's Radical Division, had revised Rule 22 of the Bureau of Immigration's *Immigration Laws and Rules*, which governed an alien's access to legal counsel.[81] On December 31, 1919, the wording was changed to read:

"*Preferably* at the beginning of the hearing under the warrant of arrest *or at any rate as soon as such hearing has proceeded sufficiently in the development of the facts to protect the Government's interests*, the alien shall be allowed to inspect the warrant of arrest and all the evidence on which it was issued and shall be apprised that thereafter he may be represented by counsel" (italics added).[82]

In the Northeast and the Midwest, where most of the government's focus lay, some of the districts arrested so many immigrants that they required additional detention facilities, many of which turned out to be abysmal. Some of those arrested in Boston were detained for months at Deer Island, where they faced awful conditions. The steam pipes heating the facility burst or were disconnected. The cells lacked sanitary facilities. At one point, the prisoners formed a de facto committee to arrange for better running of the facility, which included the orderly supply of food and distribution of mail.[83] Officials in Detroit converted the upper floors of the post office building into a prison for hundreds of men arrested during the January 2 raid. Detention conditions in Detroit were also terrible. A study conducted by the Commission on the Church and Social Service found that in addition to overcrowding and insufficient supplies, the guards were corrupt men, "who used profanity freely and who, having little sympathy with the prisoners, gave them abus[ive] treatment." At one point, the prisoners went on a hunger strike for two days to protest their treatment.[84]

Soon immigrants began to see some relief from the raids, arrests, and detention. In May 1920, 112 immigrants detained at Deer Island filed a petition for a writ of habeas corpus.[85] The lawyers for the immigrants, Lawrence G. Books and Morris Katzeff, were assisted by Felix Frankfurter and Zechariah Chafee, Jr., of Harvard Law School.[86] The District Court of Massachusetts heard their case in *Colyer v. Skeffington.*[87] The trial lasted fifteen days and produced almost 1,600 pages of transcripts. As discussed in Chapter 1, immigrants could not appeal deportation decisions except in cases where the Bureau of Immigration did not follow its own rules. The violations of civil liberties and rights, lawyers for the immigrants in *Colyer v. Skeffington*, argued, added up to gross procedural violations. The judge who heard the case, George W. Anderson, decided that the deportation hearings of the plaintiffs were "unfair and therefore lacking in due process of law."[88] "The picture of a non-English-speaking Russian peasant arrested," he wrote, "held for days in jail, then for weeks in the city prison at Deer Island,

and then summoned for a so-called 'trial' before an inspector, assisted by the Department of Justice agent under stringent instructions emanating from the Department of Justice in Washington to make every possible effort to obtain evidence of the alien's membership in one of the proscribed parties, is not a picture of a sober, dispassionate, 'due process of law' attempt to ascertain and report the true facts."[89]

Large parts of Judge Anderson's decision were exceptional. Immigration law stated that immigrants contesting deportation orders must follow a strict chain of appeals. They first must appeal the decision of the Board of Special Inquiry to the U.S. secretary of labor. After the secretary of labor ruled, immigrants could sue for habeas corpus on procedural grounds. In *Colyer v. Skeffington*, some of the initial hearings of the immigrants had not yet been completed, and many of the appeals to the secretary of labor were still outstanding. "I recognize fully that, except under extraordinary circumstances," Anderson wrote, "the court has no right to interfere in behalf of an alien until the proceedings have been completed in the Department of Labor." But, Anderson continued, "I find and rule that the extraordinary circumstances under which these aliens were arrested and detained resulted in an illegal deprivation of their liberty, requiring the court to intervene by the writ of habeas corpus without waiting final disposition of their cases in the Department of Labor."[90] Judge Anderson, therefore, found that the overzealous and exceptional abuses of the immigration raids warranted early judicial intervention. Along this vein, Judge Anderson even thanked the lawyers Frankfurter and Chafee, writing, "I desire to express my appreciation of their unselfish and highly professional endeavors to assist in the proper determination of a cause involving, directly, the fundamental rights of a large number of aliens but poorly equipped with means or knowledge to protect their rights, and, indirectly, questions of far-reaching and general importance to all, whether citizens or aliens."[91]

Taking his exceptional intervention one step further, Judge Anderson recommended that the government drop its cases against the immigrants because the government's evidence was "wholly inadequate and unreliable."[92] Under existing policy, if a court overturned a deportation on procedural grounds, the immigrant was not released from custody because the Bureau of Immigration had the option of holding another hearing. Judge Anderson, however, believed the immigrants did not come under the purview of the antiradical provision because no "scintilla of evidence" proved that they "were in any way involved, by the use of bombs, guns, or other weapons, in plans of injuring persons or property."[93] If Bureau of Immigration officials insisted on retrying the cases, Judge Anderson recommended that it should start with all-new investigations because the existing cases were so fundamentally flawed. "I think the Department of Labor should start its proceedings de novo as against these aliens," he wrote, "after a proper investigation, unaffected by the overzealous agents of any other department."[94]

Greater relief for those under arrest came from the leadership in the Department of Labor, the unit that oversaw the Bureau of Immigration. Secretary of Labor William B. Wilson became convinced that the raids represented government overreach and that not all those arrested were working with the Soviet regime. As a corrective, Wilson rescinded the Bureau of Immigration and Bureau of Investigation's expanded authority under the political radical provision. On January 26, 1920, less than a month after Commissioner General Caminetti had changed Rule 22, Secretary of Labor Wilson restored its original wording.[95] This move undercut some of the Bureau of Immigration's ability to secure deportations because it allowed immigrants legal counsel earlier in the process. Secretary Wilson also addressed abuses in the way the Bureau of Immigration had used bail. Wilson decided that, in the future, the bureau must allow an alien bail and should not use an immigrant's refusal to testify as evidence to deny bail.[96]

Wilson also canceled the deportations of three hundred members of the Communist Labor Party, which limited the reach of the antiradical provision's membership clause. On May 5, 1920, acting on the advice of Assistant Secretary Post, Wilson officially declared that the Communist Labor Party did not advocate political radicalism as outlined in the Immigration Act of 1918. Post believed the Communist Labor Party was more moderate than the Communist Party of America.[97] Individual members of the Communist Labor Party who had been arrested under the membership clause were released.[98] Immigration agents looking to deport members of the party after this point would have to prove each individual immigrant believed in anarchy, which was much harder to do.

Thousands of the members of the more radical Communist Party of America still awaited deportation when Secretary Wilson fell ill and Louis Post replaced him as acting secretary of labor. Dating back to the very first raid in November, Post had criticized their legality and what he called the Bureau of Immigration and Department of Justice's "Deportations Delirium." Post had been particularly concerned by the sharing of appropriations funding between the two agencies. He argued that Congress had allocated the funds to the Department of Justice, not the Bureau of Immigration. As Post understood it, the Department of Justice and its Bureau of Investigation were only supposed to intervene in criminal matters, not matters of immigration.[99] Post had made several of the recommendations that Secretary Wilson followed before stepping down. He suggested restoring the more robust right to counsel, allowing a broader reach of the Fifth Amendment. He also advised against applying the membership clause to the Communist Labor Party. When Post became acting secretary of labor, as a strong critic of the Palmer Raids, he set out to restore immigrants' due process rights and limit what he saw as other abuses of power, "before," as he put it, "those accidental victims of a silly delirium were deported by an authorization of mine."[100] Through his efforts over the next four months, Post changed policy and canceled about 2,700 of the remaining deportations.[101]

One of Post's first steps as acting secretary of labor was to address the fact that some detainees were still in custody months after their arrest, and in some cases, immigrants had yet to even have a deportation hearing. One such case involved a man who had been arrested in January 1920. The Bureau of Immigration set his bail at $2,500, which he was unable to pay. In February, he remained in custody and had not yet had a hearing. In another case that involved a man arrested on November 7, Post found that the immigrant had had a hearing ten days after his arrest, but that he had been neither released nor deported and remained in custody three months later.[102]

In cases like these, Post released the aliens on what he considered to be a fair bail, some on promises to appear, and others on "the promises of responsible friends; some, as at Detroit, on the word of citizens of good character interested in relieving the aliens of hardship and the community of dishonor."[103] Post lowered or waived bail in hundreds of cases. Prior to the Red Raids, bail in regular deportation cases had stood at $500, but Secretary Wilson had raised that to $1,000 in preparation for the raids.[104] During the raids, the Department of Justice convinced Commissioner General Caminetti to further increase bail in several cases. When Post began reviewing the files, he found that in some cases the Bureau of Immigration had set bail as high as $20,000. This struck Post as especially unreasonable because in many instances "there was no evidence of atrocious activities or purposes, and often none of anything more than innocent membership in a proscribed organization—in some instances not even so much as that."

The Department of Justice had requested bail, Post concluded, "out of all proportion to any cause for arrest except offenses of a high grade to be tried in court, and upon conviction to be severely punished."[105]

Much of Post's efforts to roll back the actions of the Bureaus of Immigration and Investigation focused on addressing the quality of evidence. Post disregarded evidence that had been gathered from homes and places without lawful warrants as well as testimony made before a lawyer was present (testimony that resulted from the harsher Rule 22).[106] He believed that much of the remaining evidence used to prove membership in the Communist Party of America was inconclusive. He would not deport an immigrant when the evidence was anything but "clear as crystal." Where the arrested immigrant had family in the United States, especially U.S.-born children, Post screened the membership clause even more vigorously. "In cases in which the alien is the father of children born in the United States," he wrote, "and therefore are Constitutionally American citizens, and who are dependent upon and receive from him parental support, every fair doubt regarding membership within the purview of the statute [was] accorded."[107] Post felt that the abuse of authority in the Red Raids justified that the burden of proof should be on the government rather than the immigrant.[108] In efforts to redress grave abuses in the membership clause, he even shifted the burden of proof to the government. Post dismissed most of the 2,700 remaining deportation cases due to a lack of credible evidence.

Wilson's and Post's efforts to fix what they saw as gross abuse carried out in the Red Raids included systemic changes to deportation policy. The labor secretaries restored immigrants' more robust right to counsel and provided immigrants with fairer bail. In late 1920, Post created an advisory committee in his office to prevent future deportation abuses. Two years later, this committee became known as the Secretary's Board of Review.[109] Secretary of Labor Wilson limited the reach of the membership clause by reclassifying the Communist Labor Party. Most of the efforts to roll back the Red Raids occurred on a case-by-case basis. The District Court of Massachusetts in *Colyer v. Skeffington* had released the plaintiffs. Judge George W. Anderson recommended that if the government wanted to retry the immigrants, then it should start with new investigations. New investigations were not something authorities were then in the mood to do. Post reviewed the quality of evidence and dismissed most other cases. By June 1920, of the 6,000 or so people swept up in January 2 raids and the follow-ups, 556 awaited deportation.[110]

International Limits on Political Deportations

With 556 people awaiting deportation to Soviet Russia, U.S. authorities began making plans. The larger geopolitical context complicated these decisions, even more than it had during the *Buford* deportation arrangements. The conflict growing between the United States and the new Soviet regime in Russia stalled this round of deportations for several months. Eventually, the Soviet government gave word that it would accept more deportees and U.S. immigration authorities sent off several more deportation parties. J. Edgar Hoover and Anthony Caminetti wanted to include Ludwig Martens, who was still attempting to represent the new Soviet government in New York. His case raised questions about the deportability of diplomats, who were generally protected by a variant of extraterritoriality. Louis Post stepped in and took Martens's case away from Caminetti and Hoover and handled the case through a proceeding soon known as voluntary removal. In doing so, Post navigated the diplomatic complications. By the end of 1921, after several deportation parties, Soviet authorities refused to accept more of its citizens.

In May 1920, Washington instructed the State Department official at Riga, Commissioner Evan E. Young, to discreetly approach the Estonian government about carrying in one or more parties of about five hundred, perhaps more, along with their families.[111] Young reported back to the U.S. secretary of state that the Estonians' assistance in deporting the people to Soviet Russia was doubtful at best.[112] Young's superior, Secretary of State Bainbridge Colby, inquired of Young whether the Estonians would consent to transporting the deportees through Estonia to Soviet Russia; if they agreed and wished "that party proceed under guard," the U.S. government would meet the expenses.[113] Before agreeing, the Estonians wanted assurances that the deportees had been handled fairly by U.S. authorities. Noting that in the earlier *Buford* deportations the U.S. government had been "repeatedly reproached for forcible deportations into Soviet Russia," the Estonians would not allow the transport of deportees unless they had had fair hearings.[114] The acting secretary of state cabled back, telling Young to assure the Estonians that the deportees had "all been given fair trial and, after due process of law in which at their request they have been permitted to have counsel and witnesses, were adjudged subject to deportation under American law."[115]

On July 8, the Estonian authorities verbally agreed to receive the deportees, but U.S. authorities still had the matter of Soviet approval to address. As the consular officer Young told Washington, "Admission to Soviet Russia [was] dependent on decision[s in] Moscow."[116] The Estonians suggested that U.S. officials obtain the approval of the Soviet government from Martens in the United States.[117] U.S. officials were unwilling to negotiate with Martens and so they waited. By late 1920, they still had not received word.[118]

While immigration officials waited, diplomatic tensions between the United States and the RSFSR intensified. In early 1920, the Soviets were detaining several U.S. citizens, who, the U.S. government claimed, had been arrested without cause or hearing.[119] After the second round of Red Raids in January, the RSFSR threatened that it would not release the detained U.S. citizens in Soviet Russia until the U.S. officials treated immigrants from the former Russian Empire reciprocally. To back up this threat, Bolshevik officials first defended their detention of U.S. citizens. Through Hungarian Communists, the Soviet government complained to State Department officials in Vienna, the "American view that every Russian suspected of communism is beyond the pale of law makes it impossible for the Russian Government to cancel measures taken in Russia against *bourgeois* citizens of America, they being exceedingly guilty of aiding and abetting Russian reactionaries." Yet, the Soviets stated that they "would be inclined to repatriate such citizens if their Government undertook to treat its citizens similarly."[120] The Soviet officials suggested they release U.S. citizens in Russia from detention, thereby freeing them, in an effort to negotiate for better treatment of the Russian emigrants in the United States.

For its part, the Soviet government believed that the U.S. government was hostile to the RSFSR because of its communist principles and that U.S. foreign policy was framed to further the interests of American capital. "The condition precedent for [Secretary of State Bainbridge] Colby's friendship towards Russia," Georgii Chicherin, the RSFSR commissar for foreign affairs, wrote, "is that her Government should not be a Soviet Government." The RSFSR foreign secretary communicated that his government's position was that capitulating to U.S. and larger international demands to change its government from communist to capitalist would "permit of the domination of the American financial groups in Russia." This was because, at least according the RSFSR, "any other Government [than a communist one] . . . would be a *bourgeois* or capitalist government, which in view of the present economic unity of the world, would mean a government identified with the interests of the world's dominating financial groups. The most powerful among the latter, as a consequence of the world war, are the North American financial groups."[121]

The RSFSR claimed it desired diplomatic relations with the United States, not to spread communism but rather to foster friendly relations and economic interests.[122] It wanted to secure foreign relations with countries like the United States as a way of establishing stability and stopping foreign intervention against it. This sentiment, too, is captured in the correspondence from the Soviet commissar for foreign affairs, who wrote, "That the elementary economic needs of the peoples of Russia and of other countries demand normal relations and an exchange of goods between them, is quite clear to the Russian Government, and the first condition of such relations is mutual good faith and non-intervention on both parts."[123] Martens's correspondence also echoed this message. "My mission," he wrote in a letter to Colby, "has been the attainment of friendly diplomatic and economic relations between the United States and Russia, and my activities have been strictly lawful and proper."[124] The Soviets also hoped that the Americans would change their position and recognize the RSFSR because, as the Soviet foreign affairs commissar wrote, it was good economically for both countries. "The Russian Soviet Government," Chicherin wrote, "is convinced that not only the working masses, but likewise the farsighted business men of the United States of America will repudiate the policy which is expressed in Mr. Colby's note and is harmful to American interests."[125] U.S. officials saw things very differently; they believed that the Soviets wanted to spread revolution, bringing down democracies around the world. The official U.S. position maintained that the Soviet government understood that "the maintenance of their own rule, depends, and must continue to depend, upon the occurrence of revolutions in all other great civilized nations, including the United States, which will overthrow and destroy their governments and set up Bolshevist rule in their stead." The secretary of state continued, "They have made it quite plain that they intend to use every means, including, of course, diplomatic agencies, to promote such revolutionary movements in other countries."[126]

U.S. officials would not establish diplomatic relations with the new Soviet government. "The revulsion felt by the civilized world against the tyranny now holding Russia in its power is shared by this Government," Secretary of State Bainbridge Colby wrote. "This tyranny disregards all principles upon which dealings and relations between nations are founded and is not freely chosen by any considerable part of the people of Russia."[127] Secretary Colby wrote, "It is the feeling of the American Government that recognition of the Soviet régime or negotiations with it involves sacrificing moral strength for the sake of material gains, advantages which will prove to be temporary and bought at a very high price."[128]

During this larger debate about the legitimacy of regimes and the treatment of people in either country, the Soviets eventually sent word that they would approve more deportations. On September 7, U.S. authorities heard through the Estonian minister of foreign affairs that Soviet Russia agreed to admit five hundred deportees. But the Soviets had several terms. They wanted Ludwig Martens to grant them visas first. The Soviet government also wanted permission to be granted to fifty non-Russians then in the United States to leave. In exchange, the Soviet government would approve the deportations and release one detained American in Soviet custody.[129]

With relatively little negotiation, and ignoring most of the Soviet terms, U.S. officials resumed deportations. The Bureau of Immigration sent a party through Latvia—not Estonia, with whom they had already negotiated. Why they chose this route is not clear in the records, but a ship with twenty-four deportees sailed from New York on December 23, 1920. They landed at Libau, were placed on a train to Riga, and then turned over to Soviet representatives at the Latvian-Soviet border.[130] Not long after, Young, the U.S. commissioner at Riga, sent several cables to Washington about future deportation parties through Latvia.[131] In exchange for permitting additional transit, the Latvian authorities requested a sum of three dollars per person be paid to the Latvian representative at New York to cover rail transportation through the country. Latvians were suffering from a famine after World War I, so they also requested that the U.S. government provide three days' worth of food for each deportee.[132]

Meanwhile, back in Washington, D.C., the Department of Labor and the State Department made arrangements with Latvian and Swedish consular officers in the United States. U.S. agents there hammered out an agreement with the Latvian representative regarding future transit of deportees to Soviet Russia.[133] The Department of Labor would provide the names of future deportees to the Latvian representative, who would then issue visas for travel to Soviet Russia via Latvia, at a cost to the U.S. government of five dollars each.[134] Some of the proposed routes would include a brief disembarkment in Sweden, and U.S. officials arranged for the Swedish consulate in New York to issue a visa for each deportee.[135] Deportation parties soon followed. The *Stockholm* sailed from the United States on January 22, 1921, with sixty-one passengers. The *Estonia*, with seventy deportees, departed for Libau on February 1, 1921.[136] The *Zeeland* set off in April with twenty-one passengers.[137]

Ludwig Martens was a passenger on board the *Estonia,* and how he ended up on the ship demonstrated both the aggressive policing by the Bureau of Immigration and the secretary of labor's efforts to rein them in. This case, however, followed a slightly different course than the other deportations of the Red Scare because it involved a diplomat.[138] Commissioner General of Immigration Caminetti and J. Edgar Hoover had begun looking into deporting Martens in April 1920. Hoover had discreetly approached the Department of State, inquiring into the logistics of deporting a foreign representative and the legal status of diplomatic immunity.[139] Foreign diplomats were not usually subject to immigration law. The Immigration Act of 1917 clearly stated, "Nothing in this Act shall be construed to apply to accredited officials of foreign Governments, nor to their suites, families, or guests."[140] This protection represented a different scale of extraterritoriality from what was in operation in places like China, as examined in Chapter 2. Under this variant of extraterritoriality, diplomats did not fall under the jurisdiction of the nation where they were stationed. Instead, their country's jurisdiction and law traveled with them. The State Department, however, informed Hoover that Martens was deportable because the U.S. government had not recognized him as an accredited foreign official, and he was, therefore, "not entitled by right of these diplomatic privileges recognized by international law."[141] Commissioner General of Immigration Caminetti issued a warrant of arrest and planned for Department of Justice agents to pick up Martens.

Louis Post soon got word of the plan and stepped in to prevent what might, in the future, turn out to be embarrassing diplomatically. Post first set out to prevent Caminetti and Hoover from carrying out "an abusive, lawless, indecent and scandalous" arrest and hearing.[142] Post ordered the arrest warrant transferred back to his office from Department of Justice officials. With the warrant in hand, Post arranged for Martens's arrest. He contacted Martens's lawyer, who was none other than Thomas R. Hardwick, the former senator from Georgia.[143] Hardwick, whose wife and servant had been severely injured in the wave of bombings back in 1919, was the former chair of the Commission on Immigration. Post arranged with Hardwick for Martens to turn himself in rather than submit to a public arrest. Hardwick brought Martens to Post's office, where Post arrested him, but very quickly granted bail.[144] Immigration authorities held a deportation hearing and the Bureau of Immigration found that as an official of the Soviet government of Russia, he was deportable under the membership clause. Martens appealed the decision to Secretary Wilson. Three lawyers represented Martens, while three attorneys for the attorney general, including Hoover, pushed for his deportation. Wilson found Martens in violation of immigration law, under the membership provision.[145]

With an eye to future diplomatic relations, Post then carried out the removal differently than all the other Red Scare deportations. It was a felony under the Immigration Act of 1918 for those deported under the anti-radical provision to return to the United States.[146] Law required that people wanting to return arrange approval through an appeal to the attorney general to avoid criminal charges. This section of the law meant that Martens could not easily return to the United States, if the Soviet and U.S. governments established diplomatic relations. The deportation of Martens, therefore, Post wrote, "might give rise to diplomatic embarrassments in the practical adjustment of relations between the two countries."[147] Since Martens's arrest and deportation hearing had been conducted within the law, Post could not simply cancel Martens's warrant of arrest as he had done in thousands of other Red Raid cases. Instead, Post allowed Martens to return to Russia "voluntarily" at his own expense. Despite the use of the word "voluntary," Martens's departure was compelled.[148] The voluntary removal, however, provided a way around a formal deportation, which tacked on legal consequences long afterward. The legal designation was a "voluntary removal" rather than a deportation. This meant that if he returned to the United States when diplomatic relations between the Soviets and the U.S. government were established, he would not be charged with a felony.

The deportation party aboard the *Estonia*, as with the passengers aboard the *Buford*, faced a range of delays, challenges, and bureaucratic requirements en route to Russia. One leg of the trip took them to Sweden. When the *Estonia* reached the coast, Swedish authorities stopped the boat ten miles from port and instructed the deportees to transfer to another ship. (For this transfer, all of the deportees had visas issued from the Swedish consulate in New York.) After two days, the sixty-one formal deportees and fifty-nine other passengers, including Martens, who were not "officially" deportees, left the *Estonia*. The others were most likely families of the deported. A tugboat transferred them to another ship, which was built to accommodate only thirty passengers and had no portholes or berths. As one deportee remembered, "We suffered for three days without air until we reached Libau." A Soviet commissar met the party there to arrange for their entry into the new Soviet state. These arrangements took another two days. While in process, the Soviet commissar paid the hotel expenses for those who could not afford it. Finally, Martens and the rest of the party were allowed to travel to the Soviet border.[149]

After the *Estonia* sailed, the U.S. minister in Norway cabled the U.S. secretary of state, noting a change in Soviet foreign policy. Maksim M. Litvinov, the first deputy people's commissar of foreign affairs, demanded diplomatic recognition of Soviet Russia before dealing with foreign powers.[150] On April 11, 1921, eighty-six deportees were en route to Russia when the Soviet consul at Libau stated that they would not be permitted to enter Soviet Russia prior to receipt of an official notice of deportation from the government of the United States to the Soviet government.[151] On April 28, seven of the deportees on the *Zeeland* were refused permission to land. They were eventually allowed into Russia via Danzig.[152] But, by 1922, Bureau of Immigration records note that all deportations to Russia had stopped.[153]

For almost a year and a half, officials from both the United States and the new Soviet government had cooperated in the deportations resulting from the Red Scare. Soviet officials approved them. They even aided the deportees in small ways, going so far as providing transport, as they did with the *Buford*, or putting up deportees in hotels while they waited for transit through Latvia. U.S. officials, meanwhile, negotiated with the Soviets through third-party intermediaries despite the lack of formal relations. The ways both U.S. officials and Soviet officials managed these deportations effectively reconciled them with each nations' larger foreign policy objectives. By 1922, however, the Soviet government stopped accepting the irregular deportations from the United States, and U.S. officials were unwilling to formalize relations with the Soviets to carry out more. Not until 1933 would U.S. officials open diplomatic relations with the Soviet Union.

At times between 1919 and 1922, several people and governments had made overtures to turn the deportations of the Red Scare into something else. Alexander Berkman wanted to turn his into an expulsion and go, perhaps, to Mexico. The Latvians, when negotiating transit of the *Buford* deportees, hoped they could use several deportees as part of a prisoner exchange. The Soviets offered to release detained Americans as a part of a swap for several non-Russians. U.S. officials, however, carried out each as deportations. Acting Secretary of State Norman H. Davis wrote when negotiating with the Estonians that all were "being deported under accepted principles of international law and in accordance with our own laws."[154] U.S. officials carried these out as deportations—they sent the people to Russia and obtained approval of the receiving state, even though these arrangements went through unofficial channels.

By the middle of 1921, when deportations of the Red Scare came to an end, U.S. officials did not establish an alternative destination for emigrants from the former Russian Empire in the United States awaiting deportation—as they had in some Chinese exclusion cases discussed in Chapter 2. No other country was willing to accept these deportees. It took a great deal of effort just to arrange for third-party transit of the deportation parties—arrangements that included diplomatic approval, transport, food, and, increasingly, a series of visas—with the Estonians, Latvians, and Swedes. In one of the last deportation parties to Russia, Acting Secretary of Labor Post arranged Ludwig Martens's voluntary removal. This was one of several steps taken to roll back the expansions and abuses carried out in the name of antiradicalism. By the time of Martens's arrest, one district court had released several people and questioned the quality of evidence used in the deportation cases—even though this represented an exceptional legal response. Meanwhile, Secretaries Wilson and Post also checked policy designed to expand the efficacy of the raids. They limited the applications of the membership clause. And Post, much to the ire of Caminetti and Hoover, reviewed almost every case and released thousands.

Chapter 6

From Racial to Economic Grounds

In 1913, Moola Singh, Rhagat Singh, Sundar Singh, and ninety-two other Indian men were facing deportation on grounds that they were likely to become a public charge, or "LPC" in administrative shorthand. In the text of the law, the LPC provision was written to provide immigration authorities with the grounds to deport people who at some point in the future would need support provided by public services. The Indians began their immigration to the United States by landing in the Philippines, which was then a U.S. territory. When they moved to the continental United States, immigration authorities attempted to deport them. Between 1906 and 1917, South Asians migrated lawfully to U.S. colonies and territories, but immigration officials tried to prevent their subsequent migration to the continental United States.[1] The LPC provision that Moola Singh, Rhagat Singh, Sundar Singh, and the others faced was one of three listed in 1924 under the broad heading of "those deportable on economic grounds." The other two provisions provided for the deportation of public charges—people who actually were dependent on public services—and contract laborers. Under two of these grounds, a dramatic expansion in the deportability of lawful immigrants occurred.

As illustrated in previous chapters, the status of lawful immigrant in the late nineteenth and early twentieth century was capacious. People obtained lawful status either by entering the country within the law or, for everyone but those of Chinese descent, by living in the United States from one to five years. Moreover, there were few reasons to deport lawfully resident immigrants. Congress began making these immigrants deportable for post-entry infractions by means of the antiprostitution, anarchist, and as will be taken up in the conclusion, criminal-status provisions.

Moola Singh, Rhagat Singh, and Sundar Singh spent years challenging officials' application of the LPC provision to limit Indians who were already residing in U.S. colonies, like Hawaii or the Philippines, from migrating to the western United States. Their efforts culminated in two 1917 Supreme Court cases.[2] That same year, driven by the demands of a growing group of white, western employers, policy makers developed a mostly Mexican guest worker program using the contract labor provision. With it, policy makers pegged a person's lawful status to the maintenance of the job he or she had immigrated to do with the guest worker program—something that officials had been unsuccessful in establishing under Chinese exclusion. As we shall see, it was something that policy makers had built rudimentarily in the Indian LPC cases, but that the Supreme Court restricted.

These expansions in deportability that were carried out using two of the three provisions listed under the economic grounds for deportation—the LPC and contract labor provisions—came to restrict what scholars refer to as the integration of lawfully admitted immigrants. Immigration integration, the incorporation of a person into the community or nation, is facilitated by a long list of factors; among the most important of which are a person's ability to change jobs, to improve his or her working conditions, and to access rights.[3] In contrast, public-charge deportations were most often triggered by an immigrant's *lack* of integration.

This use of the LPC and contract labor provisions forever changed the legal category of lawfully admitted immigrant in the United States: officials subdivided the capacious category of lawful status. In doing so, immigration officials were also on the vanguard of using deportability to racialize immigrants on U.S. soil, outside of an explicitly racial legal class. Deportability by then had become its own politically powerful category, which could be wielded against certain immigrant groups (particularly Mexicans) even if the deportation power was not exercised.

Deportation of "Public Charges"
and Immigrants Lacking Integration

Congress wrote its first public charge provision into the Immigration Act of 1891 and designed it to deport poor immigrants who received care at public hospitals or in some other way became dependent and unable to support themselves.[4] Enforcement of this provision took immigration officials into facilities run by states and local communities at a time when almost none existed. Not all immigrants receiving some kind of public assistance were in violation of this provision. Markers of a person's integration, which included the ways public institutions assigned eligibility for care, the time limits operated, and even the refusal of officials on the receiving end of a deportation all factored into immigration officials' determination about immigrant deportability.

From the start, several broad justifications grounded U.S. officials' efforts to deport public charges. Some of their rationale rested on humanitarian concerns. Immigration authorities asserted that deportation was a means of assisting very poor and sick immigrants. In the 1892 *Annual Report*, for instance, the commissioner general of immigration wrote, "It were a thousand times better for the alien who falls into misfortune in this country to have remained at his home, for his trouble here is doubly a burden on both mind and body."[5] In 1896, the commissioner general, commenting on the immigration budget, wrote that the public charge provision provided "relief [to] such immigrants as are in distress."[6] By the early twentieth century, an immigrant could actually request a voluntary deportation under the public charge provision, echoing the humanitarian reasoning for mandatory deportations—the assumption being that the immigrant had fallen ill and wanted to return to family and friends abroad for care.[7] This voluntary provision differed from the mandatory public charge deportation provision because it involved cases where the immigrant became a public charge from causes that arose after the immigrant landed in the United States.[8]

Concern for physically or mentally ill immigrants shows up in diplomatic correspondence, too. In 1912, German officials approached the U.S. ambassador to Germany, John G. A. Leishman, alarmed that U.S. officials were preventing dependent, ill Germans from returning home, where friends and family could care for them. He shared their concerns and wrote Huntington Wilson, the acting U.S. secretary of state, who responded that this was not the case. Wilson wrote, "The government of the United States offers no opposition to the return to this country of American citizens, whatever may be their condition or circumstances, and it does not hesitate, whenever so requested, to use its good offices to procure the return of such of its insane citizens abroad whose relatives or friends have expressed a willingness to take care of them."[9] To German and U.S. officials, deporting ill immigrants ideally could help place them in communities that could provide adequate care.

Marcus Braun, an agent with the Bureau of Immigration, described another justification for public charge deportations: they helped prevent problems of poverty in the country of emigration from becoming problems in the country of immigration. Braun wrote that the deportation of public charges stopped European countries from dumping their poorest upon the United States. "That this danger is tangible," Braun wrote in 1903, "is shown in the fact that a majority of the deportations are for the reason that the persons involved are likely to become public charges." He continued, "But for the prompt action of the Bureau in deporting a number of persons whose passages to the United States were paid by charitably inclined people, relief organizations, or even by official bodies having charge of the poor, there would have been a general movement throughout Europe to ship all native paupers to the United States as the easiest way in which to relieve the communities on which they now constitute a burden."[10] The justification to which Braun pointed had long framed other kinds of removal policies, under which the community of origin bore responsibility for impoverished members, if the cause began there.

The commissioner general of immigration articulated a different opinion on a country of emigration's responsibility for ill emigrants. In 1898 he argued for public charge deportations in cases of immigrants who, before falling ill, sent remittances home. "This practice [of sending remittances]," wrote the commissioner general, "prevails in every large city in the United States. That the alien has been steadily employed, and sending remittances to his native country through the post-office or bank up to the time of his illness, makes no difference; he applies for charity and receives it, and is therefore a burden upon the community. A significant fact is that those who resort to such practices are seldom found among the immigrants who land in the United States for the purpose of making their homes here."[11] In these cases, then, officials believed that some immigrants were not entitled to public services because rather than saving money and integrating into the United States, they had sent remittances to their country of origin. Implicit in this justification was the assumption that remittance-sending immigrants who fell ill should be the responsibility of the country to which they had sent money.

Five years after Congress created the public charge provision, the U.S. commissioner general of immigration wrote that, to the best of his knowledge, the provision was working perfectly. He noted, "[I]t is gratifying to me to be again able to report . . . that I know of no immigrant landed in this country within the past year who is now a burden upon any public or private institution."[12] The next year, he continued in a similar vein: "In every community the residents are supposed to have a home to shelter them and friends and relations to nurse them when in distress from disease, accident, or misfortune. In exceptional cases only do they become inmates of almshouses or charitable hospitals." Because of the public charge provision, though, he noted, the "foreigner . . . has no other resort in such an emergency" and "few immigrants who have landed within one year will be found in any of these institutions."[13] According to the commissioner general, then, the public charge provision prevented most immigrants from using public hospitals.

The optimistic outlook communicated by the commissioner general in his 1896 report belied the reality of enforcement. The public institutions he referred to included those that cared for the poor as well as a proliferating number of specialized facilities for the blind and deaf, mentally ill, and children.[14] These facilities had emerged out of a long tradition of care of the poor dating to the colonial era and were run by cities, counties, states, and religious organizations. Out of this tradition, long-term residence in a state or county made one eligible for public care, irrespective of citizenship. Thus, when the commissioner general wrote that the provision worked perfectly, he did not have close to accurate statistics on the number of immigrants in hospitals. When immigration officials first started enforcing the public charge provision and asked for the numbers of alien immigrants resident in public facilities, they were surprised that "up to that time no effort had been made to classify the aliens in these institutions."[15] Administrators of public hospitals, by and large, did not note the nationality of a patient because state law and policy did not place alienage restrictions on public services. Services were limited by state residence requirements, but not nativity.[16]

Two significant restrictions written into immigration law further contradicted the commissioner general's statement. In the first public charge provision in 1891, Congress made those who became a public charge only deportable within one year after immigrating; long-term residents were not deportable because they were protected by the time limit.[17] Thus, U.S. officials could only deport people who fell ill within one year of their migration. Congress passed immigration laws in 1903, 1907, and 1917 that extended the time limit, and by 1917 it stood at five years.[18] Another complication in enforcing the public charge provision came down to the cause of public dependency. U.S. law stated that a person could be deported if he or she became a public charge "from causes existing prior to his [or her] landing" in the United States.[19] Documenting that an illness preexisted immigration rather than developed after immigration was not straightforward and, with late nineteenth-century medicine, sometimes not possible. Most facilities did not even record the immigration status of inmates, never mind provide the Bureau of Immigration with numbers of immigrant inmates who lived in the United States under a year before falling ill, based on causes that preexisted immigration.

The Bureau of Immigration set up procedures for carrying out deportations of public charges over the next decade. In one of their first steps, taken in 1898, the Bureau of Immigration sent out a survey to the managers of charitable, penal, and reformatory institutions to determine just how many immigrants were public charges. The Bureau of Immigration requested that administrators of a range of institutions across the country change their record keeping and notify the federal government of immigrant patients.[20] Carrying out the public charge provision depended upon such reporting.

The Bureau of Immigration's 1911 *Immigration Laws and Rules* sketched out the rudimentary system built to coordinate enforcement with local and state institutions and hospitals in order to document the grounds for deportation. Under Rule 32, people working at public hospitals were to record the nativity of patients and report every immigrant on a particular form—Form 534—to the nearest immigration officer. Form 534, signed by the medical officer of the institution in which the alien resided, stated formally that the person was a public charge. Form 534 also required the physician to list the mental or physical disability and describe the patient's present condition as well as the probability of a cure, or the "degree to which health and ability to become self-supporting may be restored." In insanity cases, the physician filling out Form 534 needed to state whether "recurrent attacks might be expected" even if the patient recovered. This paperwork also documented the inmate's admission date, the date and port of foreign embarkation, the ship and line on which the individual had traveled to the United States and, of course, the patient's name, nationality, and citizenship.[21] When immigration authorities processed a public charge, the proceedings depended on the doctor's evidence outlined on Form 534. Other rules regulated the transportation of sick and ill public charge deportees. Rule 37, for instance, ordered steamship companies to provide deportees with a basic level of medical or psychiatric care while on board a ship. The steamship company then filed another report, Form 597, with the

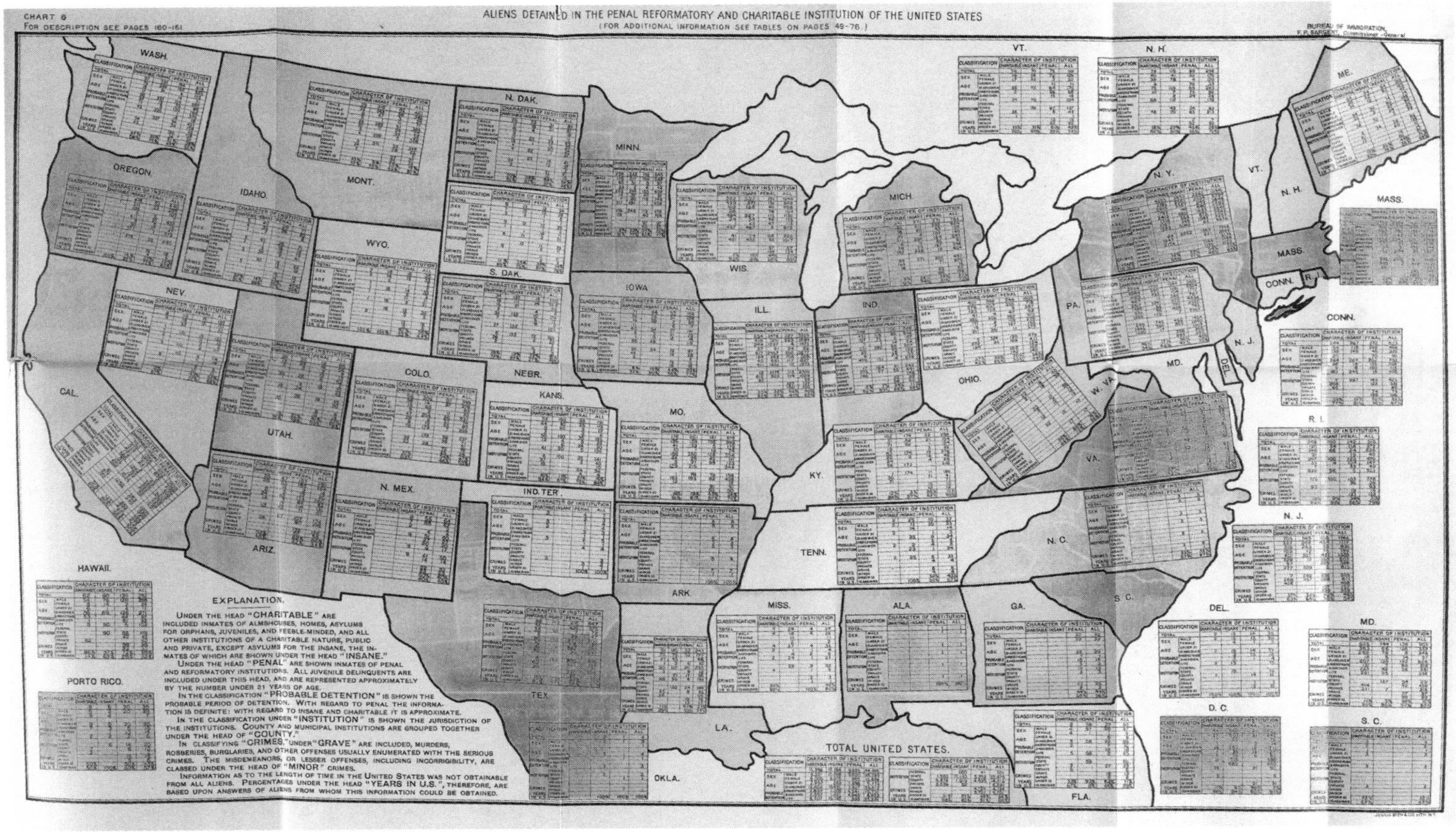

Figure 7. In 1903, immigration inspectors collected data on the number of immigrants in penal and charitable institutions across the country. "Aliens Detained in Penal, Reformatory, and Charitable Institutions of Each State," *AR-CGI* (1904), chart 6.

Immigration Bureau documenting that the shipping line did not simply drop a public charge deportee in the country of origin. Form 597 documented that the shipping company met the requirement that "[f]rom the foreign port of debarkation the steamship company must forward the alien to [her or his] destination in charge of a proper custodian."[22] Through these procedures, federal immigration authorities depended on compliance by state officials, and they worked to puzzle out whether an immigrant's public care was the responsibility of institutions in his or her country of origin or of institutions in the United States.

The multiple ways that people in the early twentieth century gained and lost citizenship complicated immigration officials' efforts to determine deportability under the public charge provision. Women's dependent citizenship is a case in point. Take, for example, the attempted deportation by Canadian authorities to the United States of Rebecca Barnett. In 1908, the Asylum for the Insane at Hamilton, Ontario, found that while Barnett, a newly admitted patient, had been born in Ontario, she had married an American and lived in the United States for several years. Thus believing that she was a U.S. citizen, the Canadians tried to deport Barnett to the United States as a public charge.[23] U.S. officials, however, refused to approve the deportation. As they told the story, Barnett, originally a Canadian, had become a U.S. citizen in 1882 when she married Alfred Barnett. Husband and wife had lived in Canada for eight months but then went to the United States and very quickly had three children. However, after about two years, the Barnetts separated, and Rebecca Barnett moved to Omaha, Nebraska, where she supported herself. Alfred Barnett moved to San Francisco, where he sued for divorce on grounds of "cruelty, absence from home, and failure to care for any of the usual household duties." While the divorce was in process, Rebecca Barnett moved herself and her children to Ontario to live with her sister. Sometime after the divorce and her return to Canada, Rebecca Barnett broke down and was admitted to the Hamilton Asylum for the Insane. U.S authorities claimed that Barnett's mental breakdown happened after her divorce, at which point Barnett's citizenship had reverted to Canadian.[24] In the end, the Province of Ontario assumed responsibility for her care.

Cases involving people who settled in one country initially, and then immigrated to another country, were even more problematic for officials. The case of Mrs. Harrison is illustrative. Many of the details of Mrs. Harrison's early life are lost to the historical record, but what is clear is that she had immigrated from Ireland to the United States in 1877. After her immigration and before marrying Harrison, she was married to a U.S. citizen, Thomas Ward, for about eleven years and had an American daughter. After her first husband's death, she married a British citizen and became Mrs. George Harrison. With this marriage, even though she continued to live in the United States, her citizenship automatically changed from American to British. By 1906, Mrs. Harrison had lived in the United States for about thirty years. Then she moved to Canada, fell ill, and Canadian authorities imprisoned her in a Montreal jail for the insane. The Montreal institution contacted immigration authorities, notifying them of a new foreign public charge. Canadian authorities ordered Harrison deported to her last country of residence and requested American approval to return her to the United States. The Americans refused to accept her. Despite her thirty-year lawful residence in that country, U.S. authorities argued, Mrs. Harrison was a British citizen, so the United States bore no responsibility for her care. They also argued that she had, during that thirty-year period, traveled between Britain, the United States, and Canada. Her marriage and her travel meant that she was not a U.S. resident and not deportable to the United States. Consequently, the Canadians could not get approval to deport her.[25]

In a small number of cases, immigration agents attempted to reassign responsibility for public care to a person's country of citizenship, rather than the country of long-term residency. In 1906, Katie McDermott, for instance, fell ill while in Canada. McDermott, a Canadian citizen, had spent years living in the United States. She returned to Canada in December 1906. Almost immediately upon arriving, McDermott was committed to the British Columbia Provincial Asylum for the Insane. The Canadians believed that her long-term residence in the United States made McDermott the responsibility of U.S. institutions, and they asked U.S. officials to allow her deportation. U.S. officials refused because McDermott was not a U.S. citizen. In trying to convince the U.S. officials to permit McDermott's deportation, the Canadian superintendent of immigration wrote, "We were not thinking of sending back to the U.S. a mere bird of passage." In cases like these, he continued, "The party concerned has had his or her bona fide and permanent domicile in the U.S. for a considerable period before coming into Canada, he or she should be sent back to the U.S. on the strength of that fact alone."[26] The U.S. authorities disagreed and refused to permit the deportation.

In a case the following year, the Canadians held U.S. officials to the older logic running through public charge provisions. In 1908, U.S. immigration officials wrote to the Canadian immigration superintendent for approval to deport a man named Ludger Simoneau. Simoneau was a long-time resident of the United States who had been a patient in a psychiatric facility for the previous three years, since at least 1905. In 1908, U.S. authorities ordered his deportation to Canada on grounds that he was a public charge. When asked for approval for the deportation, however, Canadian authorities refused. The Canadians argued that Simoneau's long-term residency in the United States made him a lawful resident there and that public services in the United States should continue to be responsible for his care. U.S. immigration authorities disputed Canada's refusal to grant approval for Simoneau's deportation. They maintained that Simoneau did not really have long-term U.S. residency because he had returned to Canada for several visits. Canadian authorities did not agree—to their reading of U.S. law, Simoneau's trips north for only a few brief visits did not represent a change in lawful residence. Since the Canadians would not permit his deportation, Simoneau remained a public charge in the United States.[27]

When officials did carry out deportations of people long gone from a community, they had to deal with a related problem—reintegration. In Canada, for instance, responsibility for care of the sick fell to provincial authorities.[28] In 1924, the assistant provincial secretary of Quebec wrote, "The hospitals, homes, asylums, orphanages of the Province of Quebec are overflowing with the indigent." And, he continued, "if we have to be called upon to take in or hospitalize Canadians who have left the country for a number of years past, it means that we are going to assume a very considerable expense and that in certain cases it will be quite impossible for us to even receive them."[29] The assistant provincial secretary of Quebec was speaking of, at most, sixteen people annually.[30] In 1913, the immigration commissioner for New York noted in his report similar challenges about U.S. citizens deported from Canada. He wrote, "Frequently cases are presented where the dependent has been absent for many years from the State of which once a citizen, affording basis for the claim by the particular State that citizenship has been relinquished, no settled residence in any State having subsequently been acquired." In resettling deported U.S. citizens, he noted, "it may be taken for granted no encouragement or aid [could be forthcoming] from any State in the United States, the practice being, [instead] regardless of how many different States the dependent may have resided in before crossing into Canada, for each State to vie with the other in disclaiming or shirking all responsibility with regard to any such dependent." Nevertheless, U.S. officials had to receive deported U.S. citizens. The commissioner of immigration in New York acknowledged this when he wrote that deportations from Canada "within the period prescribed by the Canadian act must be assented to."[31]

Some nations did not face challenges of reintegration after a deportation due to the fact that they expatriated emigrants after long-term residencies abroad. Following World War I, the newly constituted nations of Austria and Hungry wrote laws that stated that emigrants absent for more than ten years lost their citizenship. Norway, Sweden, and Germany also all expatriated citizens after an absence of more than ten years.[32] Commenting on this, one memo out of the U.S. Solicitor's Office observed, "It seems clear that, if they [people U.S. authorities wanted to deport] have lost their original nationality, they can not be furnished passports of the countries from which they came."[33] The same memo noted that it would be difficult to convince these European countries to accept deportees if the United States did not reciprocate. (U.S. citizens did not generally lose their citizenship, but during World War I, those who signed up to fight in another nation's army did.)[34] U.S. officials did not pass policy to reciprocate, however, and by 1922, the U.S. officials still had not resolved how to deal with expatriated citizens and deportation policy.[35]

Over thirty years, immigration authorities expanded their capacity to carry out deportations of public charges, and they tried to work with the administrators of what few social services existed. The cases where immigration officials carried out the deportation of a long-term resident or refused a deportation marked a new development in the much longer practice of removing and assigning responsibility for the poor. These deportations, in very small ways, elevated the importance of citizenship in determining eligibility for public care rather than an immigrant's integration. Yet, what most of the public charge deportations illustrate is that the state residence requirements, the federal time limits, and even the actions of nations on the receiving end of a deportation, made length of time in a community, rather than citizenship, elemental to entitlement to care. A lack of integration, decided by the immigration authorities, proved the trigger for public charge deportations.

Challenging Racialized LPC Deportations
and Limits to Integration

In the early twentieth century, through an ad hoc, temporary set of policies, immigration officials tried to stop the immigration of Indians or South Asians to the continental United States. Rhagat Singh, Sundar Singh, and Moola Singh faced one part of this larger racial project, the strategic use of the LPC deportation provision to limit their movements after a lawful entry. These men challenged the Bureau of Immigration's use of the LPC provision against them to the U.S. Supreme Court. A decision in favor of the Indian defendants in the nation's highest court could have had important implications. It could end the ways immigration agents were employing the deportation provision racially, in the absence of an explicitly racial class. A Supreme Court victory might also ensure Indian immigrants' freedom to move from one region of the country to another, a strategy critical to furthering their integration.

In 1906, an unprecedented six hundred people from India had applied for admission into the United States, mostly via Vancouver, British Columbia, Canada. This movement of people was a small and growing migratory flow, most of whom sought better economic opportunities, though a small minority sought political asylum from the British Raj. The South Asians who immigrated to the United States found jobs and some became wealthy farmers in California's Imperial Valley. Some of these immigrants were Muslim or Hindu, but up to 90 percent were Sikhs from the Punjab.[36] Despite the fact that most of these immigrants were Sikhs, the immigration records referred to them as "Hindus" or "Hindoos." Hindu, at the turn of the twentieth century, was a racialized identity in the United States. The term became, as historian Nayan Shah writes, "both derisive slang and the descriptive racial identity of these predominantly Punjabi migrants."[37] Building on the anti-Asian racism expressed already in Chinese exclusion and using racial knowledge passed on from Canada and other British colonies in regard to South Asians, whites in the United States incorporated Indians into an existing racial hierarchy.[38]

In 1906, when Indians started immigrating to the United States in larger numbers, Congress did not pass an Indian exclusion bill similar to the Chinese exclusion law. This was not due to widespread support for South Asians; rather, immigration authorities were trying to accomplish racial exclusion through techniques pioneered in the British Empire. Initially, they mirrored steps taken by the Canadian government, which had negotiated a cessation of immigration from India through a kind of "gentlemen's agreement" with British colonial authorities.[39] The diplomatic strategy has been described by historian Joan Jensen as "executive exclusion."[40]

This did not, however, stop immigration from India to states along the West Coast, so U.S. immigration authorities sought out proxy grounds to accomplish racial exclusion. Again, U.S. officials learned from the Canadian example. The Canadian parliament had passed a law empowering officials to exclude immigrants "[b]elonging to any race deemed unsuited to the climate or requirements of Canada, or of immigrants of any specified class, occupation or character."[41] In this law, Canadian policy makers pioneered legislation that effectively stopped certain types of immigration for economic reasons. This legislation created what became known as economic grounds for exclusion that doubled as racial exclusion.[42] This helped stop Indian immigration to the West Coast of the United States two ways. First, slowing immigration to Canada cut down immigration to the United States because most Indians immigrating into the continental United States came through Canada. Second, U.S. officials also adopted both Canadian strategies. But, in the United States, the economic grounds—particularly that immigrants would be "likely to become a pubic charge"—would have the greatest impact on U.S. deportation policy.[43]

U.S. Commissioner General Daniel J. Keefe set out to restrict what remained of Indian immigration along the West Coast. He instructed immigration officers in Seattle and San Francisco to exclude and deport Indians under existing provisions: antipolygamy, contract labor, and especially the LPC.[44] The "likely to become a public charge" provision, which would become central to Indian cases, originated in the Immigration Act of 1891, in which the LPC provision sounds like a simple preventative measure.[45] In application, however, it turned out to be far more substantial. Immigration agents used the LPC provision as a catchall category to restrict the immigration of single women, Jews, and many other groups. It was also used racially.[46] Kaoru Yamataya's case, examined in Chapter 1, was a part of an effort to exclude Japanese immigrants. U.S. immigration authorities began using the LPC provision as a part of excluding Indians, too.

Using the LPC provision against Indians turned on two versions of racist logic. On one hand, Indians fit the LPC category because, as the immigration commissioner at San Francisco Samuel W. Backus wrote, they were unable "to stand hard, laborious work." Backus maintained that one of the medical examiners reported that even the healthy "Hindus" were of "poor physique and in all likelihood would be unable to stand the hard work usually expected of aliens from other countries."[47] On the other hand, Backus argued that Indians should not be admitted because of the prejudice that existed against them there. In his mind, Euro-Americans were so prejudiced against Indians that they would not hire them. He combined these arguments thus: Indians were people "against whom there was developing a strong prejudice among the people generally because of their uncleanliness, their obnoxious habits, their unfitness for labor, etc." This prejudice "sooner or later, in one way or another, would cause those already here to become public charges."[48] Thus, racial prejudice provided the basis for the LPC claims.

By 1910, U.S. immigration officials were enforcing what amounted to Indian exclusion by proxy. As Backus put it, "The apprehension caused by the large numbers of these people [South Asians] that were gaining entrance at this port was stilled in 1910, when a stricter enforcement of the law against them was established, with the result that the number of their applications for admission became small."[49] What Backus meant by stricter enforcement was a racially applied use of other provisions of immigration law, especially the LPC provision.

Yet that year a small number of Indians discovered a loophole in the piecemeal efforts to stop Indian immigration. When the United States annexed Hawaii in 1898, Congress extended Chinese exclusion to the islands, but no law excluded Indians as a racial class. U.S. sugar growers in Hawaii wanted low-wage workers.[50] Immigration authorities supported that need in part by applying immigration rules differently: Indians could migrate to Hawaii. Immigration inspectors in the U.S. territory were not under instructions to exclude all Indians. Immigrants who lawfully entered U.S. territories could obtain certificates that allowed them to continue on to the United States without a second inspection. Thus, if an Indian man gained entrance to the U.S. territory of Hawaii, he could subsequently apply for and obtain a certificate to move lawfully to the continental United States.[51] Some Indians in Hawaii obtained these certificates and moved to the continental United States, where wages were higher. With that certificate, they avoided the immigration inspections in Seattle or San Francisco that would have excluded them as LPC.

Once the commissioner general of immigration understood the immigrants' strategy, he very quickly closed the door from Hawaii by revising immigration regulations to require all immigrants undergo a second examination before they could obtain new certificates and leave Honolulu.[52] Under the new policy, then, immigration agents did not bar Indians from Hawaii where they could work in the sugar fields; they instead barred Indians headed from Hawaii to the continental United States.[53]

This step to control Indian migration, however, only addressed the territory of Hawaii—it did not apply to other U.S. colonial possessions, such as the Philippines. In 1912, the *Immigration Laws and Rules* of the Bureau of Immigration still read:

> Aliens arriving in the Philippines bound for the continent shall be inspected and given a certificate signed by the insular collector of customs at Manila showing the fact and date of landing.
>
> Aliens who, having been manifested bona fide to the Philippines and having resided there for a time, signify to the insular collector of customs at Manila an intention to go to the continent shall be furnished such certificate, as evidence of their regular entry at an insular port.
>
> Aliens applying at continental ports and surrendering the certificate above described shall, upon identification, be admitted without further examination.[54]

Between 1910 and 1913 not more than five hundred Indians arrived in the Philippines. In 1913, some men had obtained certificates and were making their way to the continental United States without further inspection.[55] Some, including Moola Singh, landed in Washington State. Others, including Rhagat Singh and Sundar Singh, went to California.

Immigration authorities quickly took three steps to close off Indian migration to the continental United States via the Philippines. First, Anthony Caminetti, the commissioner general of immigration, met with steamship lines and persuaded them to stop carrying Indians. Second, Caminetti rewrote the rules. Just as with Hawaii two years earlier, the Bureau of Immigration began requiring an inspection to enter the Philippines and another one to land in the United States, where they would likely be excluded.[56] Third, immigration agents arrested two groups, totaling ninety-five men, and ordered their deportation as LPC. Officially, the Indians were ordered deported because they were "likely to become public charges for the reason that they are of the laboring class; that there is no demand for such labor, and there exists a strong prejudice against them in this locality."[57] Immigration authorities maintained "that the Hindoo laborers are obnoxious to very many of our people, that there exists a prejudice against them, and that comparatively few avenues are open to them in which to find employment. This showing is not made as against any particular individual petitioner, but as against the Hindoos generally as a race."[58]

Moola Singh, Rhagat Singh, and Sundar Singh led efforts to challenge the groups' deportations. In Washington State, Moola Singh and seventy-two other Indians hired lawyers. They paid a bond and were released until the outcome of the appeals. In California, Rhagat Singh, Sundar Singh, and twenty other men organized a similar appeal. They also paid a bond and were released from immigration custody.[59] These appeals first went to the commissioner general of immigration. He ruled against them. Both groups then appealed to the district courts, the circuit courts, and finally, to the Supreme Court in 1917. The appeals took four years. While the appellants were challenging their deportations on the grounds that they could not find jobs in the United States, they were all gainfully employed.

Ten years before the cases of Moola Singh, Rhagat Singh, and Sundar Singh hit the federal courts, the Supreme Court had limited the ability of immigrants to appeal their deportations in the case involving Kaoru Yamataya. The Court had ruled that immigrants could challenge deportations not on evidentiary grounds—this was part of the sweep of the plenary power—but only on procedural grounds.[60] The Court, though, had not fully defined what a procedural violation looked like. By 1913, the time of the Indian men's arrests, the definition had been partially established. The courts, for example, had determined that an immigrant's rights were violated if the government had presented no evidence or the person had not been granted a hearing.[61] To gain access to the federal courts, the lawyers for the Indians in California made two procedural challenges. First, the lawyers argued that the Indian immigrants had not been informed of the charges against them until after officials examined them and that this was a violation of procedural rights because it amounted to the denial of a fair hearing. On these grounds alone, the lawyers argued, the case should be overturned. Second, on August 20, 1913, an immigration agent told the Indians that their case was closed, but the Bureau of Immigration actually kept the investigation open until their deportation hearing in September. During this time, the defense lawyers simply waited for the hearing, whereas immigration officers continued to build a case against the Indians, adding evidence and testimony that could prove deportability on LPC grounds. Not until September 25 did the Indians' lawyers find out that the case against their clients remained open. At that point, they immediately filed additional evidence but believed they were at a distinct disadvantage.[62] This, they argued, represented another clear, procedural violation.

Once in the federal courts, the lawyers made an evidentiary challenge, even though Congress and the Supreme Court had earlier said deportees could not do so. Still, the lawyers claimed that all the evidence put forth by the government lacked any credibility because they simply recounted local racial prejudice. Moreover, the lawyers argued that the Boards of Special Inquiry ignored testimony from Indian immigrants, who confirmed that they had no problem finding work in the United States. Nor did the board pay any attention to affidavits from Indians in California, who stated that they would hire the recent immigrants.[63]

When the Indian men's deportation appeal went before district court, the case troubled Judge Maurice T. Dooling, particularly the evidentiary challenge. As he saw it, the lawyers raised a key question: "May the Department of Commerce and Labor, upon a showing satisfactory to itself and a finding not open to review that a prejudice exists in this country against aliens of any race, and that there is no demand for the labor of such race, exclude all laborers of such race on the ground that they are, for such reason, likely to become public charges?"[64] Judge Dooling debated, therefore, whether U.S. immigration authorities could make a determination that there was no demand for the labor of *one particular race* and thus exclude all members of the race on economic grounds. When Dooling understood just what "vast power" this represented, he professed himself "very unwilling to believe" it and was concerned to see such a power "lodged in any executive department of the government." Dooling feared larger implications than the Indian case as well. "[L]et there be no delusion that this power, once conceded," he warned, "can be used only in the case of Hindoos. It is equally applicable to every other race."[65] Despite his reservations, Judge Dooling found that Congress had created this power and, as the Supreme Court had upheld its constitutionality, lower courts must follow precedent and uphold it.[66] Congress had legislated that the courts could not review the findings of the Boards of Special Inquiry on evidentiary grounds, which court precedents had upheld. And in this case the government had presented evidence, including "affidavits, interviews, letters, and newspaper clippings showing the state of the public mind in California towards the Hindoos as a race or class." As the circuit court of appeals wrote, the court "will not inquire into the sufficiency of probative facts or consider the reason for the conclusions reached by the officers." The quality of that evidence did not matter.[67]

The courts also dismissed the procedural arguments. The district court never took up the issue of whether or not immigration officials had misled the defendants, which the immigration agents denied doing. The circuit court did consider it but decided there was no evidence that the immigration officers violated proper procedures. Neither court found that procedural rights had been violated. It did not matter that the defense had no chance to submit evidence in August and September. The material point for the district court was that the defendants were ultimately allowed to examine and respond to the evidence that the immigration agents had gathered. The circuit court agreed with the lower court on this point, making the deportation hearing fair and consistent with the procedural rights of immigrants.

The cases turned out to hinge on questions the lawyers raised about the different admittance procedures between the Philippines and the continental United States.[68] They argued that an "alien once landed in any territory, or other place subject to the jurisdiction of the United States, may freely go thence to any portion of the United States whether it be the mainland or any of its island possessions."[69] They, therefore, challenged the different rules that allowed the immigration of people to the colonies, but not to the continental United States. The lower courts upheld the different admittance policies by supporting the ways immigration officials could respond to local interests. The district court decreed that there "may be reasons for rejecting an alien at continental ports which would not exist if he were applying to enter the Philippines. Labor and climatic conditions and standards of living are so diverse that one going to the Philippines who would not there be likely to become a public charge might well be likely to become such if he proceeded thence to the mainland."[70] The courts, therefore, upheld limits on an immigrant's freedom of movement based on understandings of both race and labor in the context of regional demand.

After losing in the lower courts, Moola Singh, Rhagat Singh, and Sundar Singh had one last venue in which to appeal their deportations—the Supreme Court. While the cases were making their way through the lower courts, the Supreme Court decided another case, *Gegiow v. Uhl*, which unexpectedly affected their fate. *Gegiow* was not a deportation case, but in it the Supreme Court limited the government's LPC provision.[71] *Gegiow* originated at Ellis Island in 1914 when immigration agents excluded four Russian immigrants as LPC on similar grounds to those behind the Indian deportations: local community prejudice and the job market.[72] The immigration inspectors had classified these Russians as LPC for several reasons: first, they arrived in the United States with "very little money" ($25 to $40); second, they were traveling to Portland, Oregon, where the employment market was extremely tight; and third, their language and culture made them "ignorant and cliquish." The inspectors had declared the Russians to be "part of a group of illiterate laborers, only one of whom, it seems, Gegiow, speaks even the ordinary Russian tongue."[73] The government's case connected each of the concerns thus: as these immigrants arrived with little money, they would be laborers. They were unlikely to find jobs in Portland. And, even if there were jobs, community prejudices would make the employment of these men impossible. These workers, then, should be excluded. The Russians appealed and appeared before the Supreme Court in 1915. The Court overturned the Russians' exclusion, holding that Congress had not given the Bureau of Immigration the power to exclude immigrants based on local conditions or prejudices. The Court asserted that the "statute deals with admission to the United States, not to Portland." According to the language of immigration law, the Court wrote, the Russian immigrants could be excluded only on grounds of "permanent personal objections accompanying them irrespective of local conditions."[74] Immigration authorities followed the Court's ruling and admitted the four Russians into the United States.

In 1917, when the cases of Moola Singh, Rhagat Singh, and Sundar Singh finally reached the Supreme Court, it overturned their deportations by extending the logic of *Gegiow*.[75] Although neither of the decisions explained the reasons for the reversal, the Bureau of Immigration's *Annual Report* of 1917 did. The commissioner general commented, "It has been the practice to exclude by virtue of this clause aliens who for any reason whatever—physical, mental, moral, or economical—were deemed likely to be a public charge upon the community in which they might settle if permitted to enter the United States; and such persons are just as heavy a burden upon those communities if they do become public charges, no matter what the underlying cause of their becoming such may be." However, he complained, in *Gegiow*, "the Supreme Court, very much to the surprise of the bureau, held that the excluding clause, largely because of the position it occupied in the act along with other clauses excluding for personal disqualification, could not operate to exclude an alien simply because the evidence in his case showed that he would not be able to obtain employment in the place to which he intended to go."[76] These were the grounds on which the Supreme Court overturned the Indian cases, too, thus constraining immigration authorities from considering local conditions and prejudices in deportations.

Even before the Court's decision in these cases, Congress and the Bureau of Immigration had taken two steps in February 1917 to bolster their power to deport Indians in the Immigration Act of 1917. The first was to create a new racial class in law. Congress created the Asiatic barred zone, which, as legal scholar Hiroshi Motomura writes, "included everywhere from Saudi Arabia to Southeast Asia, and India, Sri Lanka, and Indonesia up through Afghanistan and the Asian parts of what soon would become the Soviet Union. The 1917 law also barred anyone who traced his or her ancestry to these countries."[77] As a result, immigrants from India and other large swaths of Asia, except Japan, were, like most Chinese immigrants, statutorily excluded as an explicit legal class. No longer did the Bureau of Immigration need to exclude Indians as a racial class by proxy. As a 1918 report from the immigration commissioner in Washington State explained, "The enactment of the present law fixing a prohibitive zone from which certain classes of aliens are not permitted to come to the United States has virtually solved our Hindu problem."[78]

Second, Congress preemptively limited the impact of the Court's ruling by rewriting another section of immigration law. The Immigration Act of 1917 effectively gave statutory authorization to the Bureau of Immigration to exclude and deport under the LPC provision based on regional demands. It did so by simply moving the LPC provision from section 2 of the law to section 3, under which temporary exclusions to deportation regulations were permitted.[79] Noting the importance of this statutory change, the commissioner general wrote in his 1917 report, "There is perhaps no feature of the new immigration law to which the bureau could point with more satisfaction than the provision in section 3 shifting the position among the excluded classes of 'persons likely to become a public charge.' "[80] In his 1918 report, he wrote, "Congress has made it clear that it is to be of general application to aliens who for any reason whatever may be deemed likely to become a charge upon the communities in which they may settle."[81]

The revised immigration law and the Supreme Court decision, therefore, preserved immigration authorities' ability to respond to local conditions and prejudices. Even though the Asiatic barred zone undermined the flexibility immigration policy provided employers in the colonies of Hawaii or the Philippines to hire racialized labor out of India, lawmakers had ensured that U.S. officials had some flexibility in applying immigration law differently between regions. And, while the Indian men had argued that hearsay evidence and the racism undergirding their designation as LPC was outrageous, the Court let it stand. The ruling did not consider the appellants' challenge to the kinds of evidence on which the deportations had rested. Both would play an important role as immigration officials took steps over the next four years to help employers worried about a labor shortage.

Contract Labor Deportations and
the Emergence of Guest Workers

In 1917, some of the nation's agribusinesses, mining companies, and railroads appealed to immigration authorities for relief from what they perceived to be a World War I–related labor crisis.[82] These firms were big businesses—western corporate farms or agribusiness alone produced 40 percent of all U.S. fruits and vegetables.[83] Immigration authorities took the unprecedented step in their response to employer demands and built a guest worker program. To do so, immigration authorities reconfigured the contract labor provision and instituted a new kind of deportability—deportation for leaving a job. Their actions represented a landmark in U.S. policy because it effectively created a formal subcategory within the larger category of lawful immigrant, the temporary migrant. Soon after the development of the guest worker program, Mexicans became the largest immigrant group deported under the contract labor provision. These numbers represented more than an outcome of the growing proportion of Mexican immigrants to overall immigrant population. They were an evolution in immigration officials' operation of the economic grounds racially.

Nearly thirty years before the World War I–era guest worker program, Congress had created the contract labor provision for a very different purpose. In 1888, it authorized federal officials to deport immigrants who entered the country with a contract to work. Many white workers in unions and some Congressmen understood this arrangement as a kind of unfree labor. This provision was only the second after Chinese exclusion, and it echoed some of the same concerns as Chinese exclusion. Those who lobbied for it argued that contract labor, like Chinese laborers, threatened the wages of white workers and, in doing so, posed a threat to freedom and democracy. By 1900, the budget for the enforcement ($150,000) was almost the same size as the budget for the enforcement of Chinese exclusion ($160,000).[84] Immigration agents operated a three-pronged policy against contract labor. First, immigration officials operated an exclusion at the borders. Second, they deported people who entered the country in violation of the exclusion. Third, immigration officials enacted employer sanctions. People who hired contracted labor could face fines. The Bureau of Immigration hired specialized officers, known as "Section 24 inspectors," to track down violators.[85]

Immigration officials' efforts to clamp down on contract labor with exclusions and deportations were largely met by failure. Employers and workers easily found ways around the exclusions at the border. Most commonly and simply, when immigrant inspectors asked a person if he or she was contracted labor, he or she denied it. Significant numbers of Greeks, Italians, Mexicans, and French Canadians all immigrated to the United States in this way.[86] The deportation provision that policy makers had intended to back up the exclusion did not work well, either. In 1911, the bureau deported twenty-one contract laborers: six from Cuba; one from England; three each from France, Germany, and Greece; two from Italy, two from Mexico, and one from Scotland (see Table 1).[87] Several factors explain this. One was the time limit—an immigrant could be deported as a contract laborer only within one year of first arrival. Beyond that, he or she was no longer deportable. In the Immigration Act of 1907, legislators extended the time limit from one to three years. Still, a person could lawfully "regularize" his or her status simply by outlasting the time limit. Another factor explaining the low numbers is that it was difficult to prove that an immigrant was, in fact, a contract laborer.

The employer sanctions, too, were almost unenforceable. For example, the Ellsworth Mining Company of Pennsylvania and the San Francisco Brick Company both faced charges of violations in 1905. Immigration authorities were certain that both companies had hired contract workers, but they had little hope for making the charges stick. In general, workers

Table 1. Deportations of Contract Laborers by Race/Ethnic Category

Year	First	n	Second	n	Third	n	Total
1909	Bulgarian, Serbian/Montenegrin	86	French	12	English	9	122
1910	Greek	49	French	6	English Polish	4	78
1911	Cuban	6	French German Greek	3	Italian Mexican	2	21
1912	Mexican	16	Dutch/Flemish Greek	4	German Turkish	2	31
1913	Bulgarian, Serbian/Montenegrin	14	Mexican	13	Greek	10	54
1914	Russian	12	Armenian English Greek	5	French German Mexican Scotch Spanish	3	51
1915	English	14	Irish	8	Mexican Spanish	7	65
1916	English	26	French	17	Mexican	15	116
1917	English	16	Irish	8	French Mexican Scotch	6	62
1918	English	13	Mexican	12	Spanish	3	33
1919	Mexican	38	English Scandinavian	8	French	7	69
1920	Mexican	52	English	9	German	3	73
1921	Mexican	74	English	26	Irish	11	152
1922	Mexican	27	French	15	English	7	71
1923	Mexican	22	English French	10	German	5	60
1924	Mexican	29	French	7	English	5	54

Source: U.S. Department of Labor, Bureau of Immigration, *Annual Report of the Commissioner General of Immigration* (Washington, D.C.: Government Printing Office, 1909–24).

either refused to testify or were not available. Some cases took up to six years to prosecute and a poor worker, especially a migrant worker, often could not remain in one place that long.[88] Often, the government allowed some employers to pay a compromise fine or settlement. Others escaped any penalty altogether. As the Bureau of Immigration's *Annual Report* noted, the government was "compelled to choose between the two equally futile courses of dismissing the proceedings or submitting to defeat."[89] In both these cases, the bureau was unable to prosecute.

In 1917, some of the nation's agribusinesses, mining companies, and railroads appealed to immigration authorities to be allowed to hire contract labor within the law. These employers argued that immigration from Europe had almost stopped since World War I's outbreak in 1914, and rural workers in the United States were moving into higher-paying urban war-time jobs. Some employers in the West also worried about the effect of a new literacy test and fees included in the Immigration Act of 1917. A grow-ing anti-immigrant coalition, made up of eugenicists, prohibitionists, aca-demics, many Protestant organizations, and even the Ku Klux Klan, had lobbied for their inclusion to significantly limit immigration.[90]

Immigration authorities agreed to the employers' requests, but they had to first figure out a way around the legal ban. Immigration authorities turned to section 3 of the 1917 Immigration Act, which permitted the department to "temporarily" admit otherwise inadmissible aliens.[91] In exchange for access to contract laborers, employers undertook the responsi-bility to provide fair housing, wages, and working conditions.[92] This pro-gram represented a new collaboration between immigration authorities and employers, and it amounted to the creation of a guest worker program.

People like Pedro Gonzalez, Jose Ruiz, and Maria Penia, all participants in the guest worker program, entered as a new subclass of lawfully admitted immigrant—the temporary or guest worker—and they had fewer rights and liberties than most other immigrants. Guest workers had to return to their country of origin after the term of their employment or risk becoming deportable. They could not leave their jobs and take another; if they did, they would become deportable.[93] General immigrant workers admitted into the United States did not face deportation if they decided to quit their job. Even those who entered in violation of exclusions—aside from most immigrants from Asia, anarchists, and prostitutes—could settle perma-nently if they lived in the United States past the deportation time limit. Furthermore, guest workers could not bring family members and most other immigrants could. Guest workers, therefore, were deportable in far more ways than other immigrants, even some outside the law.

Most of the guest workers emigrated from Mexico to jobs in the West, but some came from Canada and the Bahamas to work in the Northeast and Southeast. In 1919, for example, 20,643 immigrants from Mexico participated, along with just under 6,000 Bahamian workers.[94] In 1920, over 21,000 Mexican laborers were admitted, along with 517 workers from the Bahamas, and 89 Canadians. That year, just under 10,000 went to work in Arizona, nearly 8,000 worked in Texas and many others spread out among Colorado, California, New Mexico, Wyoming, Kansas, Idaho, Utah, Alaska, and Oklahoma.[95] This program was almost completely populated by men.

The reasons that so few Canadians participated had much to do with why Canadians were included in the first place. Officials never intended to bring in thousands of workers; instead, they initially proposed this guest worker program to manage a tight labor supply. By 1917, when the United States and Canada were allies in World War I, officials from both countries met to arrange an agreement to control the flow of laborers as one front of their mutual war effort. The resulting bilateral agreement, known as the reciprocal labor exchange policy, opened the Canadian-U.S. border to contract labor. Contract labor would be closely regulated by the two governments, as officials stated, "to prevent economic waste in the use of such skilled or experienced workmen, resulting from the desire of employers in both countries promptly to obtain sufficient employees in various lines of war activity."[96] U.S. and Canadian officials hoped the program would stabilize the workforce by strategically managing labor flows between both countries.[97]

The overwhelming focus of immigration officials was on importing labor from countries with a surplus to meet regional labor demands, and Mexico proved the critical source.[98] Massive economic dislocations caused by the programs of Mexican president Porfirio Díaz and U.S. foreign direct investment had over the previous four decades pushed millions of Mexicans off the land and subsistence farms. Rural Mexicans responded to their growing poverty by migrating. When Mexicans rose up in revolution against Díaz, millions more were unsettled. For those Mexicans fleeing economic crisis and violence, the railway lines linking Mexico to the United States facilitated immigration northward. As a result of these pressures and growing demand for their labor in the United States, over one million Mexicans moved to the United States between 1910 and 1929.[99] In 1917, then,

Mexicans were becoming a vital source of labor for U.S. employers in the West. In the guest worker program, immigration officials facilitated the entry of thousands of Mexicans (as well as the smaller group of Bahamian guest workers in the Southeast).

Race also factored into why the program was overwhelmingly Mexican. In the second half of the nineteenth century, for instance, farmers' growth in places like California had in large part come from their use of racialized labor—Chinese workers.[100] When Chinese exclusion cut off this source of labor, they found it necessary to turn to different sources for their employee needs. As immigration scholar and economist Philip Martin notes, "The economic imperative to find another source of 'nonwhite' seasonal workers was significant. In 1888, California orchard land was worth $200 to $300 per acre, reflecting in part the low wages paid to Chinese workers, $1.00 to $1.25 per day. Land used to produce grain, by contrast, was worth only $25 to $50 an acre, and the white workers on grain farms were paid $2 to $3 a day." "Without a replacement for the aging Chinese," Martin continues, "farm wages were expected to rise" and the profits of orchard owners to drop.[101] Employers first looked to Japanese immigrants, then Indians. The anti-Asian lobby, however, prevented them from using these two sources of labor. The "Gentlemen's Agreement" of 1907 (an informal agreement between the U.S. and Japanese governments in which the Japanese informally agreed to deny exit visas to laborers who wanted to enter the United States) severely restricted immigration from Japan, and the LPC and the Asiatic barred zone stopped Indian immigration. Employers then turned to Mexicans who already faced broad and growing racialization in large parts of the U.S. West. "No Mexicans allowed" signs and restrictive covenants created segregated neighborhoods. Many employers built a dual-wage system, paying people of Mexican heritage less than workers categorized as white.[102] Employers did what they could in 1917 to convince immigration authorities to help them bring in Mexicans, because they represented a source of racialized labor.

Hundreds of western employers participated in the guest worker program and hired Mexicans through it. The Los Angeles Sugar Company, for example, imported twenty-nine workers. A branch of the Spreckels Sugar Company out of Los Angeles brought in ten.[103] Some companies brought in many more workers. In 1918, the American Beet Sugar Company brought in 278 workers to its California fields in Oxnard and Chino. That year, the Utah-Idaho Sugar Company brought in 996 workers and the

Southern Pacific Railway brought in 1,700.[104] A small number of employers beyond the U.S.-Mexico borderlands, such as Alaskan canneries, looked to Mexicans as a source of labor, too.

After bringing in workers, U.S. immigration authorities used the infrastructure of the contract labor provision to help run the guest worker program. The Section 24 inspectors, once responsible for keeping contract laborers out of the country, organized and distributed contract labor into commercial agriculture, mining and construction companies, and on railways.[105] Agents stationed in the Alaskan territory reported that 75 percent of all their immigration-related arrests were of Mexicans who had been brought into Alaska by salmon packers, but who then left their employment.[106] In 1919, immigration agents in Denver issued 204 warrants of arrest for all immigration categories, of which 103 applied to Mexican agricultural and railroad laborers who had left their contract jobs.[107] Authorities' use of deportation bound these immigrants' legal status and residence in the United States to their contracted employment.

The records illustrate the changing use of deportation to manage the mostly Mexican contract laborers. Until 1917 no one immigrant group was consistently targeted. In 1913, for instance, the top three groups deported were Bulgarians, Serbians/Montenegrins, and Mexicans (see Table 1).[108] In 1914, the top four groups were Russians, Armenians, English, and Greeks.[109] During World War I, things began to change. More Mexicans faced deportation under the contract labor provision than any other racial or ethnic category. In 1918, approximately 36 percent of deported contract laborers were sent to Mexico. The following year the Bureau of Immigration deported sixty-nine workers under the contract labor provision; thirty-eight, or 55 percent, were Mexican.[110] In 1920, seventy-three workers were deported under contract labor provision; fifty-two, or 71 percent, were Mexican.[111] These relatively small numbers are evidence of immigration officials' earliest efforts to enforce the new category of deportability under the guest worker program.[112]

In at least a handful of cases, immigration authorities also used deportations to quell labor activism among the guest workers. In 1919, when the Mexican consul complained about living conditions and wages on behalf of seventy Mexicans who had been imported under contract, the Bureau of Immigration decided that the workers who were "dissatisfied" should be returned.[113] That same year, a U.S. sugar company, which had imported contract workers, brought one of its laborers to the attention of the district office of the Bureau of Immigration for Montana and Idaho. The government deported the worker, and as the immigration inspector reported, "The result was that the situation became much improved, and no complaints have been received since."[114] The collaboration in the guest worker program with employers could go further than securing labor; it could serve as a tool to manage workers' mobilization.

In 1921, a recession hit the agriculture industry, and debate swirled about ending the program. Immigration officials and employers had justified importing contracted labor in the first place to better balance labor needs with economic fluctuations. Some maintained that in light of the recession, no labor shortage existed and, consequently, there was no longer a need to bring in guest workers. (This contrasted with the view of some of the growers, who unsuccessfully lobbied Congress to continue the program by claiming that the labor shortage persisted.) Calls to end the program were also concerned with the ways in which it conflicted with the racial classes already operating in federal law. Supporters of Chinese exclusion and the new Asiatic barred zone grew concerned that sugar growers in U.S. territories like Hawaii might call for a similar program to bring in Asian guest workers. They feared it could even be used to undermine the explicit racial classes present in immigration law. Some of the opposition, therefore, worried (unnecessarily, as it would turn out) about the precedent that the largely Mexican guest worker program set in its responsiveness to regional demands for racialized labor.

Congress shut down the guest worker program. What happened to Mexican guest workers reveals much about the purpose of the new form of deportability that temporary workers faced. Some 35,000 returned to Mexico when the House Immigration and Naturalization Committee unanimously voted to end the program. At least another 15,000 remained in the United States.[115] The government responded to the latter in two ways. First, immigration officials provided a path for many to change their temporary status to permanent by paying an eight-dollar head tax. Some employers paid the fee in order to maintain their work force.[116] Second, the Mexican guest workers remaining in the United States without regularizing their status did not face widespread deportations. What little enforcement there had been proved highly discretionary; the focus of enforcement had been to hold workers to their contracts while they had them.

With the program's end, immigration officials did not roll back the ways they had fractured the capacious legal category of immigrants inside the law over the previous twenty years. Deportability under the guest worker program, as it turned out, would be adapted and expanded. In 1924, in one part of a much larger overhaul of immigration policy, lawmakers tied Chinese immigrants' Section 6 (or legal) status to the occupation that enabled their entry to the United States. Chinese immigrants who entered as merchants, for example, could thereafter be deported if they took up work as laborers.[117]

Within two decades, the use of deportability to tie people to jobs would affect millions, especially Mexican immigrants and people of Mexican heritage. Lawmakers' expansion of deportability in the first decades of the twentieth century on economic grounds carved out new mechanisms to control lawfully admitted immigrants. And it has determined the scale and scope of rights and liberties open to people on U.S. soil ever since.

Conclusion

In 1925 and 1926, two deeply troubling and little-known deportations from the United States to Mexico took place. In 1925, Captain William M. Hanson, a U.S. immigration agent stationed in Texas, deported a Mexican general named Abelardo Hinojosa, a political refugee. He turned him over to a civil official, the chief of operations of the Mexican state of Tamaulipas. Almost immediately, Mexican military authorities took custody of General Hinojosa and sent him to the Santiago Tlalteloco prison in Mexico City, as a criminal against the government. At some point, Mexican authorities shot General Hinojosa as he allegedly tried to escape.[1] Just a few months later, in 1926, the same Captain Hanson arranged the deportation of Colonel Manuel Demetrio Torres, who was also a political refugee in the United States. Sometime after Mexican authorities took custody of Torres, Mexican military officials shot and killed him, too.[2]

State Department and congressional investigations into these two cases help underscore a key argument of this book: over the previous fifty years, deportation had been built into a distinct form of removal. The destination of deportations was important, with the deportee often being sent to the country of his or her origin. Deportations were bilateral in nature. Each deportation required the approval of authorities on the receiving end. Sometimes approval was obtained through negotiations for a specific deportation; at other times, approval was obtained more generally through bilateral agreement. Officials had to provide deportees with basic rights, originating from both international law and national law.

Just after the shooting of Hinojosa, U.S. consular officers in Mexico City raised concerns over his deportation and death.[3] James Sheffield, U.S. ambassador to Mexico, sent a letter to Washington informing his superiors that he believed that Mexican military officials set General Hinojosa free, shot him, and then justified his murder as an attempted escape. This, Sheffield wrote, was the practice called *Ley Fuga*.[4] Another officer, Harry Walsh, noted in his communiqué to Washington that, before his deportation,

Hinojosa was a political refugee in the United States, so his deportation to Mexico was "equivalent to passing the sentence of death upon him."[5] That, Walsh pointed out, represented "a violation of a most settled principle of international practice."[6]

Harry Walsh and the U.S. Immigration Committee of the Senate launched investigations into the Hinojosa and Torres cases. They found evidence of corruption on the part of Hanson, and a broader, systemic violation of the rights of Hinojosa and Torres. Prior to the Mexican Revolution, Captain Hanson had owned property in Mexico, which Mexican officials confiscated during the revolution but returned to him after the deportations of Hinojosa and Torres.[7] It also came out that the Mexican government had "presented" Hanson with a gold watch appraised at $1,800.[8] When questioned by investigators, Hanson declared he had done nothing wrong. Not mentioning the real estate or the watch, he claimed that he had been unaware that both men were political refugees and had merely carried out justifiable deportations. Walsh believed differently; he saw the deportations as part of a corrupt deal between Mexican authorities and Captain Hanson.[9] The investigators also condemned Hanson for what amounted to gross violations of a central tenet of deportations. When Hanson delivered Hinojosa and Torres to Mexican officials, investigators concluded, he effectively denied them basic rights by sending the two men to their deaths.

U.S. authorities had in the previous few years removed other Mexican refugees like Hinojosa and Torres, but they had carried these out through a different form of removal, a kind of expulsion. The assistant secretary of labor Robe Carl White wrote that "the Department has frequently permitted Mexican aliens who have been ordered deported, to proceed voluntarily to other countries at their own expense. It has likewise in some cases granted stays of deportation, in order to enable aliens ordered deported to 'slip' into Mexico unnoticed."[10] Since expulsions were largely unilateral, handling the removals of Mexicans this way meant that U.S. officials did not transfer the deportees to officials on the receiving end, as required by bilateral deportation. This strategy allowed U.S. officials to follow international laws and standards of removals—not handing immigrants to government officials who would kill them but still remove the immigrants.

At the conclusion of their investigations, Hanson resigned from his position with the Immigration Service. Of far greater importance, officials were moved by the fates of Hinojosa and Torres. They stressed that any subsequent cases involving refugees like Hinojosa and Torres should be handled through expulsions rather than deportations. Assistant Secretary of Labor White recommended that "in making decisions in future cases, where in there is reason to believe that the life of a deportee would be jeopardized by his return to Mexico, consideration will be given as heretofore, with the end in view of permitting such person to voluntarily depart to other countries."[11]

Over the next twenty years, through the 1940s, nations and communities practiced forms of removals other than deportations and expulsions. Most of the major forced population movements, in fact, were handled through some other form. The final peace settlement of World War I, the Lausanne Treaty of 1923, for instance, contained provisions that moved more than one million Christians "from Anatolia to Greece and around 350,000 Muslims from Greece to Turkey."[12] These were not deportations in the formal legal sense. Instead, they were massive population exchanges aimed at making homogeneous national populations.

During the Great Depression, state and local authorities in the United States participated in the removal of as many as 1.5 million Mexican immigrants and even Mexican Americans—U.S. citizens—in what has become known as "Mexican repatriation."[13] Of the Mexican repatriations, only a small proportion of these people were formally deported. There may have been the political will to deport hundreds of thousands of Mexicans and Mexican Americans, but U.S. immigration authorities did not have the technical capacity. And, as the Supreme Court had made clear, U.S. citizens could not be deported. State and local officials accomplished the removals through other, less legal modes.

The mass removals of the Holocaust carried out by Hitler and the Nazis are often called deportations, but these, too, are different from the bilateral form of removal that this book examines. Shortly after taking power in 1933, Hitler restricted the role of international law in its jurisdiction over citizens and subjects. "The implications of this approach," as historian Mark Mazower writes, "were being drawn out in the legal and political science journals of the new Germany. Denying that international law had any validity, jurists in the Third Reich now argued that 'the nation comes before humanity.' Each racial group, according to some, possessed its own conception of law, making the idea of a global political society a nonsense."[14] Explicitly denying the role of international law and any basic rights to the removed, the authorities of the Third Reich forced millions of Jews, Poles, Gypsies, and others all over Europe to the concentration and death camps of World War II.

In the United States, formal bilateral immigrant removals—deportations—exerted an enormous impact on U.S. domestic law. One of the most important outcomes was that the cases of Fong Yue Ting, Kaoru Yamataya, and John Turner, as well as many others, drew ever more distinct lines around categories of residents in the United States: immigrants without legal residence, immigrants with legal residence, and U.S. citizens.

One of the two initial trajectories of U.S. deportation policy developed under Chinese exclusion created two groups of Chinese immigrants: those within the law and those outside the law. The purpose of the first law of Chinese exclusion in 1882 was to prevent future immigration streams of Chinese workers and to deport those who managed to enter in violation of the law. The intersection of the categories of race and class reinforced each other. For those workers who came in violation of the law, as historian Paul Kramer notes, "it makes little sense to identify this law as an exercise in either 'race' or 'class' politics." Instead, both were "understood as mutually exclusive modes of power and social differentiation. It was both race and class legislation, marking a class division that applied only to the Chinese defined as a racialized descent group."[15] Lawful immigrants, including Chinese merchants, students, and laborers already in the country before 1882, were not deportable under the new law. Under the provision denying people of Chinese heritage the right to naturalize, however, they also could never become U.S. citizens.

Over the next several decades, immigration officials systematically collapsed the categories of lawful immigrant for people of Chinese heritage into unlawful immigrant on U.S. soil through deportation policy. In the Geary Act, passed in 1892, lawmakers expanded the deportability of Chinese workers already lawfully in the country. This expansion limited the rights of people lawfully in the country who had not yet acquired certificates of residency by changing their status to unlawful. Immigration officials also arrested people with certificates of residence and well-known merchants in spite of their legal status. The status of people of Chinese heritage was thus transformed by the aggressive policing of law. Deportability had thus become a new way that people of Chinese heritage were racialized in the United States.

The hierarchical nature of the interstate system further affected the deportability of Chinese immigrants within the United States. Chinese diplomats could use the international appeal to try to defend interests of Chinese immigrants facing deportation, but not with the same strength, for instance, of U.S. officials in German and Austro-Hungarian cases. Chinese officials could not threaten to reciprocate with deportations of U.S. citizens from China as a way to prevent a deportation and protect the lines between categories of immigrants. Furthermore, embedded in the agreements signed between U.S., Canadian, and Mexican officials to facilitate deportations within North America were provisions that qualified the liberties of lawful residents of Chinese heritage to leave a country and return. Deportability enforced through the international regime, therefore, did more than enforce exclusion—it affected the power of people of Chinese heritage to stay in the country or travel abroad.

Deportability under general immigration law mattered to all immigrants, regardless of country of origin, but their experiences were often less stark and enduring than for Chinese immigrants. For example, John Turner's lawyers argued that the anarchist provision violated his First Amendment rights. The Supreme Court said that it did not. Deportability affected Turner's speech. But, under general immigration policy, immigrants who came in violation of law were protected from deportation once they lived in the United States past the time limit. General immigration policy, moreover, kept the numbers of immigrants in the country in violation of the law low because almost all people could enter lawfully. There were differences between U.S. citizens, legal residents, and immigrants outside the law, but those differences mattered far more for people of Chinese heritage than for immigrants from anywhere else.

The role deportations played in distinguishing the categories of immigrant and citizen sharpened when U.S. lawmakers expanded the grounds for deportation to include post-entry infractions in 1910. Even before that there had been times when immigration officials had deported people for what seemed like post-entry infractions. Yet these were exceptions and, for the most part, what millions of immigrants did after entering the United States did not make them deportable. Congress first created its power to deport for post-entry actions with the antiprostitution provision of 1910. This made certain actions on U.S. soil deportable offenses. Women and men who immigrated legally but were charged with prostitution or procuring could be deported at any time after their entry. This provision was framed initially as an intervention of the progressive state rather than simply a punitive turn in deportations. The provision did have a punitive side, however, which reinforced some differences between immigrants and citizens. Immigrants and citizens could both be punished for violating the criminal laws against prostitution, but immigrants could also face deportation after serving the criminal sentence. Officials hoped that the main thrust of the antiprostitution provision could be used to protect and help reform women involved in prostitution or enslaved in sex work. As the use of the antiprostitution provision declined, deportations for post-entry infractions quickly lost their humanitarian meaning and became largely punitive.[16]

A century later, immigration officials use stays of deportation to protect vulnerable immigrants. Through the T visa, created in October of 2000, victims of sex or human trafficking can regularize their status and gain legal residence in the United States. In 2008, the U.S. Congress passed and President George W. Bush signed the William Wilberforce Trafficking Victims Protection Reauthorization Act, which provides for stays of deportation for unaccompanied minors as a form of humanitarian intervention. Section 235(b) also mandates other protections for unaccompanied children from noncontiguous countries—countries other than Canada or Mexico. In 2014, when more than fifty thousand children from Honduras, El Salvador, and Guatemala fled violence, civil unrest, and dire poverty to the United States, most were processed under this law. Almost 64 percent received stays in deportation and were granted asylum.[17]

In the early twentieth century, within the category of immigrant, race shaped how officials administered deportation policy. The most overt example of this is Chinese exclusion. But officials also had the latitude to employ race outside the letter of the law. Deportation policy operated racially under the antiprostitution provision. Between 1903 and 1917, when immigration officials used the antiprostitution provision as a kind of victims' rights program, they hoped to employ it to protect white women. In quite a different way, immigration authorities employed the LPC (likely to become a public charge) provision as a proxy for racial exclusions of South Asians starting in 1906. The evidence, and the scripts behind their justifications, relied on racist stereotypes and discrimination in the job market. From 1906 through 1917, immigration authorities also employed the LPC provision to prevent the migration of South Asians into the continental United States after a lawful migration to the U.S. territories of Hawaii and the Philippines. Moola Singh and ninety-four other men challenged immigration officials' use of the economic grounds for deportation for such clearly racial reasons. They won their 1917 Supreme Court cases, but the victory did very little to undermine the power of U.S. immigration officials to use general immigration law racially.[18] That same year, in the Immigration Act of 1917, Congress folded Chinese exclusion into general immigration policy and added an explicit racial category to general immigration law when it created the Asiatic barred zone. Immigration authorities operated deportation policy with racial classes and provisions that could be used racially.

The guest worker program begun in 1917 pointed to a new way that race, class, and deportability intersected in deportation policy. The guest worker program created a class within the category of lawful immigrant: the temporary worker. Immigrants coming under this category were prevented from changing jobs and required to depart the country after the term of the contract. This new class served two objectives. One was to manage a tight labor supply between the United States and Canada, while the other, larger objective was to bring in workers from a market with a surplus to the United States. The significance of the program to race lay in the ways that it restricted liberties and rights of Mexican immigrants, adding to the ways that race already limited their opportunities to integrate into the United States.

For all its effects nationally, deportation policy expanded the ways that U.S. law mattered abroad, too. Even before Congress built policy to deport people from the United States, U.S. law was exported abroad through the international legal regime under extraterritoriality. One important outcome was to put U.S. foreign nationals beyond the reach of immigrant removal in places like China because U.S. citizens in China were processed under U.S. law rather than Chinese law. Chinese officials could not deport U.S. citizens for a century because they did not have jurisdiction over them.

In 1927, a chapter in the life of Marcus Garvey, the Jamaican-born leader of the Universal Negro Improvement Association (UNIA), illustrates that as the United States built its deportation policy, it made American law matter beyond the nation's borders in significant new ways. U.S. officials deported Garvey to Jamaica in 1926 as one who was likely to become a public charge.[19] A year later, Garvey wrote to the U.S. secretary of state to notify American officials that he intended to travel from Jamaica to Panama to do work on behalf of UNIA (see Figures 8–9). To get to where he was going, he had to be, as he wrote, "a kind of interstate passenger going from Colon on the Panama railroad to Panama City, thereby crossing the Canal

Zone which is an American territory." Garvey continued, "knowing the American laws as I do, I know there is no violation being an interstate passenger going from one point to the next without disembarking." But he asked whether the U.S. government would put any restrictions on his travel. He wanted to avoid complications, because, as he put it, he did not want "to waste time in Federal Courts."[20] U.S. authorities did have a problem with Garvey's travel. U.S. officials refused to permit it on the grounds that Garvey could not lawfully travel through the canal because of his deportation. U.S. consular officials had tracked Garvey's movements and actions when he traveled outside the United States even before his deportation.[21] His deportation gave U.S. officials grounds to limit the movement of an anticolonial activist because of the reach of U.S. law, even after his deportation.

Deportations like Garvey's also made U.S. law important to the country of a deportee's origin. Briefly following the history of the criminal status provision for deportation helps make this clear. Congress passed the first criminal status provision in 1891, and the Bureau of Immigration employed it to deport people who had criminal records before their entry into the United States.[22] For countries on the receiving end, then, the grounds for deportation amounted to violations of their own criminal law, not criminal law in the United States. In 1904, immigration officials launched a nationwide study of the imprisoned immigrant population. The Bureau of Immigration determined that there were just under 10,000 immigrants in U.S. prisons for crimes committed on U.S. soil.[23] Of these, states housed 5,259; county prisons housed 4,525; and federal prisons had only 41 in custody.[24] About 60 percent of the prisoners were located in New York, Pennsylvania, Illinois, and Massachusetts.[25] New York had the largest population, totaling just over 2,200 inmates. States in the South and the West had much smaller populations. Florida, for example, housed only 27 immigrants in its state and county jails. California's immigrant prison population was larger than that but was still relatively small at 632 inmates.[26] The federal government did not deport these immigrants from federal or state prisons for crimes committed on U.S. soil in 1904 because no federal law authorized it.

In 1917, lawmakers expanded the criminal status provision to explicitly include post-entry infractions. By then, U.S. immigration officials had been deporting some people for post-entry infractions under the antiprostitution provision or, in even smaller numbers, by proxy, as a public charge or LPC (this is eventually what happened to Marcus Garvey). The Immigration Act

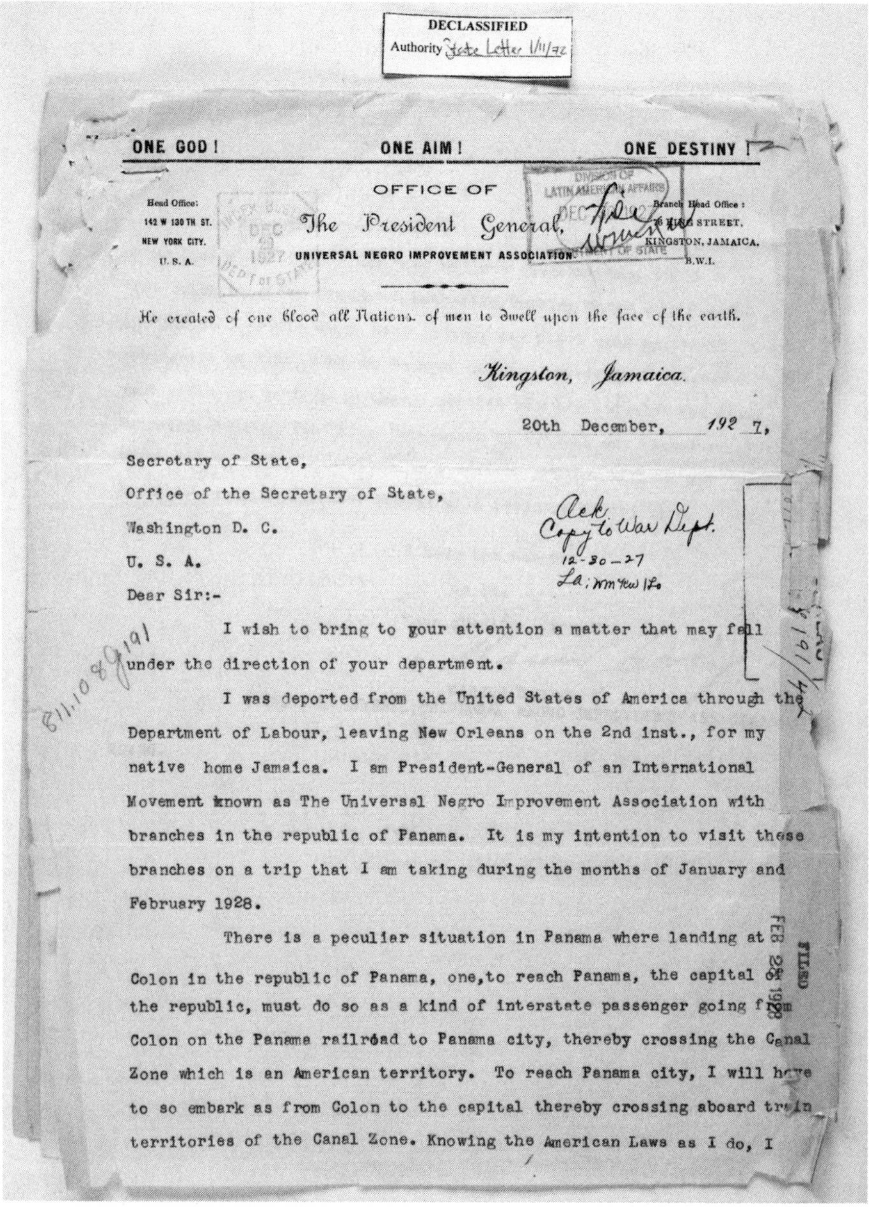

ONE GOD !   ONE AIM !   ONE DESTINY !

OFFICE OF

Head Office:
142 W 130 TH ST.
NEW YORK CITY.
U. S. A.

The President General.

Branch Head Office :
6 KING STREET,
KINGSTON, JAMAICA,
B.W.I.

UNIVERSAL NEGRO IMPROVEMENT ASSOCIATION

He created of one blood all Nations. of men to dwell upon the face of the earth.

Kingston, Jamaica.

20th December, 192 7,

Secretary of State,

Office of the Secretary of State,

Washington D. C.

U. S. A.

*Ack.
Copy to War Dept.
12-30-27
La: wm tw 1fo*

Dear Sir:-

 I wish to bring to your attention a matter that may fall
under the direction of your department.

 I was deported from the United States of America through the
Department of Labour, leaving New Orleans on the 2nd inst., for my
native home Jamaica. I am President-General of an International
Movement known as The Universal Negro Improvement Association with
branches in the republic of Panama. It is my intention to visit these
branches on a trip that I am taking during the months of January and
February 1928.

 There is a peculiar situation in Panama where landing at
Colon in the republic of Panama, one,to reach Panama, the capital of
the republic, must do so as a kind of interstate passenger going from
Colon on the Panama railroad to Panama city, thereby crossing the Canal
Zone which is an American territory. To reach Panama city, I will have
to so embark as from Colon to the capital thereby crossing aboard train
territories of the Canal Zone. Knowing the American Laws as I do, I

FILED FEB 21 1928

Figure 8. Marcus Garvey to Secretary of State, December 20, 1927, first page.
The second page of the letter is in Figure 9. National Archives and Records
Administration, College Park, Md., file 811.108, DS. Photo by Joe McCary.

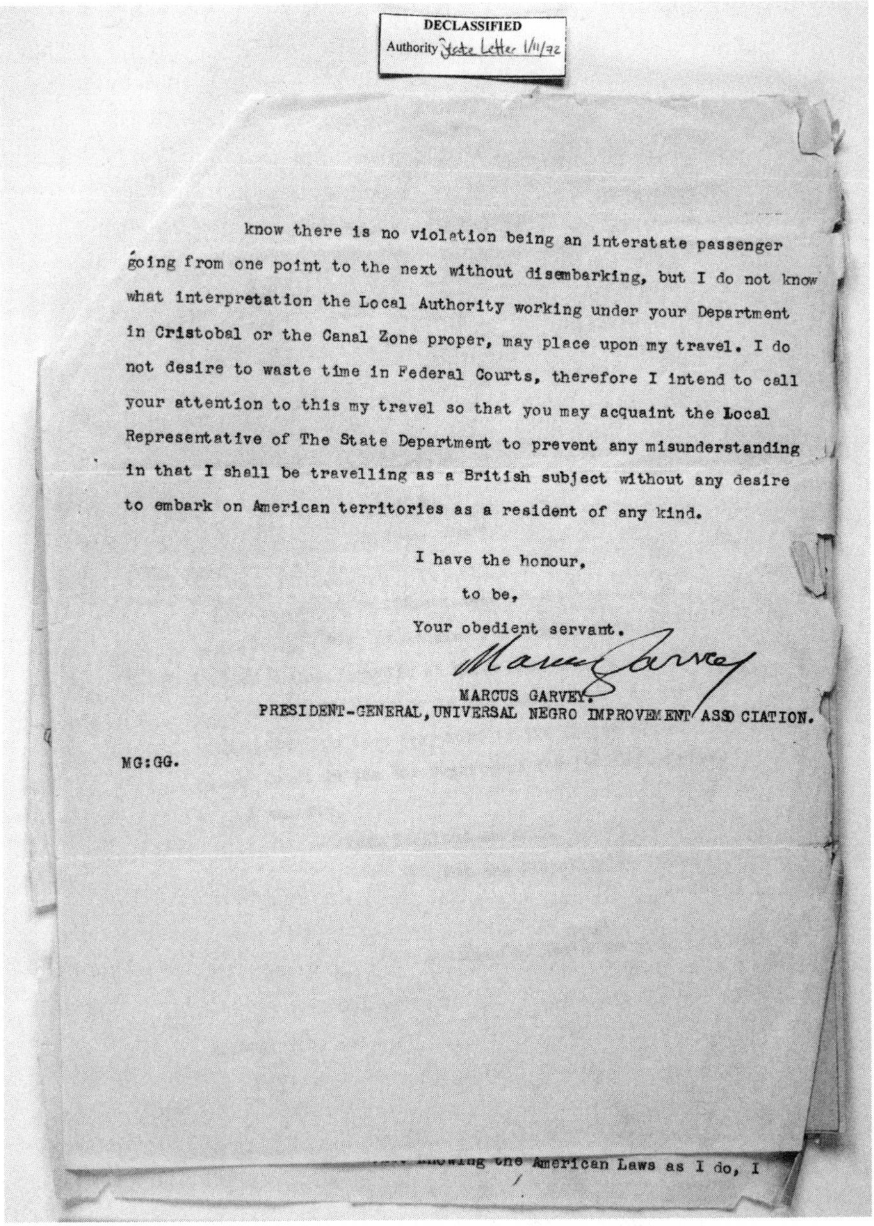

DECLASSIFIED
Authority State Letter 1/11/72

know there is no violation being an interstate passenger going from one point to the next without disembarking, but I do not know what interpretation the Local Authority working under your Department in Cristobal or the Canal Zone proper, may place upon my travel. I do not desire to waste time in Federal Courts, therefore I intend to call your attention to this my travel so that you may acquaint the Local Representative of The State Department to prevent any misunderstanding in that I shall be travelling as a British subject without any desire to embark on American territories as a resident of any kind.

I have the honour,

to be,

Your obedient servant.

Marcus Garvey

MARCUS GARVEY.

PRESIDENT-GENERAL, UNIVERSAL NEGRO IMPROVEMENT ASSOCIATION.

MG:GG.

... knowing the American Laws as I do, I

Figure 9. Marcus Garvey to Secretary of State, December 20, 1927, second page. National Archives and Records Administration, College Park, Md., file 811.108, DS. Photo by Joe McCary.

of 1917 introduced a new post-entry infraction by making those immigrants who violated laws involving "moral turpitude" deportable.[27] The definition of "moral turpitude" covered "anything done contrary to justice, honesty, principle or good morals."[28] Now, immigration officials could deport some people in jails and prisons for crimes committed on U.S. soil. Garvey's case and the small number of deportations for what amounted to post-entry infractions made emigrant-sending nations responsible for emigrants who violated any U.S. laws. In a sense, deportation for post-entry infractions made U.S. crimes important to the country of a deportee's origin through the legal regime.

Over the next forty-five years, these criminal status provisions had limited application and impact; fewer than eight hundred people were deported for moral turpitude offenses.[29] The numbers deported remained low for three reasons: the relatively small prison populations; the extremely vague nature of what constituted a deportable post-entry crime; and limited enforcement capacity. State prison and local authorities seldom initiated deportation proceedings or sought federal involvement, so the task fell almost completely on federal officials. To determine which inmates were deportable, immigration agents needed to gain access to state and local institutions and then interview the immigrants. The Bureau of Immigration would also need to send agents around the country to interview a prisoner's friends, relatives, and employers to determine whether the crime fit within the vague definition of moral turpitude—which did not parallel state and local crimes—and whether it occurred within five years of immigration. Officials then would have to assess the proper country of return and determine if that country would even take the individual back. The Bureau of Immigration had neither the budget nor the staff to carry out such elaborate investigations.[30] The impact of U.S. law abroad would remain restrained as long as U.S. officials deported small numbers of immigrants, especially those who had lived in the U.S. for many years.

The 1920s brought profound changes to U.S. policy. Lawmakers in the Immigration Act of 1924 created the new deportable category of "aliens without proper visas," and, by the late 1920s, over half of all those deported by the Bureau of Immigration fell under that category. Immigrants without proper documentation quickly became the largest class of deportees while deportations under the older, qualitative categories plummeted.[31] The Bureau of Immigration also began deporting thousands more immigrants each year. In 1922, just prior to the passage of the new law, the Bureau of

Immigration deported 4,283 immigrants. In 1923, it deported 3,546 immigrants. In 1925, the first year after Congress passed the new law, the government deported 9,402 immigrants.[32] In 1930, the government deported over 16,000 people.[33]

The numbers of immigrants deported increased every decade thereafter, and by the middle of the 1960s U.S. immigration authorities got into the business of annual mass deportations. Between 1966 and 2011, the federal government voluntarily removed or, under the nomenclature of today, "returned," over forty-one million people. For more than four decades, the United States had consistently deported close to one million people every year. For nearly all of that time, deportations via voluntary removal remained close to one million people per year.[34] The majority of all these deported men, women, and children were Mexican.

During the founding era of U.S. deportation policy, the power of deportation, deportation policy, and deportability brought new definition to constitutional rights, personal relationships, the meaning of race, and economic power in the United States. The international reach of U.S. deportation policy exported some of these consequences around the globe. With the widening of deportability and increased enforcement after the 1920s, and especially after the 1960s, the impact of deportations on law and law enforcement has become more pronounced, with new and steep costs and consequences. The historical significance of the founding years of deportation, now over a century later, remains hard to overstate.

Notes

Introduction

1. On changes in Europe, see Robin Cohen, "Shaping the Nation, Excluding the Other: The Deportation of Migrants from Britain," in *Migration, Migration History, History: Old Paradigms and New Perspectives*, ed. Jan Lucassen and Leo Lucassen (Bern: Peter Lang, 1999); Frank Caestecker, "The Changing Modalities of Regulation in International Migration Within Continental Europe, 1870–1940," in *Regulation of Migration: International Experiences*, ed. Anita Böcker et al. (Amsterdam: Het Spinhuis, 1998); Clifford Rosenberg, *Policing Paris: The Origins of Modern Immigration Control Between the Wars* (Ithaca, N.Y.: Cornell University Press, 2006); John Torpey, *The Invention of the Passport: Surveillance, Citizenship, and the State* (Cambridge: Cambridge University Press, 2000).

2. Not all of these were formal deportations, most were actually shortcut procedures, but all depended on the power of deportation. U.S. Department of Homeland Security, "Aliens Removed or Returned: Fiscal Years 1892 to 2006," Table 38, *Yearbook of Immigration Statistics: 2006*, http://www.dhs.gov/ximgtn/statistics/publications/YrBk06En.shtm (accessed July 12, 2008). As legal scholar Hiroshi Motomura states, both the recent shortcut deportations, which are now called "removals," and the more formal deportations, now called "returns," are "compelled departures." Both are defined by the Department of Homeland Security as "the compulsory and confirmed movement of an inadmissible or deportable alien out of the United States." Hiroshi Motomura, "The Discretion That Matters: Federal Immigration Enforcement, State and Local Arrests, and the Civil-Criminal Line," *UCLA Law Review* 58 (2011): 1835.

3. The term "deportation regime" is taken from Nicholas De Genova and Nathalie Peutz, eds., *The Deportation Regime: Sovereignty, Space, and the Freedom of Movement* (Durham, N.C.: Duke University Press, 2010).

4. Harold Dana Sims, *The Expulsion of Mexico's Spaniards, 1821–1836* (Pittsburgh: University of Pittsburgh Press, 1990); John Mack Faragher, *A Great and Noble Scheme: The Tragic Story of the Expulsion of the French Acadians from Their American Homeland* (New York: W. W. Norton, 2005).

5. Kunal M. Parker, *Making Foreigners: Immigration and Citizenship Law in America, 1600–2000* (Cambridge: Cambridge University Press, 2015), 73–75; Cornelia H. Dayton and Sharon V. Salinger, *Robert Love's Warnings: Searching for Strangers in Colonial Boston* (Philadelphia: University of Pennsylvania Press, 2014).

6. In 1798, Thomas Jefferson argued vehemently against this expansion of executive power. He wrote, "The same act undertaking to authorize the president to remove a person out of the United States who is under the protection of the law, on his own suspicion, without

accusation, without jury, without public trial, without confrontation of the witnesses against him, without having witnesses in his favor, without defense, without counsel, is contrary to these provisions also of the Constitution, is therefore not law, but utterly void and of no force." Thomas Jefferson, "Kentucky Resolution," as quoted by Clarence S. Darrow and Edgar L. Masters, *In the Supreme Court of the United States: United States Ex Rel. John Turner vs. William Williams, Commissioner of Immigration, Brief And Argument of Appellant* (Chicago: H. C. Darrow, 1903), 72.

7. For more information on the Alien Acts, see Hiroshi Motomura, *Americans in Waiting: The Lost Story of Immigration and Citizenship in the United States* (Oxford: Oxford University Press, 2006), 18–19; T. Alexander Aleinikoff, *Semblances of Sovereignty: The Constitution, the State, and American Citizenship* (Cambridge, Mass.: Harvard University Press, 2002); Gerald L. Neuman, *Strangers to the Constitution: Immigrants, Borders, and Fundamental Law* (Princeton, N.J.: Princeton University Press, 1996), 52–60; E. P. Hutchinson, *Legislative History of American Immigration Policy, 1798–1965* (Philadelphia: University of Pennsylvania Press, 1981), 16.

8. Hidetaka Hirota, "The Moment of Transition: State Officials, the Federal Government, and the Formation of American Immigration Policy," *Journal of American History* 99, no. 4 (March 2013): 1092–108; Aleinikoff, *Semblances of Sovereignty*; Neuman, *Strangers to the Constitution*.

9. Daniel Kanstroom, *Deportation Nation: Outsiders in American History* (Cambridge, Mass.: Harvard University Press, 2007). For a theoretical discussion of exceptional state violence, see Giorgio Agamben, *Homo Sacer: Sovereign Power and Bare Life* (Stanford, Calif.: Stanford University Press, 1998); Giorgio Agamben, *The Coming Community* (Minneapolis: University of Minnesota Press, 1993).

10. Katherine Unterman, *Uncle Sam's Policemen: The Pursuit of Fugitives Across Borders* (Cambridge, Mass.: Harvard University Press, 2015); Nan Goodman, *Banished: Common Law and the Rhetoric of Social Exclusion in Early New England* (Philadelphia: University of Pennsylvania Press, 2012); Daniel S. Margolies, *Spaces of Law in American Foreign Relations: Extradition and Extraterritoriality in the Borderlands and Beyond, 1877–1898* (Athens: University of Georgia Press, 2011).

11. For information on why the United States received so many immigrants in this period, see Jose C. Moya and Adam McKeown, "World Migration in the Long Twentieth Century," in *Essays on Twentieth-Century History,* ed. Michael Adas (Philadelphia: Temple University Press, 2010), 9–52.

12. Erika Lee uses the term to refer to this new role of the federal government. Erika Lee, *At America's Gates: Chinese Immigration During the Exclusion Era, 1882–1943* (Chapel Hill: University of North Carolina Press, 2003). For other scholarship on Chinese exclusion that tracks the rise of federal immigration restriction, see, for example, Beth Lew-Williams, "Before Restriction Became Exclusion: America's Experiment in Diplomatic Immigration Control," *Pacific Historical Review* 83, no. 1 (February 2014): 24–56; Moon-Ho Jung, *Coolies and Cane: Race, Labor, and Sugar in the Age of Emancipation* (Baltimore: Johns Hopkins University Press, 2008); Adam McKeown, *Chinese Migrant Networks and Cultural Change: Peru, Chicago, Hawaii, 1900–1936* (Chicago: University of Chicago Press, 2001); Andrew Gyory, *Closing the Gate: Race, Politics, and the Chinese Exclusion Act* (Chapel Hill: University of North Carolina Press, 1998); Lucy E. Salyer, *Laws Harsh as Tigers: Chinese Immigrants and the Shaping of*

Modern Immigration Law (Chapel Hill: University of North Carolina Press, 1995). On U.S. immigration policy and nation building more broadly, see Deirdre M. Moloney, *National Insecurities: Immigrants and U.S. Deportation Policy Since 1882* (Chapel Hill: University of North Carolina Press, 2012); Margot Canaday, *The Straight State: Sexuality and Citizenship in Twentieth-Century America* (Princeton, N.J.: Princeton University Press, 2009); Anna Pegler-Gordon, *In Sight of America: Photography and the Development of U.S. Immigration Policy* (Berkeley: University of California Press, 2009); Motomura, *Americans in Waiting*; Aristide R. Zolberg, *A Nation by Design: Immigration Policy in the Fashioning of America* (Cambridge: Cambridge University Press, 2006); Roger Daniels, *Guarding the Golden Door: American Immigration Policy and Immigrants Since 1882* (New York: Hill and Wang, 2004); Kevin R. Johnson, *The "Huddled Masses" Myth* (Philadelphia: Temple University Press, 2004); Eithne Luibhéid, *Entry Denied: Controlling Sexuality at the Border* (Minneapolis: University of Minnesota Press, 2002).

13. Nicholas De Genova and Nathalie Peutz, "Introduction," *The Deportation Regime*, 2.

14. Scholars interested in the international legal regime focus on the consequences of deportations for the receiving end of a deportation. Scholars are studying, for example, how Mexico, Honduras, El Salvador, and Guatemala—the four states receiving the majority of all removals from the United States—are currently experiencing problems of reintegration. Others scholars are examining the social history, how many of the removed or returned are legally tied to their country of citizenship, but feel more cultural and social belonging to the United States. See Daniel Kanstroom, *Aftermath: Deportation Law and the New American Diaspora* (New York: Oxford University Press, 2012); David C. Brotherton and Luis Barrios, *Banished to the Homeland: Dominican Deportees and Their Stories of Exile* (New York: Columbia University Press, 2011); Bill Ong Hing, *Deporting Our Souls: Values, Morality, and Immigration Policy* (Cambridge: Cambridge University Press, 2006).

15. Recent scholarship examines immigration policy internationally during the late nineteenth and early twentieth century, but it does not focus specifically on the international regime facilitating deportations. See David Scott FitzGerald and David Cook-Martín, *Culling the Masses: The Democratic Origins of Racist Immigration Policy in the Americas* (Cambridge, Mass.: Harvard University Press, 2014); David Cook-Martin, *Scramble for Citizens: Dual Nationality and State Competition for Immigrants* (Stanford, Calif.: Stanford University Press, 2013); Kornel Chang, *Pacific Connections: The Making of the U.S.-Canadian Borderlands* (Berkeley: University of California Press, 2012); Donna R. Gabaccia, *Foreign Relations: American Immigration in Global Perspective* (Princeton, N.J.: Princeton University Press, 2012); Adam McKeown, *Melancholy Order: Asian Migration and the Globalization of Borders* (New York: Columbia University Press, 2008); Marilyn Lake and Henry Reynolds, *Drawing the Global Colour Line: White Men's Countries and the International Challenge of Racial Equality* (Cambridge: Cambridge University Press, 2008).

16. Getting into the business of deportation, as historian Mae Ngai notes, brought federal authorities into new kinds of law enforcement within the United States. Mae M. Ngai, *Impossible Subjects: Illegal Aliens and the Making of Modern America* (Princeton, N.J.: Princeton University Press, 2004). For other scholarship that focuses on the impact of immigration policy on law enforcement within the United States, see Kanstroom, *Deportation Nation*; Mary Bosworth and Jeanne Flavin, eds., *Race, Gender, and Punishment: From Colonialism to the War on Terror* (New Brunswick, N.J.: Rutgers University Press, 2007); Kenneth D. Ackerman,

Young J. Edgar: Hoover, the Red Scare, and the Assault on Civil Liberties (New York: Carroll & Graf, 2007); Hing, *Deporting Our Souls*; Mark Dow, *American Gulag: Inside U.S. Immigration Prisons* (Berkeley: University of California Press, 2004); Nancy Morawetz, "*INS v. St. Cyr*: The Campaign to Preserve Court Review and Stop Retroactive Application of Deportation Laws," in *Immigration Stories*, ed. David A. Martin and Peter H. Schuck (New York: Foundation Press, 2005), 279–309. For strong coverage of immigration law as a part of the federal government's plenary power, see Gabriel J. Chin, "*Chae Chan Ping* and *Fong Yue Ting*: The Origins of Plenary Power," in Martin and Schuck, *Immigration Stories*, 7–30; Burt Neuborne, "*Harisiades v. Shaughnessy*: A Case Study in the Vulnerability of Resident Aliens," in Martin and Schuck, *Immigration Stories*, 87–112; Aleinikoff, *Semblances of Sovereignty*; Neuman, *Strangers to the Constitution*.

17. As legal scholar Hiroshi Motomuro notes, "immigration law starts with Congress but in practice it is made in the field." Hiroshi Motomura, *Immigration Outside the Law* (New York: Oxford University Press, 2014), 121.

18. This book draws on a rich variety of sources for this history, including deportation files and hearing records, court cases, congressional reports, immigration legislation, and the annual reports published by the Bureau of Immigration. For some recent scholarship examining the ways law and constitutionalism were shaped beyond the courts, in places like administrative bureaucracy or in the efforts of people to navigate law, see Sophia Z. Lee, *The Workplace Constitution from the New Deal to the New Right* (Cambridge: Cambridge University Press, 2014); Tomiko Brown-Nagin, *Courage to Dissent: Atlanta and the Long History of the Civil Rights Movement* (New York: Oxford University Press, 2011). See also Jeremy K. Kessler, "The Administrative Origins of Modern Civil Liberties Law," *Columbia Law Review* 5 (2014): 1083–166; and Christopher Capazzola, *Uncle Sam Wants You: World War I and the Making of the Modern American Citizen* (New York: Oxford University Press, 2008).

19. Motomura uses this term in *Immigration Outside the Law*.

Chapter 1

1. Act of May 5, 1892, § 3, 27 Stat. 25 (1892).

2. *Fong Yue Ting v. United States*, 149 U.S. 698 (1893).

3. Lee, *At America's Gates*, 25.

4. Estelle T. Lau, *Paper Families: Identity, Immigration Administration, and Chinese Exclusion* (Durham, N.C.: Duke University Press, 2006); Lee, *At America's Gates*; McKeown, *Chinese Migrant Networks*; Karen Leong, "'A Distinct and Antagonistic Race': Constructions of Chinese Manhood in the Exclusionist Debates, 1869–1878," in *Across the Great Divide: Cultures of Manhood in the United States West*, ed. Matthew Basso, Laura McCall, and Dee Garceau (New York: Routledge, 2001); Madeline Yuan-yin Hsu, *Dreaming of Gold, Dreaming of Home: Transnationalism and Migration Between the United States and South China, 1882–1943* (Stanford, Calif.: Stanford University Press, 2000); Salyer, *Laws Harsh as Tigers*; Charles J. McClain, *In Search of Equality: The Chinese Struggle Against Discrimination in Nineteenth-Century America* (Berkeley: University of California Press, 1994).

5. As quoted in Lee, *At America's Gates*, 29.

6. Gyory, *Closing the Gate*, 187. On electoral and congressional bipartisan support, see also Alexander Saxton, *The Indispensable Enemy: Labor and the Anti-Chinese Movement in California* (Berkeley: University of California Press, 1971), 104–12, 172–78. As Saxton writes, the reasons anti-Chinese bigotry was effective in eastern politics were several:

That the enactment [of Chinese exclusion] was due to massive agreement in the West on the Chinese question is unmistakable. Yet the origins of that consensus were not primarily western. Patterns of thought and organization which shaped the anti-Chinese movement had stemmed from the Jacksonian era in the East. The resurgence of these patterns in California politics deeply affected the national debate on Reconstruction. Abandonment of Reconstruction by the Republicans, together with the erosion of the abolitionist line within the party, had in effect given permission for the bipartisan anti-Chinese alliance. And there was one other factor as well. Steam transportation, especially the completion of the transcontinental railroad and the Southern Pacific network to the Gulf of Mexico, assured investors interested in the Pacific slope alternative sources of labor supply. (*Indispensable Enemy*, 178)

7. For work on state expulsions and some of the ways that state governments sometimes worked with the federal government, see Hirota, "The Moment of Transition"; Aleinikoff, *Semblances of Sovereignty*; Neuman, *Strangers to the Constitution*.

8. Act of May 6, 1882, § 12, 22 Stat. 58 (1882).

9. Act of July 5, 1884, § 12, 23 Stat. 115 (1884); Act of Sept. 13, 1888, § 12, 25 Stat. 476 (1888).

10. For a discussion of the way that the categories of class and race were mutually constitutive, see Paul A. Kramer, "Imperial Openings: Civilization, Exemption, and the Geopolitics of Mobility in the History of Chinese Exclusion, 1868–1910," *Journal of the Gilded Age and Progressive Era* 14, no. 3 (2015): 317–47, esp. 322.

11. Salyer, *Laws Harsh as Tigers*, 46; Lee, *At America's Gates*, 42.

12. Lee, *At America's Gates*, 41.

13. Lee, *At America's Gates*, 123.

14. Brief for the Appellant at 1–3, Fong Yue Ting v. U.S., 149 U.S. 698 (1893), *USSCRB*.

15. *Fong Yue Ting*, 149 U.S.

16. Joseph H. Choate, J. Hubley Ashton, and Maxwell Evarts, Brief for the Appellant, 72–73.

17. Brief for the Appellant, 72–73.

18. Brief for the Appellant, 11.

19. Brief for the Appellant, 7–8.

20. Brief for the Appellant, 7.

21. Brief for the Appellant, 7.

22. Brief for the Appellant, 57.

23. *Chae Chan Ping v. United States*, 130 U.S. 581 (1889); *Nishimura Ekiu v. United States*, 142 U.S. 651 (1892).

24. *Fong Yue Ting*, 149 U.S. at 705.

25. Sarah Cleveland, "Powers Inherent in Sovereignty: Indians, Aliens, Territories, and the Nineteenth Century Origins of Plenary Power over Foreign Affairs," *Texas Law Review* 81 (November 2002): 280.

26. *Fong Yue Ting*, 149 U.S. at 713.

27. *Fong Yue Ting*, 149 U.S. at 706.

28. *Fong Yue Ting*, 149 U.S. at 724.

29. *Fong Yue Ting*, 149 U.S. at 730.

30. *Fong Yue Ting*, 149 U.S. at 730. The court further distinguished deportation from punishment in 1896 when it decided *Wong Wing v. United States*. The court found the Geary Act's section that imposed a year of hard labor on Chinese, if found unlawfully in the United States, as a punishment. *Wong Wing v. United States*, 163 U.S. 228 (1896); Salyer, *Laws Harsh as Tigers*, 171; Motomura, *Americans in Waiting*, 65–66.

31. *Fong Yue Ting*, 149 U.S. at 730. For more on the legal history of banishment, see Peter D. Edgerton, "Banishment and the Right to Live Where You Want," *University of Chicago Law Review* 74, no. 3 (Summer 2007): 1023–55; William Garth Snider, "Banishment: The History of Its Use and a Proposal for Its Abolition Under the First Amendment," *New England Journal on Criminal and Civil Confinement* 24 (Summer 1988): 455–509.

32. *Fong Yue Ting*, 149 U.S. at 730.

33. Thomas Alexander Aleinikoff, David A. Martin, and Hiroshi Motomura, *Immigration and Citizenship: Process and Policy*, 5th ed. (St. Paul, Minn.: Thomson/West, 2003), 710. For more on the plenary power, see Cleveland, "Powers Inherent in Sovereignty"; John S. W. Park, *Elusive Citizenship: Immigration, Asian Americans, and the Paradox of Civil Rights* (New York: New York University Press, 2004), 96–97.

34. As legal scholar Teemu Ruskola writes in his commentary on the case, "the dissenting justices understood perfectly well what was at stake, announcing that it gave rise to an 'unlimited and despotic power' over aliens." Teemu Ruskola, *Legal Orientalism: China, the United States, and Modern Law* (Cambridge, Mass.: Harvard University Press, 2013), 8, 145–46.

35. *Fong Yue Ting*, 149 U.S. at 762.

36. *Fong Yue Ting*, 149 U.S. at 738.

37. "Is it within legislative capacity to declare the limits?" Brewer asked. "If so, then the mere assertion of an inherent power creates it, and despotism exists. May the courts establish the boundaries? Whence do they obtain the authority for this? Shall they look to the practices of other nations to ascertain the limits?" *Fong Yue Ting*, 149 U.S. at 737.

38. *Fong Yue Ting*, 149 U.S. at 740.

39. *Fong Yue Ting*, 149 U.S. at 740.

40. *Fong Yue Ting*, 149 U.S. at 759.

41. *Fong Yue Ting*, 149 U.S. at 754.

42. Jean Pfaelzer, *Driven Out: The Forgotten War Against Chinese Americans* (New York: Random House, 2007), 291, 307–19.

43. Act of Nov. 3, 1893, 28 Stat. 7 (1893). On compliance, see Pfaelzer, *Driven Out*, 330–35.

44. *Fong Yue Ting*, 149 U.S. at 730–31. For more on the administrative competency of executive officials determining hearings, see Patricia Russell Evans, " 'Likely to Become a Public Charge': Immigration in the Backwaters of Administrative Law, 1882–1933" (Ph.D. diss., George Washington University, 1987).

45. Act of May 5, 1892, § 2, 27 Stat. 25 (1892). The commissioners were a part of the broader growth of administrative law in the late nineteenth century. The circuit courts were abolished in 1911. Salyer, *Laws Harsh as Tigers*, 261 n. 102; Jeffrey Lehman and Shirelle Phelps, *West's Encyclopedia of American Law*, 2nd ed. (Detroit: Thomson/Gale, 2005), 3:465, 6:391; U.S. National Archives and Records Administration, "Chinese Immigration and the Chinese in the United States," http://www.archives.gov/locations/finding-aids/chinese-immigration.html (accessed July 3, 2008).

46. If a U.S. commissioner found against a defendant, he or she could appeal the ruling to the district courts by suing for a writ of habeas corpus within ten days of the initial deportation order. Act of Sept. 13, 1888, § 13, 25 Stat. 476; see also Salyer, *Laws Harsh as Tigers*, 75.

47. *United States v. Lee Huen*, 118 F. 442, 456 (D.N.D.N.Y. 1902).

48. *Lee Huen*, 118 F. at 457.

49. *United States v. Hung Chang*, 134 F. 19, 26 (6th Cir., 1904).

50. As historian Charles McClain notes, this was "the first and only time that a federal statute sought to put a racial limitation on the right to testify in federal court." McClain, *In Search of Equality*, 203.

51. Tsui Kwo Yin to James G. Blaine, Secretary of State, May 5, 1892, *MS Notes from the Chinese Legation in the United States to the Department of State, 1868–1906*, 3:26–30, National Archives (United States). *Nineteenth Century Collections Online*, http://tinyurl.galegroup.com/tinyurl/VMHL1.

52. *Fong Yue Ting*, 149 U.S. at 730.

53. According to the Supreme Court, one reason for the white witness requirement stemmed from previous problems with Chinese testimony. "The enforcement of former acts, under which the testimony of Chinese persons was admitted to prove similar facts, was attended with great embarrassment," the Court wrote, "from the suspicious nature, in many instances, of the testimony offered to establish the residence of the parties, arising from the loose notions entertained by the witnesses of the obligation of an oath." *Fong Yue Ting*, 149 U.S. at 730.

54. *Fong Yue Ting*, 149 U.S. at 759.

55. For more on the belief held by many immigration agents and court employees that people of Chinese heritage were especially dishonest, see Lee, *At America's Gates*, 91–92, 211; Adam McKeown, "Ritualization of Regulation: The Enforcement of Chinese Exclusion in the United States and China," *American Historical Review* 108 (2003): 377–403.

56. *Lee Huen*, 118 F. at 464.

57. *Lee Huen*, 118 F. at 464.

58. The immigration agents also agreed that having an interpreter gave the witness additional time to prepare false testimony. "In our courts a witness who does not understand or who cannot speak our language, but who speaks through an interpreter, if at all, has the time and opportunity to prepare his answers to each question with care, and hence the force of a cross-examination is broken, if not destroyed." *Lee Huen*, 118 F. at 463.

59. As historian Lucy Salyer points out, at this stage of proceedings, "the customary evidentiary principles—the consistency of the testimony, the weight of the evidence, and so forth—applied in the deportation case and made it easier for Chinese to establish their claims." Salyer, *Laws Harsh as Tigers*, 90.

60. *AR-CGI* (1901), 46.

61. Salyer, *Laws Harsh as Tigers*, 87.

62. As historian Jean Pfaelzer notes, the confusion and inconsistency in enforcement fueled vigilantism against Chinese immigrants in the West. Pfaelzer, *Driven Out*, 291–335. See also Salyer, *Laws Harsh as Tigers*, 86–87.

63. Congress did this in the McCreary Amendment, Act of Nov. 3, 1893, 28 Stat. 7 (1893).

64. Salyer, *Laws Harsh as Tigers*, 88.

65. *AR-CGI* (1904), 137. For more information on the centralization and enforcement of Chinese exclusion under Commissioner General Powderly and his successor Frank P. Sargent, see Lee, *At America's Gates*, 66–67; Delber L. McKee, "'The Chinese Must Go!' Commissioner General Powderly and Chinese Immigration, 1897–1092," *Pennsylvania History* 44, no. 1 (January 1977): 37–51.

66. Powderly went on to say that that customs officers were "not always able personally to give that attention to the enforcement of the Chinese exclusion laws which is indispensable, nor in the multiplicity of their duties as collectors are they often able to acquire and maintain that familiarity with the laws and decisions and regulations hereunder which is so necessary to officers clothed with such a large authority." *AR-CGI* (1902), 80.

67. Act of Feb. 14, 1903, § 7, 32 Stat. 825 (1903). The shift had begun under earlier legislation. In 1900, Congress transferred the administration of the exclusion laws to centralize and strengthen their enforcement. However, everyday enforcement remained with the officials of the U.S. Customs Service. Act of June 6, 1900, 31 Stat. 588 (1900). In 1901, Congress passed another act, which allowed a U.S. district attorney to assign more cases to U.S. commissioners, who tended to rule in favor of the government. Act of Mar. 3, 1901, § 1, 31 Stat. 1093 (1901); *AR-CGI* (1903), 7. For instance, in 1903, J. B. Rodgers, a U.S. commissioner in northern New York, ordered deportations in 75 percent of his cases, while another commissioner in the same district, J. Corbin, ordered deportations in only 10 percent of his cases. The other U.S. commissioners for that district deported between 12 and 30 percent of all Chinese defendants. These numbers are misleading, however, because Rodgers heard only 4 cases, while Corbin heard 376. *AR-CGI* (1903), 109.

68. The Bureau of Immigration also hoped that centralization would help improve the consistent application of Chinese exclusion throughout the country. The bureau saw the centralization of records as important to improving enforcement by establishing a system that could more efficiently, professionally, and accurately supply information to U.S. commissioners and courts throughout the country. *AR-CGI* (1904), 137, 140–41. This mattered because the bureau had reported that some U.S. commissioners had received "half-hearted support on the part of a few of the United States attorneys" and that there was inconsistency, especially in the northern New York district. *AR-CGI* (1903), 109. For a strong examination of enforcement and identity documents, see Pegler-Gordon, *In Sight of America*, 67–103.

69. The increased restrictions contributed to the reasons behind a boycott of U.S. goods in China. See Kramer, "Imperial Openings," 326, 332–33.

70. Erika Lee, "Enforcing the Borders: Chinese Exclusion Along the U.S. Borders with Canada and Mexico, 1882–1924," in *American Dreaming, Global Realities: Rethinking U.S. Immigration History*, ed. Donna R. Gabaccia and Vicki L. Ruíz (Urbana: University of Illinois Press, 2006), 158–89.

71. For information on facilitative payments, see Nicholas R. Parrillo, *Against the Profit Motive: The Salary Revolution in American Government, 1780–1940* (New Haven, Conn.: Yale University Press, 2013).

72. This is a list of the most common fees. There were additional fees for drawing a bond of defendant and sureties, for "issuing a commitment," and for "recognizance of all witnesses," and so on. J. H. Carpenter, January 1, 1901, to May 18, 1906, Box 76, USC-AZ.

73. J. W. Crenshaw, July 3, 1891, to June 29, 1896, p. 270, Box 75, USC-AZ; J. W. Crenshaw, August 7, 1900, pp. 48–49, Box 75, USC-AZ.

74. C. W. Johnstone, September 30, 1909, pp. 98–99, Box 76, USC-AZ.

75. Funding came out of the Chinese exclusion budget of $160,000. *AR-CGI* (1901), 52. Until 1907, appropriations for the expenses of Chinese exclusion came from the U.S. Treasury. From 1907 to 1911, annual appropriations of $500,000 were made from the immigrant fund. In 1912 and 1913, there was no specific amount allocated, but the expenses were approximately the same as in earlier years. During the twenty years between 1894 and 1913, the government spent over three million dollars enforcing Chinese exclusion, which came out of the immigrant fund, paid by immigrants applying for admission. *AR-CGI* (1913), 32–33.

76. The exact total for deportations near the Canadian border was $64,965.71. That year, the total budget for Chinese exclusion came to $250,000. The actual costs came to $268,632.63. *AR-CGI* (1903), 110, 112.

77. "The larger per capita expense," the bureau reported, was "due to the greater distance from China of those in New York and the New England States." *AR-CGI* (1904), 164. In 1905, 55 Chinese immigrants were deported from northeastern states, 112 from the northwestern region, and 454 from other parts of the nation, for a total of 621 Chinese deportations. The deportations cost $67,730.61, or an average cost of $109.07 for each person deported. *AR-CGI* (1905), 102.

78. Salyer, *Laws Harsh as Tigers,* 90.

79. Ngai, *Impossible Subjects,* 18.

80. Act of Feb. 26, 1885 (Foran Act), 23 Stat. 332 (1885).

81. Catherine Collomp, "Immigrants, Labor Markets, and the State, a Comparative Approach: France and the United States, 1880–1930," *Journal of American History* 86, no. 1 (June 1999), 36. See also Amy Dru Stanley, *From Bondage to Contract: Wage Labor, Marriage, and the Market in the Age of Slave Emancipation* (Cambridge: Cambridge University Press, 1998).

82. Knights of Labor, *Proceedings of the General Assembly* (1884), 575–77, as quoted in Collomp, "Immigrants, Labor Markets, and the State," 56.

83. The Foran Act followed a precedent set during the Civil War, when the U.S. Congress passed two laws about contracted labor. In 1862, Congress banned the importation of contracted workers from China. These workers were popularly known as "coolies." In 1864, Congress passed a different law specifically allowing employers to contract with other immigrant workers abroad. Act of Feb. 19, 1862, 12 Stat. 340 (1862); Act of July 4, 1864, 13 Stat. 385 (1864). For information on contracted, indentured labor under this law, see Jung, *Coolies and Cane.*

84. Act of Feb. 26, 1885, 23 Stat. 332 (1885).

85. This was how the earlier indentured servants operated. For more information on guest workers, see Cindy Hahamovitch, *No Man's Land: Jamaican Guestworkers in America and the Global History of Deportable Labor* (Princeton, N.J.: Princeton University Press, 2011).

86. Act of Feb. 23, 1887, 24 Stat. 414 (1887); Act of Oct. 19, 1888, 25 Stat. 566 (1888).

87. Act of Mar. 3, 1891, § 11, 26 Stat. 1084 (1891).

88. Act of Mar. 3, 1891, § 1, 26 Stat. 1084 (1891).

89. The warrant of deportation would be canceled after the immigrant was removed from national territory.

90. *Yamataya v. Fisher (Japanese Immigrant Case),* 189 U.S. 86 (1903).

91. Petition for writ of habeas corpus, *Japanese Immigrant Case,* 1–2, USSCRB; Traverse of Return, *Japanese Immigrant Case,* 6–8, USSCRB.

92. Brief of Appellant, *Japanese Immigrant Case*, 10–16, *USSCRB*; Salyer, *Laws Harsh as Tigers*, 172.

93. Traverse of Return, 6; Brief of Appellant, 3.

94. Brief of Appellant, 5–9; Salyer, *Laws Harsh as Tigers*, 172.

95. *Yamataya*, 189 U.S. at 101; since no words in the act invested "executive or administrative officers with . . . absolute, arbitrary power," the Court held the law constitutional. See also Salyer, *Laws Harsh as Tigers*, 173.

96. Brief of Appellant, 16–20.

97. *Yamataya*, 189 U.S. at 102. In *Nishimura Ekiu*, an earlier exclusion case, the Court had found in favor of the government's argument that immigration law provided sufficient trial and appellate tribunals. In *Yamataya*, the Court once again agreed with the government's assertion of administrative competency.

98. Motomura, *Americans in Waiting*, 67–68; Hiroshi Motomura, "The Curious Evolution of Immigration Law: Procedural Surrogates for Substantive Constitutional Rights," *Columbia Law Review* 92 (November 1992): 1624–704.

99. *Yamataya*, 189 U.S. at 100.

100. *Yamataya*, 189 U.S. at 101.

101. *Yamataya*, 189 U.S. at 98.

102. *Yamataya*, 189 U.S. at 102.

103. As legal scholar Hiroshi Motomura describes the Court's decision, "the Supreme Court said . . . that deportation procedures had to meet a minimum constitutional standard, but then found that the procedures in question were sufficient." Motomura, *Americans in Waiting*, 104.

104. *AR-CGI* (1913), 183.

105. Ngai, *Impossible Subjects*, 18.

106. Motomura, *Immigration Outside the Law*.

107. Act of Mar. 3, 1891, § 11, 26 Stat. 1084 (1891), Act of Mar. 3, 1903, § 20, 32 Stat. 1213 (1903); Act of Feb. 20, 1907, § 20, 34 Stat. 898 (1907); Act of Feb. 5, 1917, § 19, 39 Stat. 874 (1917).

108. For an article exploring these procedural challenges through the twentieth century, see Motomura, "Curious Evolution of Immigration Law."

109. The courts upheld this. As the Ninth Circuit wrote in its decision in the case of *Low Wah Suey v. Backus*, "In order to successfully attack by judicial proceedings the conclusions and orders made upon such hearings it must be shown that the proceedings were manifestly unfair, that the action of the executive officers was such as to prevent a fair investigation, or that there was a manifest abuse of the discretion committed to them by the statute. In other cases the order of the executive officers within the authority of the statute is final." *Low Wah Suey v. Backus*, 225 U.S. 460, 468 (1912).

110. *AR-CGI* (1912), 39.

111. *AR-CGI* (1911), 143.

112. *United States v. Wong You*, 223 U.S. 67 (1912).

113. Act of Mar. 3, 1891, § 1, 26 Stat. 1084 (1891).

114. Act of Mar. 3, 1893, § 10, 27 Stat. 569 (1893).

115. *Wong You*, 223 U.S. at 67.

116. While the numbers of Chinese immigrants were very small in relation to the overall numbers of immigrants, the small stream of migration from China continued to matter to

U.S. immigration authorities. In 1910, 5,330 Chinese were admitted to Canada, and American authorities worried that most of these immigrants would migrate south into the United States. *AR-CGI* (1911), 143.

117. *Wong You*, 223 U.S. at 69.

118. *AR-CGI* (1914), 346.

119. *AR-CGI* (1914), 344. Only fifty-seven warrants had been canceled. Eleven of the defendants died or escaped custody. *AR-CGI* (1914), 347–48.

120. *AR-CGI* (1913), 183.

121. *AR-CGI* (1913), 25.

122. *AR-CGI* (1914), 348.

123. *AR-CGI* (1913), 183.

124. The report noted that "[t]he year has seen the handling of probably the largest number of immigration 'warrant' cases ever initiated in this district in a single year—414—an increase of over 300% as against last year, which in turn showed an increase of 200% over the year previous. Deportation was accomplished in 134 cases, and 181 cases remained pending at the close of the year." *AR-CGI* (1914), 282–83.

125. *AR-CGI* (1914), 281.

126. The government that year deported about 60 percent of all Chinese arrested on executive warrants under Chinese deportation policy. On departmental warrants under general immigration policy, the rate was just over 80 percent. However, the 60 percent deportation rate is misleadingly high because the government only proceeded under Chinese exclusion laws when it believed it had a strong case. Therefore, it can be assumed that if the government tried to deport all Chinese immigrants identified for deportation under Chinese exclusion laws, the percentage of persons actually deported would have been much lower. *AR-CGI* (1916), 228.

127. *AR-CGI* (1918), 318.

128. *AR-CGI* (1917), 140.

129. Act of Feb. 5, 1917, § 19, 39 Stat. 874 (1917); in section 38, Congress stated that the unamended sections of the previous Chinese exclusion law remained standing.

Chapter 2

1. John A. Kasson to Count Paul von Hatzfeldt, April 6, 1885, *FRUS* (1886), 415.

2. H. C. Squiers to Edwin F. Uhl, April 17, 1897, *FRUS* (1897), 211–12.

3. Between 1868 and 1897, U.S. consular officers intervened in 447 cases. Squiers to Uhl, April 17, 1897. From Germany, these were a small subgroup of a much larger series of mass expulsions, especially of Poles. Others expelled from Germany and German colonies included Jesuits, French agitators, Danes, and gypsies. Matthew P. Fitzpatrick *Purging the Empire: Mass Expulsions in Germany, 1871–1914* (New York: Oxford University Press, 2015); Matthew P. Fitzpatrick, "A State of Exception? Mass Expulsions and the German Constitutional State, 1871–1914," *Journal of Modern History* 85, no. 4 (2013): 772–800.

4. Foreign offices, as historian Kal Raustiala notes, represented "small plots of foreign territory projected into the domain of the host state," which facilitated national interests and relations between nation-states. "These special extraterritorial zones allowed each sovereign to maintain their territorial sovereignty, while simultaneously enabling interaction between them." Kal Raustiala, *Does the Constitution Follow the Flag? The Evolution of Territoriality in American Law* (Oxford: Oxford University Press, 2009), 12–13.

5. For more on German citizenship, see Krista O'Donnell, Renate Bridenthal, and Nancy Reagin, eds., *The Heimat Abroad: The Boundaries of Germanness* (Ann Arbor: University of Michigan Press, 2005), 15.

6. The question of American citizenship abroad was a larger one than just the military cases. Just after the American Civil War, citizenship issues came up with the United Kingdom over Irish Americans. Christian G. Samito, *Becoming American Under Fire: Irish Americans, African Americans, and the Politics of Citizenship During the Civil War Era* (Ithaca, N.Y.: Cornell University Press, 2009), 194–216.

7. Diplomats from Spain and Italy, for example, tried to prevent the denaturalization of their citizens by protesting liberal naturalization policies in Brazil or Argentina. David Cook Martin, *Scramble for Citizens: Dual Nationality and State Competition for Immigrants* (Stanford, Calif.: Stanford University Press, 2013). Similarly, the imperial Japanese and Italian governments worked through state-promotional efforts to maintain ties with their emigrants abroad. Mark Choate, *Emigrant Nation: The Making of Italy Abroad* (Cambridge, Mass.: Harvard University Press, 2008); Eiichiro Azuma, *Between Two Empires: Race, History, and Transnationalism in Japanese America* (New York: Oxford University Press, 2005).

8. For an article on broader ways U.S. citizens used consular officers as a resource, see Nancy L. Green, "Americans Abroad and the Uses of Citizenship: Paris, 1914–1940," *Journal of American Ethnic History* 31, no. 3 (Spring 2012): 5–32.

9. Edwin M. Borchard, *Diplomatic Protection of Citizens Abroad; or, The Law of International Claims* (New York: Banks Law Publishing Co., 1915), 347.

10. On flexible citizenship, see Aihwa Ong, *Flexible Citizenship: The Cultural Logics of Transnationality* (Durham, N.C.: Duke University Press, 1999); and Lisa Lowe, *Immigrant Acts: On Asian American Cultural Politics* (Durham, N.C.: Duke University Press, 1996). This was not a term used in the nineteenth century, but the act of using multiple citizenships was an issue. In 1869, President Ulysses Grant noted in his opening message to Congress that some immigrants naturalized in the United States in order to evade military service elsewhere. E. P. Hutchinson, *Legislative History of American Immigration Policy, 1798–1965* (Philadelphia: University of Pennsylvania Press, 1981), 56. Eileen Scully also notes that during the U.S. Civil War "conscription convinced some naturalized Americans to return to their native lands; they then used [this] instance to avoid one call to arms, and their U.S. citizenship another. The U.S. minister to Paris reported in 1865 at least 500 of these cases. U.S. diplomatic officers received instructions to guard against this abuse when protecting Americans from deportation." Eileen Scully, *Bargaining with the State from Afar: American Citizenship in Treaty Port China, 1844–1942* (New York: Columbia University Press, 2001), 55.

11. Bartlett Tripp to W. Q. Gresham, August 13, 1894, *FRUS* (1894), 32.

12. Tripp to Gresham, August 13, 1894, 32.

13. Tripp to Gresham, August 13, 1894, 32.

14. Edmund Jussen to the Imperial Royal Police Directory, January 18, 1889, *FRUS* (1889–90), 32.

15. George H. Pendleton to T. F. Bayard, November 2, 1885, *FRUS* (1886), 434.

16. Jussen to the Imperial Royal Police Directory, January 18, 1889, 32. In a letter defending a naturalized citizen in Austria from deportation for lack of military service, the U.S. State Department outlined the rules under which Austria-Hungary could arrest and punish former citizens for nonfulfillment of military duty. Those conditions included: "If he has emigrated

after having been drafted, at the time of conscription, and thus having become enrolled as a recruit for service in the standing army. . . . If he has emigrated whilst he stood in service under the flag . . . if, having a leave of absence for an unlimited time. . . . If . . . he has emigrated after having received a call into service or after a public proclamation requiring his appearance, or after war has broken out." James G. Blaine to F. D. Grant, October 8, 1889, *FRUS* (1889–90), 27–29.

17. T. F. Bayard to George H. Pendleton, July 7, 1885, *FRUS* (1886), 420–21; Pendleton to Bayard, November 2, 1885, 429, 436. U.S. officials even defended young men who emigrated closer to the age of eighteen, when military service was required.

18. John A. Kasson to Frederick T. Frelinghuysen, February 27, 1885, *FRUS* (1886), 404.

19. John A. Kasson to Frederick T. Frelinghuysen, January 6, 1885, *FRUS* (1886), 392; T. F. Bayard to George H. Pendleton, March 12, 1886, *FRUS* (1888), 369–71.

20. Count Paul von Hatzfeldt to Chapman Coleman, May 16, 1885, *FRUS* (1886), 418.

21. John A. Kasson to Dr. [Clemens] Busch, February 25, 1885, *FRUS* (1886), 405; Hatzfeldt to Coleman, May 16, 1885, 418.

22. Based on the treaties of 1828 and 1868, the State Department argued, "a two years' residence in his native country of a citizen naturalized in the United States of America does not of itself divest him of his adopted citizenship. The treaties provide that when a citizen of either country naturalized in the other shall renew his residence in the country of his birth without the intent to return to his adopted country, he shall be held to have renounced his naturalization, and further that the intent not to return '*may* be held to exist' after the residence in the native country shall exceed two years." Frederick T. Frelinghuysen to John A. Kasson, January 15, 1885, *FRUS* (1886), 397.

23. For information on ascriptive citizenship, see Rogers Smith, *Civic Ideals: Conflicting Visions of Citizenship in U.S. History* (New Haven, Conn.: Yale University Press, 1999).

24. Kasson to Busch, February 25, 1885, 405.

25. Kasson to Busch, February 25, 1885, 405.

26. Hatzfeldt to Coleman, May 16, 1885, 418.

27. Hatzfeldt to Coleman, May 16, 1885, 417.

28. Frederick T. Frelinghuysen to John A. Kasson, February 7, 1885, *FRUS* (1886), 400.

29. Kasson to Busch, February 25, 1885, 405.

30. Frelinghuysen to Kasson, February 7, 1885, 400–401.

31. Kasson to Busch, February 25, 1885, 405.

32. Wu Ting-Fang continued, "I and the Chinese official representative in the United States have exerted our influence to have the registration laws observed by Chinese laborers, and I am not disposed to complain of the severe enforcement of these laws; but I feel sure you will agree with me that they should not be so enforced as to bring loss, inconvenience and terror to the whole body of peaceful and innocent Chinese population, in marked contrast with the treatment extended to other foreign residents." To conclude his letter, Wu Ting-Fang expressed his hope that the U.S. State Department would issue instructions to U.S. Treasury officials to refrain from such raids as those that occurred in Denver. Wu Ting-Fang to John Sherman, Secretary of State, January 4, 1898, *MS Notes from the Chinese Legation* 4:2–4.

33. Yang Yu to Alvey A. Adee, Acting Secretary of State, September 27, 1893, *MS Notes from the Chinese Legation* 3:180–81.

34. Shen Tung to John Jay, June 8, 1899, *MS Notes from the Chinese Legation* 4:202–3.

35. Wu Ting-Fang to John Hay, July 10, 1899, 4:205–7.

36. Jussen to the Imperial Royal Police Directory, January 18, 1889, 32.

37. Jussen to the Imperial Royal Police Directory, January 18, 1889, 32–33. The claims of the consular officials perhaps overstated the U.S. context because, as scholarship on the Civil War notes, immigrants did feel pressure to enlist and serve. But they did not face expulsion for not serving.

38. By World War I, the U.S. State Department had closed the last of the formal extraterritorial courts in Morocco and Tangier. Scully, *Bargaining with the State*, 4–5, 65; Ruskola *Legal Orientalism*, 135–36, 138–39.

39. Leti Volpp, "Imaginings of Space in Immigration Law," *Law, Culture and the Humanities* 9, no. 3 (2012): 461.

40. Ruskola, *Legal Orientalism*, 115; Scully, *Bargaining with the State*, 4–6; Teemu Ruskola, "Colonialism Without Colonies: On the Extraterritorial Jurisprudence of the U.S. Court for China," *Law and Contemporary Problems* 71 (2008): 217–42; Teemu Ruskola, "Canton Is Not Boston: The Invention of American Imperial Sovereignty," in *Legal Borderlands: Law and the Construction of American Borders*, ed. Mary L. Dudziak and Leti Volpp (Baltimore: Johns Hopkins University Press, 2006), 267–92. This included U.S. citizens and U.S. nationals. "Filipinos in China," as Ruskola notes, "were American enough to bring them under America's extraterritorial empire . . . even if they were not deserving of U.S. citizenship." Ruskola, *Legal Orientalism*, 179.

41. Ruskola, "Colonialism Without Colonies," 218, 238. Some of the qualitative categories for deportation in the United States were important in China. As Ruskola notes, prostitution was a major concern of Lebbeus Wilfley, first judge of the U.S. Court for China. "'America' had in fact become synonymous with prostitution in Shanghai; brothels were generally called 'American houses,' prostitutes were referred to as 'American girls,' and going to the red light district was described as 'going to America.'" Vagrants, as Ruskola finds, were an issue, too. Ruskola, *Legal Orientalism*, 177–79.

42. As legal scholar Kal Raustiala describes, extraterritoriality drew lines about what was "inside and outside the scope of a sovereign's law." Raustiala, *Does the Constitution Follow*, vii.

43. For a larger treatment of the campaign, see Scully, *Bargaining with the State*, 114–16.

44. Officials turned to Alaska code, which provided for the prosecution of "[a]ll persons who live in houses of ill repute" and "all idle or dissolute persons who have not . . . lawful occupation or employment by which to earn a living." Charles Sumner Lobingier, ed., *Extraterritorial Cases Including the Decisions of the United States Court for China from Its Beginning, Those Reviewing the Same by the Court of Appeals, and the Leading Cases Decided by Other Courts on Questions of Extraterritoriality*, 2 vols. (Manila: Bureau of Printing, 1920–28), 1:190.

45. *Sexton v. United States* (1909), in Lobingier, *Extraterritorial Cases*, 1:180–94.

46. *Sexton v. United States*, in Lobingier, *Extraterritorial Cases*, 1:194.

47. *United States v. Hadley* (1910), in Lobingier, *Extraterritorial Cases*, 1:207–11 (see esp. 209–11).

48. "If sentenced to prison, treaty port Americans served their time in the local American consular jail; longer terms were served in the U.S. prison in the Philippines or in a federal penitentiary in the continental United States." Scully, *Bargaining with the State*, 7.

49. Borchard, *Diplomatic Protection of Citizens Abroad*; L. Oppenheim, *International Law: A Treatise*, 2nd ed., vol. 1 (London: Longmans, Green, 1912); see also Francis Wharton, ed., *A Digest of the International Law of the United States* (Washington, D.C.: Government Printing Office, 1887).

50. Borchard, *Diplomatic Protection*, 102. For historical work on the civilization discourse, see, for example, Paul A. Kramer, *The Blood of Government: Race, Empire, the United States, and the Philippines* (Chapel Hill: University of North Carolina Press, 2006); Gail Bederman, *Manliness and Civilization: A Cultural History of Gender and Race in the United States, 1880–1917* (Chicago: University of Chicago Press, 1996).

51. Borchard, *Diplomatic Protection*, 346. Borchard wrote that "when a local [government] fails to fulfill [its] duties, 'when it is incapable of ruling, or rules with patent injustice,' the right of diplomatic protections inures to those states whose citizens have been injured by the governmental delinquency." *Diplomatic Protection*, 27.

52. Borchard, *Diplomatic Protection*, 25–26.

53. Scully, *Bargaining with the State*, 25. See also Gerrit W. Gong, *The Standard of "Civilization" in International Society* (Oxford: Clarendon Press, 1984).

54. Oppenheim, *International Law*, 395.

55. Scully, *Bargaining with the State*, 25–26.

56. The history of extraterritoriality and jurisdiction over foreigners in the Ottoman Empire goes as far back as the pre-Westphalian period. Ruskola, *Legal Orientalism*, 120. For larger efforts to undermine extraterritorialty, see Lauren Benton, *Law and Colonial Cultures: Legal Regimes in World History, 1400–1900* (Cambridge: Cambridge University Press, 2002), 244–46. For the Japanese case, F. C. Jones, *Extraterritoriality in Japan and the Diplomatic Relations Resulting in Its Abolition, 1853–1899* (New Haven, Conn.: Yale University Press, 1931), 47. On the Ottoman case, see Nasim Sousa, *The Capitulatory Regime of Turkey: Its History, Origin, and Nature* (Baltimore: Johns Hopkins Press, 1933).

57. Oppenheim, *International Law*, 33 n. 1. Eileen Scully notes that Ottoman officials "were able to parlay that gain into more indigenous control over mixed cases, real estate, and protégé questions." Scully, *Bargaining with the State*, 48. See also Halil Inalcik, "Imtiyāz," in *The Encyclopaedia of Islam*, 2nd ed., ed. P. Bearman et al. (Leiden: Brill, 2012), 3:1178; Isa Blumi, "Capitulations in the Late Ottoman Empire: The Shifting Parameters of Russian and Austrian Interests in Ottoman Albania, 1878–1912," *Oriente Moderno* 83, no. 3 (2003): 635–47; Feroz Ahmed, "Ottoman Perceptions of the Capitulations, 1800–1914," *Journal of Islamic Studies* 11, no. 1 (2000): 1–20; Susa, *The Capitulatory Regime of Turkey*.

58. *In the late nineteenth century, as historian Eileen Scully notes, "Ottoman rulers endeavored to narrow and rationalize foreign privileges . . . [and] foreigners lost a significant percentage of their immunities." Scully, Bargaining with the State, 48.*

59. Within two years, the Ottomans would prohibit foreign Jews from moving to Palestine and limit visits to three months. John Bassett Moore, *A Digest of International Law* (Washington, D.C.: Government Printing Office, 1906), 4:130–32.

60. Earlier in the century, U.S. diplomats might have refused. A treaty signed between Switzerland and the United States in 1850 had, for instance, provided for the protection of only Christian emigrants. By the 1880s, though, policy had changed somewhat. Naomi W. Cohen, *Jews in Christian America: The Pursuit of Religious Equality* (New York: Oxford University Press, 1992), 53–55, 98.

61. G. H. Heap to John T. Robeson, August 6, 1885, *FRUS* (1885), 865.

62. G. H. Heap to S. S. Cox, September 21, 1885, *FRUS* (1885), 864–65; Heap to Robeson, August 6, 1885, 865.

63. S. S. Cox to T. F. Bayard, October 24, 1885, *FRUS* (1885), 873–75.

64. Turkish officials stood by their interpretation of nullification. Samuel S. Cox, the U.S. minister to Turkey, wrote to Secretary of State Thomas F. Bayard that "the Ottoman Government insists on going behind the record to give vigor to its own law, or as you say, 'participate in or make the naturalization of its subjects conditional, a doctrine which was never acknowledged by the United States, and probably never will be.'" Cox to Bayard, October 24, 1885, 875.

65. Cox to Bayard, October 24, 1885, 873.

66. Moore, *Digest of International Law*, 4:130.

67. Cohen, "Shaping the Nation, Excluding the Other," 355, 357.

68. As historian Frank Caestecker notes, "Providing expellees with a choice of border . . . respected the principle of individual liberty," which also was built into logic upholding the international appeal and extraterritoriality. Frank Caestecker, "The Transformation of Nineteenth-Century West European Expulsion Policy, 1880–1914," in *Migration Control in the North Atlantic World*, ed. Andreas Fahrmeir, Olivier Faron, and Patrick Weil (New York: Berghahn Books, 2003), 122–24. See also Caestecker, "Changing Modalities of Regulation," 74.

69. Caestecker, "West European Expulsion Policy," 126.

70. Frank Caestecker, *Alien Policy in Belgium, 1840–1940: The Creation of Guest Workers, Refugees and Illegal Aliens* (New York: Berghahn Books, 2000), 38–40.

71. Caestecker, *Alien Policy in Belgium*, 38–42; elsewhere Caestecker writes that "these treaties stipulated that every country had to accept its own nationals who had emigrated or give free passage to those who had to pass through their territory. The issue of the transit fare for third-country nationals, in most cases, was not mentioned in these agreements and continued to pose problems. The agreements made it impossible for the expelling state to force third-country nationals onto the territory of neighbouring states without the consent of that state. Expulsions were no longer a unilateral affair. Constraints were imposed by the neighbouring countries." "West European Expulsion Policy," 127–28.

72. Act of Feb. 10, 1855, 10 Stat. 604 (1855). This act established that foreign women automatically became U.S. citizens upon marriage to a U.S. citizen, or upon the naturalization of their husbands. See also Ian F. Haney López, *White by Law: The Legal Construction of Race* (New York: New York University Press, 1996), 46. For more information on the paternalism of U.S. citizenship and marriage law, see Nancy F. Cott, *Public Vows: A History of Marriage and the Nation* (Cambridge, Mass.: Harvard University Press, 2000); Pamela Haag, *Consent: Sexual Rights and the Transformation of American Liberalism* (Ithaca, N.Y.: Cornell University Press, 1999); Amy Dru Stanley, *From Bondage to Contract: Wage Labor, Marriage, and the Market in the Age of Slave Emancipation* (Cambridge: Cambridge University Press, 1998); Carole Pateman, *The Sexual Contract* (Stanford, Calif.: Stanford University Press, 1988).

73. John Sargent, Inspector in Charge, to Commissioner General of Immigration, January 5, 1909, File 52241/19, INS.

74. Flora was born in the United States and she married a Canadian. (She actually told agents that she did not know if he was a Canadian.) Flora Gendron to the Secretary of State, December 20, 1915, File 54012/11, INS.

75. Gendron to the Secretary of State, December 20, 1915.

76. John H. Clark, Commissioner at Montreal, to Commissioner General of Immigration, January 13, 1909, File 52241/19, INS.

77. Act of Sept. 13, 1888, § 12, 25 Stat. 476 (1888); Lee, *At America's Gates*, 79; Act of May 5, 1892, § 2, 27 Stat. 25 (1892).

78. *AR-CGI* (1911), 162. The supervising inspector for District 23 made similar comments again in 1916. He wrote that "[t]he practice of deporting to Mazatlan, Mexico, those Chinese persons who cross the [U.S.-Mexican] boundary for the purpose of being apprehended and sent to China at the expense of this Government has had the anticipated effect. A number of such 'free trippers,' upon learning that they were destined to Mazatlan, promptly offered to defray their further expenses if permitted to go to China." *AR-CGI* (1916), 228.

79. The Canadian government passed a law similar to U.S. exclusion in 1923. Lee, "Enforcing the Borders," 161. See also Patricia E. Roy, *A White Man's Province: British Columbia Politicians and Chinese and Japanese Immigrants, 1858–1914* (Vancouver: University of British Columbia Press, 2003).

80. *Yuen Pak Sune v. United States*, 191 F. 825, 826–28 (2d Cir. 1911).

81. *Yuen Pak Sune*, 191 F. at 826–28.

82. *United States v. Hen Lee*, 236 F. 794, 794–98, (S.D.N.Y. 1916).

83. Barbara Roberts, *Whence They Came: Deportation from Canada, 1900–1935* (Ottawa: University of Ottawa Press, 1988), 12–13. Roberts found that between the 1890s and 1906, the Canadians had a "long-standing rule" of sending back public charges. This policy was sometimes referred to as the return of "failed" immigrants. However, these removals were not sanctioned by any law. Roberts, *Whence They Came*, 53–54, 58.

84. J. H. Clark to W. D. Scott, Superintendent of Immigration, April 29, 1909, vol. 513, file 800129, CAN.

85. A. L. Jolliffe, Commissioner, to the Secretary, Department of Immigration and Colonization, July 10, 1920, vol. 514, file 800129, CAN.

86. W. D. Scott to W. W. Cory, memorandum, March 28, 1912, vol. 513, file 800129, CAN.

87. Sims, *Expulsion of Mexico's Spaniards*; Stanley C. Green, *The Mexican Republic: The First Decade* (Pittsburgh, Pa.: University of Pittsburgh Press, 1987).

88. Clement L. Bouvé, *A Treatise on the Laws Governing the Exclusion and Expulsion of Aliens in the United States* (Washington, D.C.: John Byrne, 1912), 752.

89. Bouvé, *Treatise on the Laws*, 758–59.

90. To Mr. Secretary (regarding Hugo Dickson), April 10, 1922, 312.1124, DF. See also Roland Harrison, Assistant Secretary of State, to George H. Wilkins, August 5, 1925, 312.1124, FSP. In 1916, when Mexico was embroiled in revolution, U.S. officials got word that a new constitution might change the operations of deportations from Mexico. The secretary of state sent an inquiry to the American consul in Querétaro, Mexico, after he heard that the new Mexican constitution might revise a section that "foreigners considered pernicious may be deported by the Chief Executive without forming a cause and without giving any account thereof to the foreign government concerned." Wilbur J. Carr to John R. Silliman, American Consul, Querétaro, Mexico, January 25, 1916, 812.111/8, Roll 107, FSP.

91. H. F. Arthur Schoenfeld, American Chargé d'Affaires, Mexico, to the Secretary of State, July 22, 1925, 312.1124, FSP; Aarón Sáenz to Mr. Chargé d'Affaires, July 20, 1925,

Enclosure 2 (Translated) in H. F. Arthur Schoenfeld, to the Secretary of State, July 22, 1925. Roland Harrison to George H. Wilkins, August 5, 1925.

92. American Vice Consul in Charge, Nuevo Laredo, Mexico, March 20, 1920, "Closing of a house of prostitution conducted by Americans in Nuevo Laredo and the return of proprietor and inmates to the American side," 812.1151/2, FSP.

93. H. C. von Struve, American Consul, Mexicali, Mexico, to the Secretary of State, "Deportation of Thomas A. Green," October 29, 1923, 312.1125, FSP; Secretary of State to H. C. von Struve, November 7, 1923, 312.1124 (Green), FSP.

94. H. C. von Struve, American Consul, to the Secretary of State, October 29, 1923, 312.1124 (Guaderrama), FSP.

95. Secretary of State to James B. Stewart, American Consul, Tampico, Mexico, December 19, 1923, 312.1124 (Leach), FSP. The United States did not recognize Mexico and had no ambassador between 1921 and 1923, though George T. Summerlin carried out ambassadorial functions. For more information on Leach's case, see Dan La Botz, "Mexican Workers Fire the Boss: The Use of Article 33 to Attempt to Expel Supervisors, 1922–1936" (August 1998), http://lasa.international.pitt.edu/LASA98/LaBortz.pdf; see also W. F. Buckley, American Association of Mexico, to the Secretary of State, February 4, 1924, 312.1124 (Leach), FSP. Leach's case seems to be one of at least thirty cases in which members of an organization of U.S. citizens named the American Association of Mexico tried to intervene.

96. George T. Summerlin to the Secretary of State, Mexico, December 29, 1923, Embassy of the United States of America, 312.1124 (Leach), FSP.

97. Daniels, *Guarding the Golden Door*, 5. During these years, millions of immigrants landed in other countries, too. For instance, between 1881 and 1910, 2.4 million immigrants went to Brazil and 2.1 million to Argentina. Between 1852 and 1901, 1.3 million immigrants went to Australia. Immigration to Australia peaked between 1911 and 1913, when an average of 150,000 immigrants landed per year. Thomas Dublin, ed., *Immigrant Voices: New Lives in America, 1773–1986* (Urbana: University of Illinois Press, 1993), 3.

98. Bruno Ramirez, *Crossing the 49th Parallel: Migration from Canada to the United States, 1900–1930* (Ithaca, N.Y.: Cornell University Press, 2001), 37.

99. Ramirez, *Crossing the 49th Parallel*, 35.

100. Ramirez, *Crossing the 49th Parallel*, xiii.

101. Memorandum of Conference with Mr. Sargent, Commissioner-General of Immigration, December 12, 1905, vol. 513, file 800129, CAN.

102. Because U.S. officials had signed an agreement with the transportation lines and the Canadian government regarding the second type, those cases were also relatively simple. This agreement was known as the Canadian Agreement. For more information, see Marian L. Smith, "The Immigration and Naturalization Service (INS) at the U.S.-Canadian Border, 1893–1993: An Overview of Issues and Topics," *Michigan Historical Review* 26, no. 2 (Fall 2000): 127–47.

103. W. D. Scott, Canadian Superintendent of Immigration, to John H. Clark, U.S. Commissioner of Immigration, September 15, 1908, vol. 513, file 800129, CAN; John H. Clark, U.S. Immigration Commissioner, to the Canadian Superintendent of Immigration, December 7, 1909, vol. 513, file 800129, CAN; John. L. Zurbrick, Inspector in Charge, to Malcolm R. J. Reid, Dominion Immigration Agent, August 23, 1912, vol. 513, file 800129, CAN.

104. W. D. Scott to John H. Clark, January 5 1914, vol. 513, file 800129, CAN; W. D. Scott to W. W. Cory, memorandum, October 19, 1914, vol. 513, file 800129, CAN.

105. R. W. F., Office of the Solicitor, Department of State, to Mr. Baker, May 23, 1925, RG 59, 711.125/4, M314, Roll 27, DS; Merrill, Consul, El Paso, Texas, to U.S. Secretary of State, El Paso, Texas, May 18, 1925, RG 59, 711.125/3, Roll 27, DS; Article VII, Convention Between the United States of America and Mexico, December 23, 1925, Papers relating to the foreign relations of the United States, Serial Set Vol. No. 8585–2, Session Vol. No. 24, 69th Congress, 1st Session, H.Doc. 476, vol. 2. For more on anti-Chinese policy in Mexico, see Grace Peña Delgado, *Making the Chinese Mexican: Global Migration, Localism, and Exclusion in the U.S.-Mexico Borderlands* (Stanford, Calif.: Stanford University Press, 2012); Julía María Schiavone Camacho, *Chinese Mexicans: Transpacific Migration and the Search for a Homeland, 1910–1960* (Chapel Hill: University of North Carolina Press, 2012); Gerardo Re'nique, "Race, Mestizaje and Nationalism: Sonora's Anti-Chinese Movement and State Formation in Post-Revolutionary Me'xico," *Political Power and Social Theory* 14 (2000): 91–140.

Chapter 3

1. See William Preston, Jr., *Aliens and Dissenters: Federal Suppression of Radicals, 1903–1933*, 2nd ed. (Urbana: University of Illinois Press, 1994); Philip S. Foner, *History of the Labor Movement in the United States*, vols. 1–6 (New York: International Publishers, 1947–88), esp. vol. 4, *The Industrial Workers of the World, 1905–1917*.

2. *Turner v. Williams*, 194 U.S. 279, 280 (1904).

3. Darrow and Masters, *Brief and Argument of the Appellant*, 5.

4. Later in the twentieth century, the meaning of "civil liberties" and "civil rights" became roughly distinct, with "civil rights" often referring to government regulation to prevent discrimination and "civil liberties" referring to freedoms and rights protected against government regulation. But during the nineteenth century and into the twentieth, this division did not yet exist. For lawmakers in the post–Civil War era considering the rights of African Americans, as legal scholar Christopher W. Schmidt writes, "the central issue was not differentiating 'civil rights' from 'civil liberties,' as the two terms were used interchangeably. Rather, the key lines of distinction and discussion for lawmakers were between three categories of rights: civil rights (sometimes referred to as civil liberties), social rights, and political rights." He writes, "the origins of the modern distinction between civil rights and civil liberties can be traced to the late 1940s, when liberal anticommunists sought to distinguish their incipient interest in the cause of racial equality from their belief that national security demanded limitations on the speech and due process rights of suspected subversives." Christopher W. Schmidt, "The Civil Rights–Civil Liberties Divide," *Stanford Journal of Civil Rights and Civil Liberties* 12 (2016): 6–7 and 4.

5. As with other free speech advocacy of the first decade of the twentieth century, attorneys Clarence Darrow and Edgar Lee Masters, representing Turner before the Supreme Court, argued for First Amendment rights "as a vehicle for working-class power, a back door for a more just society." Laura Weinrib, "The Sex Side of Civil Liberties: *United States v. Dennett* and the Changing Face of Free Speech," *Law and History Review* 30, no. 2 (2012): 325–86, quote at 383. See also David M. Rabban, *Free Speech in Its Forgotten Years, 1870–1920* (Cambridge: Cambridge University Press, 1999), 46–47.

6. Arthur O. Pleydell Affidavit, February 4, 1904, at 13, Motion of Appellant to be Admitted to Bail, Turner v. Williams, 194 U.S. 279 (1904), *USSCRB*.

7. Plydell Affidavit, 13–14; Samuel Gompers, Affidavit of Samuel Gompers in Support of Motion to Admit to Bail, February 11, 1904, at 1–3, Turner v. Williams, 194 U.S. 279 (1904), *USSCRB*.

8. For more on the Free Speech League, see David M. Rabban, "The Free Speech League, the ACLU, and Changing Conceptions of Free Speech in American History," *Stanford Law Review* 45, no. 1 (1992): 47–114.

9. Plydell Affidavit, 14; *Turner v. Williams*, 194 U.S. at 283.

10. Darrow and Masters, *Brief and Argument of the Appellant*, 90–100.

11. Darrow and Masters, *Brief and Argument of the Appellant*, 95.

12. Darrow and Masters, *Brief and Argument of the Appellant*, 80–83.

13. Darrow and Masters, *Brief and Argument of the Appellant*, 83–107.

14. Darrow and Masters, *Brief and Argument of the Appellant*, 86.

15. Darrow and Masters, *Brief and Argument of the Appellant*, 108–187.

16. Darrow and Masters, *Brief and Argument of the Appellant*, 22, 25.

17. *Turner v. Williams*, 194 U.S. at 291.

18. Darrow and Masters, *Brief and Argument of the Appellant*, 33.

19. Darrow and Masters, *Brief and Argument of the Appellant*, 26–55.

20. Motion of Appellant to Advance Cause, Louis F. Post Affidavit, February 8, 1904, Turner v. Williams, 6–7, *USSCRB*. See also Rabban, *Free Speech in Its Forgotten Years*, 46–47.

21. Gompers Affidavit, 2–3.

22. Darrow and Masters, *Brief and Argument of the Appellant*, 5–6.

23. Darrow and Masters, *Brief and Argument of the Appellant*, 26–55.

24. Darrow and Masters, *Brief and Argument of the Appellant*, 41.

25. Darrow and Masters, *Brief and Argument of the Appellant*, 48; the brief also stated, "To be able to repress beliefs but not to prevent their utterance is an empty power, and one which never could suit the sponsors of this law or any similar law."

26. Justice David J. Brewer wrote a concurring decision in which he agreed with the Court, but he once again noted that he had problems with the government's power to deport. *Turner v. Williams*, 194 U.S. at 295–96.

27. *Turner v. Williams*, 194 U.S. at 292.

28. Act of Mar. 3, 1903, § 21, 32 Stat. 1213, 1218 (1903).

29. The opinion stated, "It is, of course, true that if an alien is not permitted to enter this country, or, having entered contrary to law, is expelled, he is in fact cut off from worshipping or speaking or publishing or petitioning in the country, but that is merely because of his exclusion therefrom. He does not become one of the people to whom these things are secured by our Constitution by an attempt to enter forbidden by law." *Turner v. Williams*, 194 U.S. at 292.

30. Alice Wexler, *Emma Goldman in Exile: From the Russian Revolution to the Spanish Civil War* (Boston: Beacon Press, 1989), 100–101.

31. *Turner v. Williams*, 194 U.S. at 291.

32. "In re Chan Leong Hee," Office of Inspector in Charge, U.S. Bureau of Immigration, Los Angeles, February 19, 1909, File 163, Box 11, CCF-CA.

33. Kramer, "Imperial Openings," 322. There were fluctuations in this number. As Kramer notes, during the years that Terence Powderly and Frank Sargent served as commissioner general, they cut down on those admitted through administrative discretion. Theodore Roosevelt reversed some of their actions in 1906. Kramer, "Imperial Openings," 339.

34. Act of Nov. 3, 1893, § 1, 28 Stat. 7 (1893). Men and women with U.S. criminal records faced deportation with no avenue of appeal. In California, the state with the largest

community of Chinese immigrants, leaders of the Chinese community initially assisted authorities in identifying criminals for deportation. They hoped that doing so would help combat broader anti-Chinese sentiment and shore up the rights of the larger community of lawful residents. Salyer, *Laws Harsh as Tigers*, 89–90.

35. *United States v. Ah Fawn*, 57 F. 591, 592 (S.D. Cal. 1893).

36. *Ah Fawn*, 57 F. at 592.

37. *Ah Fawn*, 57 F. at 596.

38. *Ah Fawn*, 57 F. at 595.

39. *Lee Ah Yin v. United States*, 116 F. 614, 615–16 (9th Cir. 1902). Five months later, another court decision, *Wong Ah Quie v. United States*, 118 F. 1020 (9th Cir. 1902), confirmed that Chinese prostitutes fell into the legal category of laborers. Sucheng Chan, "The Exclusion of Chinese Women, 1870–1943," in *Entry Denied: Exclusion and the Chinese Community in America, 1882–1943*, ed. Sucheng Chan (Philadelphia: Temple University Press, 1991), 133.

40. For the above discussion of the Chan case, see "In re Chan Leong Hee." U.S. Department of Commerce and Labor, Bureau of Immigration, *Treaty, Laws, and Regulations Relating to Exclusion of Chinese* (Washington, D.C.: Government Printing Office, 1905), 62.

41. "In re Chan Leong Hee."

42. "In re Chan Leong Hee."

43. *United States v. Ng Park Tan*, 86 F. 605 (N.D. Cal. 1898).

44. This quote opened with, "Now, construing all the legislation on this subject in the light of our internal policy as already stated, I am disposed to hold that the law, properly and effectually construed, contemplates that a merchant of China may enter this country only for the purpose of prosecuting his business as a merchant here. He may not, under pretense of being a merchant, secure entry as such, intending immediately to become and continue a laborer." *United States v. Yong Yew*, 83 F. 832 (E.D. Mo. 1897).

45. "In re Chan Leong Hee."

46. The report further noted that "no authoritative decision has as yet been rendered, but the different United States attorneys are vigorously prosecuting the Government's interests, and it is hoped that within a short time, from the haze of uncertainty which now envelops the question, a precedent may issue which will serve to clarify the legal atmosphere." *AR-CGI* (1914), 346.

47. Sisson added that since Section 6 immigrants had the right to bring their families, their children could also lawfully take up laboring. He wrote, "applicants admitted as the minor sons of domiciled merchants are permitted to engage immediately in laboring pursuits." *AR-CGI* (1920), 302.

48. Lee, *At America's Gates*, 155–56, 201–3.

49. For a strong treatment of the changing practices of home births and citizenship rights, see Natalia Molina, *Fit to Be Citizens: Public Health and Race in Los Angeles, 1879–1939* (Berkeley: University of California Press, 2006).

50. *Moy Suey v. United States*, 147 F. 697, 698 (7th Cir. 1906).

51. *United States v. Sing Tuck*, 194 U.S. 161 (1904); *United States v. Ju Toy*, 198 U.S. 253 (1905).

52. The Immigration Act of 1892 laid this out in section 3, determining "that any Chinese person or person of Chinese descent arrested under the provisions of this act or the acts

hereby extended shall be adjudged to be unlawfully within the United States unless such person shall establish, by affirmative proof, to the satisfaction of such justice, judge, or commissioner, his lawful right to remain in the United States." Act of May 5, 1892, § 3, 27 Stat. 25 (1892).

53. *Moy Suey*, 147 F. at 698.

54. *Moy Suey*, 147 F. at 698.

55. *Moy Suey*, 147 F. at 698–99.

56. Salyer, *Laws Harsh as Tigers*, 91. See also *AR-CGI* (1916), 211.

57. *AR-CGI* (1911), 142.

58. *AR-CGI* (1911), 142.

59. *AR-CGI* (1914), 311; see also *AR-CGI* (1916), 211, which states, "One of the main difficulties in the judicial cases is the great length of time appeals are permitted to remain upon the dockets, some cases having been pending for as much as three years between the time of arrest and the hearing on appeal before the district judge."

60. *AR-CGI* (1911), 142; see similar complaints in *AR-CGI* (1912), 19.

61. *AR-CGI* (1914), 346. Nonetheless, immigration officials succeeded in deporting only 52 percent of all people of Chinese heritage they arrested in 1911 and only 44 percent of all those arrested in 1912. *AR-CGI* (1911), 142–43; *AR-CGI* (1912), 19.

62. *AR-CGI* (1916), 201.

63. *AR-CGI* (1916), 201. The submission of anonymous tips is also discussed in the bureau's reports in 1919. *AR-CGI* (1919), 309.

64. These cases placed the burden of proof on the defendant: *Yee King v. United States*, 179 F. 368 (2d Cir. 1910); *Kum Sue v. United States*, 179 F. 370 (2d Cir. 1910); *United States v. Too Toy*, 185 F. 838 (S.D.N.Y. 1911); *Yee Ging v. United States*, 190 F. 270 (W.D. Tex. 1911); *Bak Kun v. United States*, 195 F. 53 (6th Cir. 1912); *United States v. Hom Lim*, 223 F. 520 (2d Cir. 1915); *Fong Ping Ngar v. United States*, 223 F. 523 (2d Cir. 1915); *Ng You Nuey v. United States*, 224 F. 340 (6th Cir. 1915); *Chin Ah Yoke v. White*, 244 F. 940 (9th Cir. 1917); *Sit Sing Kum v. United States*, 277 F. 191 (2d Cir. 1921).

65. *Yee Ging*, 190 F. at 272–73.

66. *Yee Ging*, 190 F. at 272. Judge Maxey had decided an earlier case important to citizenship that involved race and citizenship in applying to Mexicans; in the 1897 case of *In re Rodriguez*, he ruled that Mexicans were legally eligible to naturalize. For more on *In re Rodriguez*, see Ngai, *Impossible Subjects*, 43–54; Haney López, *White by Law*, 43–44.

67. The New York judge wrote, "It is quite true that in Moy Suey . . . a distinction is taken between a Chinese person entering the United States and so covered by United States v. Ju Toy . . . and a Chinese person who has got in and is arrested here, but, that decision not being binding upon me, I cannot follow it." *Too Toy*, 185 F. at 840.

68. The court also stated, "If the government were called on to make a case, the result would be doubtful, but I am distinctly proceeding upon the theory that it is not, and that the defendant has the burden." *Too Toy*, 185 F. at 841.

69. *Ng Fong Ho v. White*, 259 U.S. 276 (1922).

70. *Ng Fong Ho*, 259 U.S. at 281.

71. Motomura, "Curious Evolution of Immigration Law."

72. *Ng Fong Ho*, 259 U.S. at 284.

73. *Ng Fong Ho*, 259 U.S. at 284–85.

74. *Soo Hoo Yee v. United States*, 3 F.2d 592 (1924).

75. *Soo Hoo Yee*, 3 F.2d at 595.

76. The court also noted, "It is also true that on his arrival in Canada from China he told the Canadian Immigration officials that he was on his way to Cuba, although he was in fact on his way to the United States. But the fact that he misrepresented his intentions, while it impairs his own testimony, does not impair that of the witnesses who corroborate him." *Soo Hoo Yee*, 3 F.2d at 597.

77. *Soo Hoo Yee*, 3 F.2d at 594.

78. *Soo Hoo Yee*, 3 F.2d at 597.

Chapter 4

1. Memorandum for the Acting Secretary from the Acting Commissioner General, August 26, 1915, File 54012/33, INS.

2. *AR-CGI* (1913), 226.

3. Barbara Meil Hobson, *Uneasy Virtue: The Politics of Prostitution and the American Reform Tradition* (Chicago: University of Chicago Press, 1990), 140.

4. On the difficulties defining white slavery and the panic, see Jessica R. Pliley, *Policing Sexuality: The Mann Act and the Making of the FBI* (Cambridge, Mass.: Harvard University Press, 2014); David J. Langum, *Crossing over the Line: Legislating Morality and the Mann Act* (Chicago: University of Chicago Press, 1994). On the concept of a moral panic, see Stuart Hall et al., *Policing the Crisis: Mugging, the State and Law and Order*, 2nd ed. (New York: Palgrave Macmillan, 2013).

5. Donna Guy, *Sex and Danger in Buenos Aires: Prostitution, Family, and Nation in Argentina* (Lincoln: University of Nebraska Press, 1991), 12.

6. For more on the international congresses and meetings on white slavery, see Guy, *Sex and Danger*, 24–28.

7. Hutchinson, *Legislative History of American Immigration Policy*, 131.

8. Chan, "Exclusion of Chinese Women," 132–33. For information on the Page Act, see George Anthony Peffer, *If They Don't Bring Their Women Here: Chinese Female Immigration Before Exclusion* (Urbana: University of Illinois Press, 1999). On general immigration as applied to women, see Martha Gardner, *The Qualities of a Citizen: Women, Immigration and Citizenship, 1870–1965* (Princeton, N.J.: Princeton University Press, 2005).

9. Act of Mar. 3, 1903, §§ 2 and 21, 32 Stat. 1213 (1903).

10. Katharine M. Donato and Donna Gabaccia, *Gender and International Migration from the Slavery Era to the Global Age* (New York: Russell Sage Foundation, 2015), 84–92; Walter F. Willcox, ed., *International Migrations*, vol. 2 (New York: National Bureau of Economic Research, 1931), 90.

11. Meeting of the Board of Special Inquiry, Ellis Island, December 14, 1906, File 52241/10, INS.

12. Acting Supervising Inspector to the Commissioner General, July 15, 1915, File 54012/26, INS.

13. Salyer, *Laws Harsh as Tigers*, 232.

14. Meeting of the Board of Special Inquiry, December 14, 1906.

15. Meeting of the Board of Special Inquiry, December 14, 1906.

16. For instance, in 1920 the Bureau of Immigration employed about 1,700 officers and employees. The inspectors, of which there were three classes, made between $1,380 and $2,500

annually. The clerical employees, of which there were also three classes, made between $1,320 and $2,120. The agency also employed watchmen, laborers, and other members to do "subclerical" work. *AR-CGI* (1920), 55. The commissioner of immigration stationed at Boston stated that per annum watchmen made an average of $960; firemen, $930; laborers, $840; and matrons, $830. On the lower wages for matrons, the agent at Boston noted, "In spite of the fact that the laborers are greatly underpaid as compared with those in private employ, it will be noted that they are receiving more than the matrons. It must be admitted, however, that the latter class of employees, occupying positions of responsibility, serving as deporting officers and in many ways performing duties akin to those of a trained nurse, are entitled to compensation in excess of that paid unskilled laborers. Perhaps this and other discrepancies will be cleared up in the reclassification of the civil service to be considered during the next session of Congress." *AR-CGI* (1920), 327.

17. In 1920, a report from the inspector in charge stationed at Cleveland stated that employees were allowed four dollars per diem for travel expenses. He argued that, in 1920, "hardly anywhere can a room be obtained for less than $2.50 to $3, and the cheapest sort of meals cost two or even three times as much as they did five years ago." The employees paid their travel expenses and then waited in excess of thirty days to be reimbursed by the government. *AR-CGI* (1920), 390.

18. Acting Commissioner to Hon. J. Keefe, Commissioner General of Immigration, April 28, 1909, File 52241/14, INS.

19. E. J. Wallace, Acting Commissioner, to Commissioner General of Immigration, November 5, 1913, File 53678/19–53678/20, INS.

20. F. H. Larned, Acting Commissioner General, to Supervising Inspector, Immigration Service at San Antonio, Texas, November 6, 1908, File 52241/2, INS.

21. Immigrant Inspector to the Commissioner of Immigration at Montreal, July 5, 1915, File 54012/3–8, INS.

22. Travel, whether paid for by the transportation company or the government, was in third class and often at discounted government rates provided by train or steamship companies. Commissioner General to Commissioner of Immigration at Boston, Mass., January 16, 1913, File 53574/9, INS.

23. Immigrant Inspector to the Commissioner of Immigration at Montreal, July 5, 1915, File 54012/3–8, INS.

24. Fileto Lorenzo, December 6, 1909, File 752, "Fileto Lorenzo/Keeping, Supporting and Harboring an Alien Woman for Prostitution," Box 8, CCF-AZ.

25. Reverend Emil Kauten, chancellor of the Diocese of Seattle, and Rev. Hugh P. Gallagher, S.J., president, Seattle College, and pastor, Church of the Immaculate Conception, to Inspector in Charge, U.S. Immigration Service at Seattle, Washington, November 30, 1908, File 52241/4, INS.

26. Acting Commissioner, Memorandum for the Acting Secretary, August 4, 1915, File 54012/28, INS.

27. Acting Commissioner-General of Immigration, Memorandum for the Acting Secretary, September 2, 1915, File 54012/30, INS.

28. For precedents to this, see *AR-CGI* (1914), 286.

29. Immigrant Inspector to the Commissioner of Immigration at Montreal, July 5, 1915, File 54012/3–8, INS.

30. *AR-CGI* (1920), 307.

31. *AR-CGI* (1920), 308. In 1921, the department arranged nine coast-to-coast deportation parties, carrying 1,176 aliens. *AR-CGI* (1921), 15–16. In 1923, the department arranged eight coast-to-coast deportation parties, seven from Chicago to New York, five from Kansas City to the Mexican border, and several smaller parties from the Canadian and Mexican borders, carrying about 2,500 deportees. *AR-CGI* (1923), 14–15.

32. *AR-CGI* (1923), 14–15.

33. Pliley, *Policing Sexuality*; Langum, *Crossing over the Line*.

34. Langum, *Crossing over the Line*, 38. See also Pliley, *Policing Sexuality*, 33, 66.

35. Cott, *Public Vows*, 146–47. See also Pliley, *Policing Sexuality*, 35–37.

36. Langum, *Crossing over the Line*, 36, 37; Cott, *Public Vows*, 145–47.

37. Gardner, *Qualities of a Citizen*, 65.

38. Nancy Foner et al., eds., *New York and Amsterdam: Immigration and the New Urban Landscape* (New York: New York University Press, 2014), 11.

39. Gardner, *Qualities of a Citizen*, 69–70.

40. Mark Thomas Connelly, *The Response to Prostitution in the Progressive Era* (Chapel Hill: University of North Carolina Press, 1980), 56–57; Immigration Act of 1907, 34 Stat. 898.

41. Haag, *Consent*, 63, 65, 67.

42. Haag, *Consent*, 65.

43. Haag, *Consent*, 63.

44. For information on this beyond immigration history, see Haag, *Consent*, 69.

45. Acting Immigration Inspector to Inspector in Charge, Immigration Service, Los Angeles, July 9, 1913, File 53678/21–33, INS.

46. Acting Immigration Inspector to Inspector in Charge, Immigration Service, Los Angeles, July 9, 1913.

47. Langum, *Crossing over the Line*, 34.

48. *AR-CGI* (1916), 180. As historian Martha Gardner notes, in the application of white slavery law, racialization did not always serve as a "code for sexual deviance." Gardner, *Qualities of a Citizen*, 68.

49. On the category of whiteness, see Katherine Benton-Cohen, *Borderline Americans: Racial Division and Labor War in the Arizona Borderlands* (Cambridge, Mass.: Harvard University Press, 2009); Haney López, *White by Law*; Ngai, *Impossible Subjects*; Daniels, *Guarding the Golden Door*. On the broader racialization of Mexican immigrants, see Natalia Molina, *How Race Is Made in America: Immigration, Citizenship, and the Historical Power of Racial Scripts* (Berkeley: University of California Press, 2013); Matt Garcia, *A World of Its Own: Race, Labor, and Citrus in the Making of Greater Los Angeles, 1900–1970* (Chapel Hill: University of North Carolina Press, 2001); Neil Foley, *The White Scourge: Mexicans, Blacks, and Poor Whites in Texas Cotton Culture* (Berkeley: University of California Press, 1997); George J. Sánchez, *Becoming Mexican American: Ethnicity, Culture and Identity in Chicano Los Angeles, 1900–1945* (New York: Oxford University Press, 1993); and David Montejano, *Anglos and Mexicans in the Making of Texas, 1836–1986* (Austin: University of Texas Press, 1987).

50. *AR-CGI* (1914), 14–15.

51. *AR-CGI* (1914), 15.

52. *AR-CGI* (1914), 14–16.

53. Barrett's trip, which lasted from April 15 to June 30, 1914, was also about prevention. For more information on the prevention tasks, see *AR-CGI* (1914), 16, 365–66.

54. *AR-CGI* (1914), 14.

55. *AR-CGI* (1914), 359. In terms of reception and cooperation, Barrett anecdotally wrote that she was well received at the International Council of Women meeting in Rome, stating that at the close of the meeting many women "expressed their appreciation of the international attitude of our country." Barrett also wrote that two notable women specifically thanked her: "Queen Helena [of Italy] expressed her pleasure at the United States Government sending a special representative to this conference and also her interest in the efforts of this Government. . . . Queen Marguerita, the Queen mother, also personally expressed to me her interest in similar terms." *AR-CGI* (1914), 367.

56. To add to their case that Bissonette was "immoral," the mother and brother also alleged that Bissonette had lived with a man in Canada for a number of years, without marriage. In the Matter of Bissonette, Josephine D., at a Meeting of the Board of Special Inquiry, January 23, 1909, File 52241/21, INS; John H. Clark, Commissioner, to Commissioner General of Immigration, January 2, 1909, File 52241/21, INS.

57. Affidavit, Calite Clement, February 3, 1909, File 52241/20, INS; Affidavit, Julian Brisebois February 3, 1909, File 52241/20, INS; Affidavit, Napoleon Guindon, February 3, 1909, File 52241/20, INS; Affidavit, Calixte Montsion, February 3, 1909, File 52241/20, INS; Affidavit, Alexis Groulx, February 3, 1909, File 52241/20, INS; In the Matter of Bissonette, Josephine, Canadian French, Memorandum on Behalf of Josephine D. Bissonette, Alien, for Dismissal of Department Warrant, William Blau and Charles L. Hoffman, Attorneys for Miss Bissonette, p. 11, File 52241/20, INS.

58. Bissonette had moved to New York when she was thirteen. After several years of working as a nanny, Bissonette moved in with her married sister and for eighteen years worked as her maid and caretaker, earning forty dollars a month. Acting Commissioner R. Dobler to Hon. Daniel J. Keefe, Commissioner General of Immigration, New York, January 22, 1909, File 52241/21, INS; In the Matter of Bissonette, Josephine, Canadian French, at a Meeting of a Board of Special Inquiry Held at Ellis Island, New York Harbor, January 21, 1909, File 52241/21, INS.

59. This had become a deportable category within the Immigration Act of 1907.

60. As seen in Chapter 1, immigration officials did this when first deporting people of Chinese heritage under general immigration law. For more on this, see also Gardner, *Qualities of a Citizen*; Roberts, *Whence They Came*.

61. Berthe Olivice, the French prostitute, had entered the United States on a second-class ticket, and the records imply that because of that she was not closely inspected as a potential excludable immigrant. Meeting of the Board of Special Inquiry, December 14, 1906, File 52241/10, INS.

62. Daniel J. Keefe, Commissioner General, to Commissioner of Immigration, February 19, 1909, File 52241/21, INS; Secretary to Hon. William Sulzer, February 6, 1909, File 52241/21, INS; Unknown to Hon. Oscar S. Straus, Secretary Department Commerce and Labor, February 3, 1909, File 52241/21, INS.

63. It was at this point that the brother and mother requested Bissonette's deportation to Canada. Bissonette's lawyer testified to the Bureau of Immigration that the brother had approached him and stated that "the control of the estate should be transferred to Canada, where it would be near his mother and himself, and if that was not done, he proposed to bring suit, and he made all kinds of threats against her in particular, unless things were done

as he wanted it." In the Matter of Bissonette, Josephine D., at a Meeting of the Board of Special Inquiry, January 23, 1909, p. 7, File 52241/21, INS. The lawyer also pointed out discrepancies in the affidavits that had been used to secure the initial warrant of arrest. For instance, one of the brothers testified that he had seen his sister in the Canadian town of Alfred every day. The brother, however, could not physically have seen Bissonette in Alfred because during thirteen of the eighteen years under question, he lived hundreds of miles away in Montreal. In the Matter of Bissonette, Josephine, Canadian French, Memorandum on Behalf of Josephine D. Bissonette, Alien, for Dismissal of Department Warrant, William Blau and Charles L. Hoffman, Attorneys for Miss Bissonette, pp. 16–19, File 52241/20, INS.

64. Each witness testified to Bissonette's morality and her respectability, swearing that she did not operate a house of prostitution. In the Matter of Bissonette, Josephine, Canadian French, Memorandum on Behalf of Josephine D. Bissonette, 16–19.

65. In the Matter of Bissonette, Josephine D., at a Meeting of the Board of Special Inquiry, January 23, 1909, File 52241/21, p. 7, INS; Oath of Signer of Bond, John Miller, File 52241/21, INS; Oath of Signer of Bond, Bruno C. Rothenburg, File 52241/21, INS.

66. Commissioner to Hon. Daniel J. Keefe, Commissioner General of Immigration, January 26, 1909, File 52241/21, INS.

67. For use of the term "unmake" in relation to deportability of aliens, see Ngai, *Impossible Subjects*, 56–95.

68. As a result, the commissioner wrote, "there is every reason to believe she will henceforth lead an honest, useful, and moral life." *AR-CGI* (1917), 201–2. In immigration records Berthe Sainsot is listed as Bertha. Claudine Basile, her niece, provided more information on her aunt, whose correct name is Berthe Sainsot. Claudine Basile, e-mail message to author, November 13, 2014.

69. The records state that Gau had originally bought this ticket for another single young woman, but that that woman's brother had found out that she was being lured into prostitution. The brother showed up and saved his sister. This left Gau with a ticket, which she then persuaded Schetter to use. Memo for the Assistant Secretary, In re deportation of Marie Schetter, from Acting Commissioner General, December 22, 1908, File 52241/4, INS.

70. Schetter also testified that when she arrived at the brothel, she refused for weeks to practice prostitution and instead worked as a door person. Eventually she was finally "broken" and engaged in prostitution. According to her testimony, Schetter felt sick about this. The records state that Gau not only forced her into prostitution but also kept Schetter's wages. Testimony of Marie Schetter, December 10, 1908, File 52241/4, INS.

71. John H. Sargent, Inspector in Charge, to the Commissioner General, December 15, 1908, File 52241/4, INS.

72. Sargent to the Commissioner General, December 15, 1908.

73. Memo for the Assistant Secretary, In re deportation of Maria Schetter, from Acting Commissioner General, December 22, 1908, File 52241/4, INS; Sargent to the Commissioner General, December 15, 1908.

74. Memo for the Assistant Secretary, In re deportation of Maria Schetter, from Acting Commissioner General, December 22, 1908.

75. Kauten and Gallagher to Inspector in Charge, November 30, 1908.

76. Assistant Commissioner to Commissioner General of Immigration, November 20, 1915, File 54012/30, INS.

77. Her file does not indicate whether she was able to remain in the United States past 1921. Assistant Commissioner, In Charge of B.S.I and Appeals, to Commissioner General of Immigration, October 17, 1921, File 54012/30, INS.

78. Motomura, *Americans in Waiting*, 9–12.

79. *AR-CGI* (1911), 80–83.

80. *AR-CGI* (1914), 108–11; (1916), 86–89; (1917), 84–87; (1918), 152–55.

81. Criminals, under the Page Act, were defined as "persons who are undergoing a sentence for conviction in their own country of felonious crimes . . . or whose sentence had been remitted on condition of their emigration." 18 Stat. 477 (1875). Colonies and states did try to remove migrants classified as criminals prior to the establishment of the federal administration of immigration law. For more information, see Neuman, *Strangers to the Constitution*; and Aleinikoff, *Semblances of Sovereignty*.

82. 22 Stat. 214 (1882). E. P. Hutchinson writes, "Any crime involving an act intrinsically and morally wrong, or an act done contrary to justice, honesty, principle, or good morals is a crime involving moral turpitude." Hutchinson, *Legislative History of American Immigration Policy*, 451.

83. 26 Stat. 1084 (1891); Hutchinson, *Legislative History of American Immigration Policy*, 408.

84. In comparison, that year the federal government deported 238 immigrants as public charges. *AR-CGI* (1896), 10.

85. *AR-CGI* (1900), 8.

86. The 1907 law, therefore, made it illegal to directly or indirectly import a woman for prostitution. The new text of the law forbid anyone to "keep, maintain, control, support or harbor in any house or other place, for the purpose of prostitution, or for any other immoral purpose, any alien woman or girl, within three years after she shall have entered the United States." Act of Mar. 3, 1903, § 21, 32 Stat. 1213 (1903); Act of Feb. 20, 1907, § 3, 34 Stat. 898 (1907).

87. Susan J. Pearson, *The Rights of the Defenseless: Protecting Animals and Children in Gilded Age America* (Chicago: University of Chicago Press, 2011), 158. For more on the transition in policing, see Rebecca M. McLennan, *The Crisis of Imprisonment: Protest, Politics, and the Making of the American Penal State, 1776–1941* (Cambridge: Cambridge University Press, 2008); Eric H. Monkkonen, *The Local State: Public Money and American Cities* (Stanford, Calif.: Stanford University Press, 1995); Eric H. Monkkonen, *Police in Urban America, 1860–1920* (Cambridge: Cambridge University Press, 1981).

88. See Gardner, *Qualities of a Citizen*, 76. Included in these efforts was also a white slavery squad, which operated in nineteen cities, from March to July 1909. Pliley, *Policing Sexuality*, 41–45.

89. "Deportation of Anarchists and Aliens of the Criminal Classes Under the Immigration Act of Feb. 20, 1907," Department Circular 163, March 3, 1908, File 51924/30, INS.

90. "Deportation of Anarchists and Aliens," March 3, 1908.

91. Everett Wallace, Acting Commissioner, to Honorable F. P. Sargent, Commissioner General of Immigration, June 4, 1908, File 51924/30, INS.

92. Immigration Report, June 1908, File 51924/30, INS.

93. *Keller v. United States*, 213 U.S. 138 (1909).

94. Connelly, *Response to Prostitution*, 52–53.

95. *Keller*, 213 U.S. at 147.

96. Benjamin C. Bachrach and Mr. Elijah N. Zoline, Brief and Argument for Plaintiffs in Error at 9, Keller v. United States, 213 U.S. 138 (1909), *USSCRB*.

97. Brief and Argument for Plaintiffs, 4–5; Connelly, *Response to Prostitution*, 52–53.

98. Mr. Assistant Attorney General Fowler, Brief for the United States at 8–9, Keller v. United States, 213 U.S. 138 (1909), *USSCRB*.

99. *Keller*, 213 U.S. at 148–49.

100. Daniel J. Keefe, Commissioner General, to Supervising Inspector, Immigration Service, San Antonio, Texas, April 23, 1909, File "Sara Cervantez Imported by Simon Chavez," 52241/20, INS; Luther B. Stewart to the Commissioner General of Immigration, April 23, 1909, File 52241/20, INS.

101. Keefe to Supervising Inspector, Immigration Service, San Antonio, April 23, 1909.

102. Couzin, as it turned out, was deportable after his prison sentence because he was an immigrant procurer. At the time of Couzin's release from prison, no warrant of deportation had been filed with the prison authorities. Consequently, Couzin was set free. The woman with whom he was arrested and whom he was charged with procuring had already been deported on December 18, 1908. Police Commissioner of New York to Hon. Wm. Williams, Commissioner of Immigration, Ellis Island, New York, November 22, 1909, File 55241/10, INS.

103. Changes in the antiprostitution provision of deportation law were part of a larger change in immigration policy. The timing of the act's passage was closely connected to the release of the Dillingham Commission's report. For further information, see Robert F. Zeidel, *Immigrants, Progressives, and Exclusion Politics: The Dillingham Commission, 1900–1927* (DeKalb: Northern Illinois University Press, 2004), 115.

104. White Slave Traffic Act, 36 Stat. 825 (1910). Historian Pamela Haag shows that the Mann Act, and its regulation of sexuality, was hailed by the *New York Tribune* as "one of the most significant interpretations of the Constitution as a grant of national power." The Supreme Court upheld this expansion of power. Haag, *Consent*, 72–73. For more on the reach of the Mann Act, see Chan, "Exclusion of Chinese Women," 132–33; Moloney, *National Insecurities*; Grace Peña Delgado, "Border Control and Sexual Policing: White Slavery and Prostitution Along the U.S.-Mexico Borderlands, 1903–1910," *Western Historical Quarterly* 43, no. 2 (Summer 2012): 157–78.

105. In a coincidence, a major Mann Act prosecution and Supreme Court case involved Drew Caminetti, the son of Woodrow Wilson's commissioner general of immigration, Anthony Caminetti. The case led to a scandal involving accusations that Anthony Caminetti used his position to try to postpone the trial against his son. Langum, *Crossing over the Line*, 104, 112–13. For information on laying the groundwork on the interstate commerce use, see Pliley, *Policing Sexuality*, 67–69.

106. Over time, the Mann Act had less and less direct impact on the deportation of foreign prostitutes and procurers. The more important historically significant sections dealt with domestic regulation of prostitution and "immorality." Langum, *Crossing over the Line*, 64. By 1911, the Bureau of Immigration already noted that section 6 was not working. *AR-CGI* (1911), 126.

107. As quoted in Langum, *Crossing over the Line*, 42.

108. Haag, *Consent*, 63, 65. The Mann Act also was in force in China, under extraterritoriality. See *United States v. W. H. Thompson* (1912), in Lobingier, *Extraterritorial Cases*, 1:261–63.

109. Act of Mar. 26, 1910, § 3, 36 Stat. 263 (1910).

110. Robert Watchorn, Commissioner, to Hon. Daniel J. Keefe, Commissioner General of Immigration, March 22, 1909, "Re the Assumption of False Identities by White Slavers," File 52423/30, INS.

111. The Immigration Act of 1903 also made importing immigrant women into the United States for the purposes of prostitution a felony. Act of Mar. 3, 1903, § 3, 32 Stat. 1213 (1903). This was not unique to those deported under the antiprostitution provision; the deportation of some other immigrants—like criminals, anarchists, and polygamists—had a three-year time limit, too.

112. As quoted in Connelly, *Response to Prostitution,* 57.

113. *AR-CGI* (1911), 82; Act of Mar. 26, 1910, § 3, 36 Stat. 263 (1910).

114. In 1908, President Theodore Roosevelt created an investigative bureau within the Department of Justice, which President William Howard Taft named the Bureau of Investigation in 1909. In 1932, it was renamed the Federal Bureau of Investigation. Langum, *Crossing over the Line,* 48–49.

115. Langum, *Crossing over the Line,* 48–49.

116. Pliley, *Policing Sexuality,* 91.

117. *AR-CGI* (1913), 192–93.

118. Motomura, *Immigration Outside the Law,* 4.

119. For the term "discretion that matters," see Motomura, "The Discretion That Matters," 1819–58.

120. "In re Pekka Turumem and Hilda Huhuarmiemi or Hilda Huimaimeni, alias Hilja Niemi," Supplemental Memorandum for the Acting Secretary, September 8, 1915, File 54012/19, INS.

121. Gardner, *Qualities of a Citizen,* 85.

122. *AR-CGI* (1920), 418. These numbers refer to women deported and excluded, but they illustrate that not all women were being treated under the Barrett-recommended policy.

123. On respectability along lines of race, class, and gender, see Glenda Elizabeth Gilmore, *Gender and Jim Crow: Women and the Politics of White Supremacy in North Carolina, 1896–1920* (Chapel Hill: University of North Carolina Press, 1996), esp. chaps. 2 and 3; Barbara Young Welke, *Recasting American Liberty: Gender, Race, Law, and the Railroad Revolution, 1865–1920* (Cambridge: Cambridge University Press, 2001), esp. chap. 8; Priscilla Murolo, *The Common Ground of Womanhood: Class, Gender, and Working Girls' Clubs, 1884–1928* (Urbana: University of Illinois Press, 1997); Carole Srole, *Transcribing Class and Gender: Masculinity and Femininity in Nineteenth-Century Courts and Offices* (Ann Arbor: University of Michigan Press, 2010).

124. *AR-CGI* (1919), 315.

125. Gardner, *Qualities of a Citizen,* 56; and 66, where Gardner cites a 1909 report from a San Antonio district inspector who wrote that along the Mexican borders many cases involve women who "are merely prostitutes . . . practicing prostitution . . . of their own volition" and not white slaves.

126. Memorandum for Mr. Larned, June 2, 1913, File 53575/291, INS.

127. He then suggested, "I believe that a test case involving this point should be carried to the higher courts in order that this question may be settled." *AR-CGI* (1914), 284.

128. Cott, *Public Vows,* 149.

129. Memorandum for the Acting Secretary, U.S. Department of Labor, October 30, 1908, File 52241/5, INS.

130. *AR-CGI* (1911), 126.

131. Memorandum for the Acting Secretary, U.S. Department of Labor, October 7, 1915, File 52241/5, INS.

132. At this time, there was also an interrelated discussion of the nullification of arranged marriages, especially in the case of Japanese picture brides, but also in the case of the Russians and Jews, and the validity of polygamous marriages. For further discussion, see Cott, *Public Vows*, 137–46; and Haag, *Consent*, 99–101, 114, 116–17.

133. Memorandum for the Acting Secretary, U.S. Department of Labor, October 30, 1908, File 52241/5, INS.

134. This question of jurisdiction of citizenship was also raised in the 1883 circuit court case in the Eastern District of Michigan, *Pequignot v. City of Detroit*. Memorandum for the Acting Secretary, U.S. Department of Labor, October 30, 1908, File 52241/5, INS.

135. Office of the Commissioner, Montreal, to Commissioner General of Immigration, May 19, 1916, File 54012/9–11, INS. See Tuttle's position also in Unknown to Commissioner of Immigration, September 27, 1915, File 53713/178, INS.

136. The deportation file documents that Heyndrekx entered the United States in April 1908 from Canada into Blaine, Washington. The Bureau of Immigration issued a warrant for her arrest, on grounds that she was practicing prostitution in violation of the Immigration Act of 1907. J. C. Nardini, Acting Immigrant Inspector United States Service, "In the Matter of the Application of Sicilia DeBeelde Heyndrekx Alias Sicilia DeBeelde Alias Alice Martin for Writ of Habeas Corpus," August 17, 1909, Box 11, File 175, CCF-CA.

137. In an affidavit and supplemental petition for the writ, Joseph Charles Heyndrekx testified that he was a citizen of the United States, that he and Sicilia had been married in New York in November 1905, and that they had been living together as husband and wife at the time of Sicilia Heyndrekx's arrest. Affidavit and Supplemental Petition for Writ of Habeas Corpus in the Matter of the Application of Sicilia DeBeelde Heyndrekx alias Sicilia DeBeelde alias Alice Martin, August 17, 1909, Box 11, File 175, CCF-CA.

138. W. A. Hammel, Sheriff of the County of Los Angeles, State of California, to D. Crowley, Deputy Sheriff, "In the matter of the Application of Sicilia DeBeelde Heyndrekx Alias Sicilia DeBeelde Alias Alice Martin for Writ of Habeas Corpus," August 17, 1909, Box 11, File 175, CCF-CA.

139. While it is not entirely clear, it appears that Heyndrekx was deported as an alien and her marriage not recognized. Judge of the District Court of the United States, "In the Matter of the Application of Sicilia DeBeelde Heyndreks Alias Sicilia DeBeelde Alias Alice Martin: Order of Dismissal," August 25, 1909, Box 11, File 175, CCF-CA.

140. Cott, *Public Vows*, 148–49.

141. Act of Feb. 5, 1917, § 19, 39 Stat. 874 (1917). After the passage of the Cable Act in 1922, this law became moot because a woman no longer acquired the citizenship of her husband by marriage. Jane Perry Clark, *Deportation of Aliens from the United States to Europe* (New York: Columbia University Press, 1931), 239–40.

142. Pliley, *Policing Sexuality*, 203.

143. Pliley, *Policing Sexuality*, 66. This collaboration had initially sparked opposition, especially from Southern Democrats, who criticized the involvement of federal police forces at the local and state levels. Pliley, *Policing Sexuality*, 71–74.

144. *AR-CGI* (1914), 7.

Chapter 5

1. Stanley Coben, *A. Mitchell Palmer: Politician* (New York: Columbia University Press, 1963), 203–4; Louis F. Post, *The Deportations Delirium of Nineteen-Twenty* (Chicago: Charles H. Kerr, 1923), 18–19, 37–38.

2. Authorities also anticipated a third wave of bombings, which did not happen. Post, *Deportations Delirium*, 39–40.

3. Alice Wexler, *Emma Goldman in Exile: From the Russian Revolution to the Spanish Civil War* (Boston: Beacon Press, 1989), 13–14.

4. The U.S. government first passed a provision making anarchists deportable in the Immigration Act of 1903. During World War I, Bureau of Immigration officials tried at an administrative level to expand their ability to deport under the anarchist provision in a campaign against the radical labor union International Workers of the World (IWW). These efforts were relatively unsuccessful. On this deportation campaign and how it set precedents for the Red Raids, see Preston, *Aliens and Dissenters*.

5. Act of Feb. 5, 1917, § 19, 39 Stat. 874 (1917). As Assistant Secretary of Labor Louis F. Post noted, this change made peaceful anarchists deportable for the first time. While John Turner, a peaceful anarchist, had been deported back in 1904, Post suggested that after that the Bureau of Immigration applied the anarchist provision only when it could prove that the anarchist advocated violence. But, as Post wrote, "Although the immigration law of 1903 did not exclude alien 'anarchists' of the non-resistant and orderly school, the revised immigration law of 1917 did." Post, *Deportations Delirium*, 61–62.

6. Officials from the Bureau of Immigration and the Department of Justice actually drafted the clause, which Congress included in the Immigration Act of 1918. *AR-CGI* (1919), 33.

7. Act of Oct. 16, 1918, § 1, 40 Stat. 1012 (1918).

8. In 1917, Goldman and Berkman were arrested for obstructing the Selective Service Act, an offense under the Espionage Act of 1917. They both were found guilty, fined, and sentenced to two-year prison terms. Post, *Deportations Delirium*, 18–19.

9. Candace Falk, *Love, Anarchy, and Emma Goldman: A Biography* (New Brunswick, N.J.: Rutgers University Press, 1990), 166, 177; Post, *Deportations Delirium*, 13.

10. Wexler, *Emma Goldman in Exile*, 13–14; Post, *Deportations Delirium*, 14.

11. Falk, *Love, Anarchy, and Emma Goldman*, 176.

12. Falk, *Love, Anarchy, and Emma Goldman*, 181.

13. The government had revoked the now dead Kershner's citizenship ten years earlier on the grounds that it had been granted illegally, before he was twenty-one. In building this case, the government also uncovered a grand larceny charge against him in June 1894, which also undermined his citizenship claims. Kershner pleaded guilty to having embezzled $680 from the Lodge of Oddfellows, for which he served a prison term. (This occurred after Goldman left him.) In building its case against Goldman's citizenship, the government also questioned the legitimacy of her marriage to Kershner. Falk, *Love, Anarchy, and Emma Goldman*, 177–78.

14. Post, *Deportations Delirium*, 14. On denaturalization in U.S. history, see Patrick Weil, *The Sovereign Citizen: Denaturalization and the Origins of the American Republic* (Philadelphia: University of Philadelphia Press, 2013).

15. Falk, *Love, Anarchy, and Emma Goldman*, 178; Wexler, *Emma Goldman in Exile*, 12; Emma Goldman, *Living My Life*, 2 vols. (New York: Dover Publications, 1970), 2:714.

16. Post, *Deportations Delirium*, 22. Seven other passengers were being deported for violating other provisions of immigration law. *AR-CGI* (1920), 32.

17. As quoted in Coben, *A. Mitchell Palmer*, 209. Historian Salvatore Salerno notes that the Justice Department also suspected labor activists and anarchists from the Italian community in Paterson in the bombings. In the end, the federal government brought no charges. Salvatore Salerno, "*I Delitti Della Razza Bianca* (Crimes of the White Race): Italian Anarchists' Racial Discourse as Crime," in *Are Italians White? How Race Is Made in America*, ed. Jennifer Guglielmo and Salvatore Salerno (New York: Routledge, 2003).

18. Coben, *A. Mitchell Palmer*, 209.

19. Coben, *A. Mitchell Palmer*, 210.

20. For more on the history of Jewish radicalism in the United States, see Hasia Diner, *The Jews of the United States* (Berkeley: University of California Press, 2004); Gerald Sorin, *The Prophetic Minority: American Jewish Immigrant Radicals, 1880–1920* (Bloomington: Indiana University Press, 1985); Jonathan Frankel, *Prophecy and Politics: Socialism, Nationalism, and the Russian Jews, 1862–1917* (Cambridge: Cambridge University Press, 1981).

21. Coben, *A. Mitchell Palmer*, 218.

22. As quoted in Coben, *A. Mitchell Palmer*, 219.

23. Of these 650, the Bureau of Immigration deported only 43. Coben, *A. Mitchell Palmer*, 219–20.

24. Post, *Deportations Delirium*, 28.

25. Coben, *A. Mitchell Palmer*, 221.

26. Coben, *A. Mitchell Palmer*, 218.

27. Coben, *A. Mitchell Palmer*, 219; Post, *Deportations Delirium*, 22–24.

28. In March 1919, Martens presented himself to the U.S. secretary of state as the representative of the RSFSR in the United States. He lived and worked in New York and also opened an office in Washington, D.C. L. Martens to the Secretary of State, March 31, 1920, *FRUS* (1920), 3:455.

29. Secretary of State to the Attorney General (Palmer), April 8, 1920, enclosure, "Memorandum Regarding the Diplomatic Status of Mr. L. Martens," April 6, 1920, *FRUS* (1920), 3:457–61. The United States continued to recognize Bakhmeteff until the summer of 1922. Post, *Deportations Delirium*, 284. On the U.S. decision to intervene, see George Kennan, *Soviet-American Relations, 1917–1929*, 3 vols. (Princeton, N.J.: Princeton University Press, 1958), esp. vol. 2.

30. L. Martens to the Secretary of State, November 15, 1919, *FRUS* (1920), 3:687–90.

31. He wrote, "They have been arrested without warrant and subjected to oppressive treatment against which they have no adequate protection, as citizens of a country whose Government is not recognized by the Government of the United States." Martens to the Secretary of State, November 15, 1919.

32. L. Martens to the Italian Ambassador (Avezzana), October 4, 1920, *FRUS* (1920), 3:476–77.

33. Martens to the Secretary of State, November 15, 1919.

34. Martens to the Secretary of State, November 15, 1919.

35. When Louis F. Post directed, for instance, that Emma Goldman "be deported to Soviet Russia," he specified that she should be sent to "'Red Russia' as that part of Russia was then commonly called—and not to 'White Russia,' where at that time she would have probably fared worse." Post, *Deportations Delirium*, 18.

36. Martens to the Secretary of State, November 15, 1919.

37. *AR-CGI* (1920), 32.

38. *AR-CGI* (1920), 32.

39. Post, *Deportations Delirium*, 7.

40. The secretary of state noted that, since there was "no port to which they can now be sent which will admit them directly to such territory . . . in these circumstances it will be necessary to arrange . . . their transit . . . perhaps through the port of Libau or Windau." Secretary of State (Lansing) to the Commissioner at Riga (Gade), December 11, 1919, *FRUS* (1920), 3:690.

41. Commissioner at Riga (Gade) to the Secretary of State, December 17, 1919, *FRUS* (1920), 3:691.

42. Secretary of State (Lansing) to the Commissioner at Riga (Gade), December 19, 1919, *FRUS* (1920), 3:691.

43. Secretary of State (Lansing) to the Commissioner at Riga (Gade), December 24, 1919, *FRUS* (1920), 3:693.

44. Commissioner at Riga (Gade) to the Secretary of State, December 21, 1919, *FRUS* (1920), 3:692.

45. Commissioner at Riga (Gade) to the Secretary of State, December 17, 1919, *FRUS* (1920), 3:691.

46. Secretary of Labor Wilson had no funds to send families along with the deportees; he sent out a directive ordering that "no deportee having wife or child in this country be placed on board the 'Buford.'" As Post noted, Wilson's instructions were followed in all the immigration stations except New York, where many of the deportees were being detained. Post, *Deportations Delirium*, 4–5.

47. Post noted, "It is not strange, therefore, that the deportations seemed to bereaved families left behind, and to their friends, to have been vicious kidnappings instead of regular, even if harsh, administrative proceedings according to law." Post, *Deportations Delirium*, 5–6.

48. Post, *Deportations Delirium*, 9–10.

49. Commissioner at Riga (Gade) to the Secretary of State, January 5, 1920, *FRUS* (1920), 3:693.

50. Secretary of State (Lansing) to the Commissioner at Helsingfors (Haynes), January 7, 1920, *FRUS* (1920), 3:694.

51. In contrast to the tone of the communications from Latvia, this cable stated that the result of this attack would "have no probably permanent effect." Commissioner at Helsingfors (Haynes) to the Secretary of State, January 9, 1920, *FRUS* (1920), 3:694.

52. The Finns would cover the expenses of the ten retained. Commissioner at Helsingfors (Haynes) to the Secretary of State, January 10, 1920, *FRUS* (1920), 3:695–96.

53. Secretary of State (Lansing) to the Commissioner at Helsingfors (Haynes), January 10, 1920, *FRUS* (1920), 3:694.

54. Secretary of State (Lansing) to the Commissioner at Helsingfors (Haynes), January 13, 1920, *FRUS* (1920), 3:696.

55. Post, *Deportations Delirium*, 6.

56. Secretary of State to the Commissioner at Helsingfors (Haynes), January 10, 1920, *FRUS* (1920), 3:694.

57. Post, *Deportations Delirium*, 6.

58. Wexler, *Emma Goldman in Exile*, 19–20.

59. Wexler, *Emma Goldman in Exile*, 19–20.

60. These organizations also included Polish, Lithuanian, Croatian, and Ukrainian members. *AR-CGI* (1920), 383.

61. *AR-CGI* (1919), 371.

62. Post, *Deportations Delirium*, 96.

63. Coben, *A. Mitchell Palmer*, 227.

64. *AR-CGI* (1920), 394.

65. Colyer v. Skeffington, 265 F. 17, 38 (D. Mass. 1920).

66. *AR-CGI* (1920), 389–90.

67. Yong Chen, *Chinese San Francisco, 1850–1943: A Trans-Pacific Community* (Stanford, Calif.: University of Stanford Press, 2000), 191.

68. *AR-CGI* (1919), 352.

69. *AR-CGI* (1919), 378.

70. *AR-CGI* (1920), 406–7.

71. *AR-CGI* (1920), 411.

72. *AR-CGI* (1920), 355.

73. This report, unlike the reports from the South and other western offices, made it appear as if the office had been very busy. The commissioner in charge of the Washington office wrote that its agents had investigated and considered 7,628 cases of anarchists and members of the radical classes. It applied for 230 warrants of arrest and served 93. However, only nineteen immigrants were actually deported that year. *AR-CGI* (1920), 372.

74. *AR-CGI* (1919), 336.

75. *AR-CGI* (1920), 355.

76. For example, the study reported that "one of these [men] had given power of attorney to a fellow-countryman who had taken all the money and disappeared." Constantine M. Panunzio, *The Deportation Cases of 1919–1920* (New York: Commission on the Church and Social Service, Federal Council of the Churches of Christ in America, 1921), 21–22.

77. Panunzio, *Deportation Cases*, 20–21.

78. *AR-CGI* (1920), 394.

79. *AR-CGI* (1920), 383.

80. Panunzio, *Deportation Cases*, 65–68.

81. In November 1919, J. Edgar Hoover, who would bear the major burden of organizing the January raids, wrote to Caminetti recommending a change in Rule 22. He again urged revision on December 17: "In view of the difficulty in proving the cases against persons known to be members of the Union of Russian Workers, due to the arbitrary tactics of persons employed by such members, I would appreciate an early reply to my letter . . . in order that the same condition may not arise when future arrests are made of undesirable aliens." Caminetti presented a memorandum to John Abercrombie, Secretary Wilson's officer in charge of deportation matters, calling for the modification of Rule 22, and on December 31 Abercrombie agreed. Coben, *A. Mitchell Palmer*, 223. Preston dates the change to December 30, when Secretary Wilson was away, and the decision fell to Acting Secretary John Abercrombie. Preston, *Aliens and Dissenters*, 217–18.

82. Panunzio, *Deportation Cases*, 36–37.

83. Finally, the government transferred the detainees to converted barracks at Fort Wayne, Indiana, which were better equipped. *Colyer*, 265 F. at 45.

84. Panunzio, *Deportation Cases*, 81–82. In contrast, the commissioner general of immigration noted that conditions in Chicago were good. He wrote, "In this city it was fortunately possible to get the use of one whole cell wing at the house of correction, made vacant by the operation of the prohibition law, and aliens arrested in this vicinity were detained in comparative comfort until their friends could arrange bail." *AR-CGI* (1920), 394.

85. Post, *Deportation Delirium,* 103.

86. For more on this case, see Alan Rogers "Judge George W. Anderson and Civil Rights in the 1920s," *Historian* 54, no. 2 (Winter 1992): 288–304.

87. *Colyer,* 265 F. at 21.

88. *Colyer,* 265 F. at 71.

89. *Colyer,* 265 F. at 47.

90. *Colyer,* 265 F. at 79.

91. *Colyer,* 265 F. at 22.

92. *Colyer,* 265 F. at 48. This actually excluded the cases of four defendants who were not arrested as a part of the raid. The court treated these immigrants differently from the emigrants from the Russian Empire. *Colyer,* 265 F. at 69.

93. *Colyer,* 265 F. at 21.

94. *Colyer,* 265 F. at 77.

95. Preston, *Aliens and Dissenters,* 221–22. Panunzio dates the change to Jan. 28. Panunzio, *Deportation Cases of 1919–1920,* 37.

96. Preston, *Aliens and Dissenters,* 222–23.

97. Post, *Deportations Delirium,* 84. Coben states that they did not differ significantly. Coben, *A. Mitchell Palmer,* 223.

98. Post, *Deportations Delirium,* 154–59; *AR-CGI* (1920), 33.

99. Post, *Deportations Delirium,* 52.

100. Post, *Deportations Delirium,* 187.

101. Post, *Deportations Delirium,* 167–68. As he understood it, the secretary of labor "was not a perfunctory reviewing officer, but . . . he had exclusive responsibly [over deportations]—primary, intermediate and final." Post, *Deportations Delirium,* 196.

102. Post, *Deportations Delirium,* 190–91.

103. Post, *Deportations Delirium,* 190.

104. Post, *Deportations Delirium,* 69–71.

105. Post, *Deportations Delirium,* 70–71.

106. Post, *Deportations Delirium,* 185.

107. Post, *Deportations Delirium,* 187.

108. Post, *Deportations Delirium,* 221.

109. This committee was initially composed of experts in different areas of immigration. In 1920, Walter D. Davidge was its chairman, and its members included George W. Stillson, Bryce Edwards, an expert in contract labor cases, and Charles E. Booth, an expert in Chinese cases. The committee was temporarily disbanded, but under legislation in 1922, it was reconstituted. Post, *Deportations Delirium,* 196–97.

110. Post did not believe these immigrants had been a part of the bombings, but they were deportable under the membership clause. Post, *Deportations Delirium,* 167, 192.

111. Washington instructed Young to "[m]ake no inquiries of Estonians but telegraph whether such deportees could proceed freely and safely into Soviet Russia without previous

arrangement with the Soviet authorities." Secretary of State (Colby) to the Commissioner at Riga (Young), Washington, May 26, 1920, *FRUS* (1920), 3:697; Secretary of State (Colby) to the Commissioner at Riga (Young), June 7, 1920, *FRUS* (1920), 3:698.

112. Commissioner at Riga (Young) to the Secretary of State, May 28, 1920, *FRUS* (1920), 3:697.

113. Secretary of State (Colby) to the Commissioner at Riga (Young), June 7, 1920, *FRUS* (1920), 3:698.

114. Commissioner at Riga (Young) to the Secretary of State, June 21, 1920, *FRUS* (1920), 3:698.

115. Acting Secretary of State to the Commissioner at Riga (Young), June 28, 1920, *FRUS* (1920), 3:698–99.

116. Commissioner at Riga (Young) to the Secretary of State, May 28, 1920, *FRUS* (1920), 3:697.

117. Commissioner at Riga (Young) to the Secretary of State, July 6, 1920, *FRUS* (1920), 3:699.

118. The commissioner general of immigration wrote in late 1920, "The bureau has made consistent and persistent efforts extending over many months to bring about arrangements for the transportation to Soviet Russia of the aliens . . . unlike the first effort [with the *Buford*], no signs of encouragement have been visible, but information supposedly authoritative indicated the futility of attempting to transport to the borders of Soviet Russia." *AR-CGI* (1921), 33.

119. As their due process rights had been violated, the U.S. Department of State could have intervened but did not because that would open diplomatic relations. The acting U.S. secretary of state actually maintained that the Soviets were using the detained Americans "as hostages to force this Government into direct negotiations from which general political advantages are expected." Acting Secretary of State (Davis) to the Commissioner at Vienna (Halstead), July 2, 1920, *FRUS* (1920), 3:675.

120. Commissioner at Vienna (Halstead) to the Secretary of State, June 15, 1920, *FRUS* (1920), 3:673.

121. Georgii Chicherin, People's Commissar for Foreign Affairs, dispatch in reply to the note of the Secretary of State Bainbridge Colby, enclosed in L. Martens to the Italian Ambassador (Avezzana), October 4, 1920, *FRUS* (1920), 3:474–78, quotes here at 475.

122. Chicherin dispatch, 475.

123. Chicherin dispatch, 477.

124. L. Martens to the Secretary of State, March 31, 1920, *FRUS* (1920), 3:455.

125. Chicherin dispatch, 477–78.

126. Secretary of State to the Italian Ambassador (Avezzana), August 10, 1920, *FRUS* (1920), 3:463–68.

127. Secretary of State to the Ambassador in Great Britain (Davis), August 2, 1920, *FRUS* (1920), 3:461–63.

128. Secretary of State to the Ambassador in Great Britain, August 2, 1920.

129. Commissioner at Riga (Young) to the Secretary of State, September 7, 1920, *FRUS* (1920), 3:700.

130. The acting secretary of state asked Young, the U.S. commissioner at Riga, if he had any objections to this process. He did not, but soon more complications arose. Acting Secretary of State to the Commissioner at Riga (Young), January 12, 1921, *FRUS* (1921), 2:802–3.

131. On January 15 Young notified officials in Washington, that "pending my further telegraphic report no further deportations should be made via Latvia and if any [are] now en route please cable me immediately full information." Commissioner at Riga (Young) to the Acting Secretary of State, January 15, 1921, *FRUS* (1921), 2:803.

132. Commissioner at Riga (Young) to the Acting Secretary of State, January 19, 1921, *FRUS* (1921), 2:803.

133. *AR-CGI* (1921), 14. See also Commissioner of Immigration, Ellis Island, January 18, 1921, File 55110/2, INS; Memorandum for the Acting Commissioner General from Leo B. Russell, Immigrant Inspector in Charge of Transportation and Deportation, January 25, 1921, File 55110/2, INS.

134. On January 7, Russell received instructions to pay John J. Kalnin, the Latvian representative, $325 for issuing visas for sixty-five deportees. The funds were payable from the appropriation for "Enforcement of Laws Against Alien Anarchists, 1921." Leo B. Russell, Inspector in Charge of Transportation and Deportation, Bureau of Immigration, to Alfred Hampton, Acting Commissioner General, "Approved Louis F. Post, Assistant Secretary of Labor," January 7, 1921, File 55110/3, INS. On January 20, 1920, Russell received instructions to pay Kalnin $305 for issuing visas for sixty-one more deportees to Soviet Russia. Alfred Hampton, Acting Commissioner General, to Leo B. Russell, Inspector in Charge of Transportation and Deportation, Bureau of Immigration, "Approved Louis F. Post, Assistant Secretary of Labor," January 20, 1920, File 55110/3, INS.

135. Memorandum for the Acting Commissioner General by Leo B. Russell, Immigration Officer of Transportation and Deportation, January 25, File 55110/03, INS. Russell paid a consular agent of the Swedish consulate in New York $122 for issuing visas for sixty-one deportees. Alfred Hampton, Acting Commissioner General, to Mr. Leo B. Russell, Inspector in Charge of Transportation and Deportation, Bureau of Immigration, "Approved Louis F. Post, Assistant Secretary of Labor," January 20, 1921, File 55110/3, INS.

136. Commissioner General from J. J. Skeffington, Commissioner of Immigration, April 18, 1921, File 55110/3; Secretary of State to the Commissioner at Riga (Young), February 7, 1921, *FRUS* (1921), 2:804. The Baltic American Line charged the U.S. government $9,000 for the *Estonia* deportations. Commissioner General W. W. Husband to Claude N. Bernette, Manager, Congressional Information Bureau, April 15, 1921, File 55120/3, INS.

137. F. M. Dearing, Associate Secretary for the Secretary of State, to the Secretary of Labor, "Attention Commissioner of Immigration," April 28, 1921, File 55110/04, INS.

138. Husband to Bernette, April 15, 1921.

139. Secretary of State to the Attorney General (Palmer), April 8, 1920, *FRUS* (1920), 3:457.

140. Act of Feb. 5, 1917, § 3, 39 Stat. 874 (1917).

141. Secretary of State to the Attorney General (Palmer), April 8, 1920, enclosure, "Memorandum Regarding the Diplomatic Status of Mr. L. Martens," April 6, 1920, *FRUS* (1920), 3:457–61; Secretary of State to the Attorney General (Palmer), November 30, 1920, *FRUS* (1920), 3:478–79.

142. Post, *Deportations Delirium*, 288.

143. Hardwick had since been elected governor of Georgia. He had been one of the targets of the June bombings of 1919, which had precipitated the Red Raids. Post, *Deportations Delirium*, 288–89.

144. They had to wait until March 29, 1920, when Martens, who was under congressional investigation on other charges, was released from congressional custody. Post, *Deportations Delirium*, 289–91.

145. Post, *Deportations Delirium*, 289–91; L. Martens to the Secretary of State, March 31, 1920, *FRUS* (1920), 2:455–57.

146. Act of Oct. 16, 1918, § 8 (b), 40 Stat. 1012 (1918).

147. Post, *Deportations Delirium*, 292.

148. For a larger discussion of compelled departures as a form of deportation, see Motomura, "The Discretion That Matters," 1835.

149. Department of State to W. W. Husband, Commissioner General of Immigration, Enclosure, Gregory Gorbich, May 6, 1921, File 55110/4, INS.

150. Minister in Norway (Schmedeman) to the Secretary of State, February 26, 1921, *FRUS* (1921), 2:792; Minister in Czechoslovakia (Crane) to the Secretary of State, March 30, 1921, *FRUS* (1921), 2:792–93.

151. Charles E. Hughes to Secretary of Labor, April 11, 1921, File 55110/04, INS.

152. F. M. Dearing, Associate Secretary for the Secretary of State, to the Secretary of Labor, April 28, 1921, File 55110/04, INS.

153. By 1922, the Bureau of Immigration's *Annual Report* stated that it deported only sixty-four aliens that year "due, in a measure, to a reduction in alien radical activities and to an inability to deport aliens to Russia . . . although a number of the subjects of that country of established radical tendencies have been placed under orders of deportation during the year." *AR-CGI* (1922), 13.

154. Acting Secretary of State to the Commissioner at Riga (Young), June 28, 1920, *FRUS* (1920), 3:698–99.

Chapter 6

1. *Healy v. Backus*, 243 U.S. 657 (1917); *Marshall v. Backus*, 243 U.S. 657 (1917).

2. *Healy v. Backus*, 243 U.S.; *Marshall v. Backus*, 243, U.S.

3. Looking at immigrant integration in the twenty-first century, scholars link jobs as an especially important part of immigrant integration. Scholars Richard Alba and Nancy Foner, for instance, write that immigrants employed in the United States "are to some degree integrated into American society through work. This observation acknowledges the opportunities opened up by paid employment, which often involves regular interactions with non-coethnics along with the possibilities to develop potentially useful social networks and additional skills." Richard Alba and Nancy Foner, *Strangers No More: Immigration and the Challenges of Integration in North America and Western Europe* (Princeton, N.J.: Princeton University Press, 2015), 59. On the importance of mobility to immigrant efforts to improve work and wages in the early twentieth century—critical parts of integration—see Gunther Peck, *Reinventing Free Labor: Padrones and Immigrant Workers in the North American West, 1880–1930* (Cambridge: Cambridge University Press, 2000); Ronald Takaki, *Strangers from a Different Shore: A History of Asian Americans* (Boston: Little, Brown, 1998), 147–48.

4. The law stated that any alien who became a public charge within one year after his arrival in the United States "from causes existing prior to his landing therein shall be deemed to have come in violation of law" and could be deported. Act of Mar. 3, 1891, § 11, 26 Stat. 1084 (1891). In the Immigration Act of 1882, Congress stated, "Any person unable to take care of himself or herself without becoming a public charge . . . shall not be permitted to

land," but the law did not include a deportation provision. Act of Aug. 3, 1882, § 2, 22 Stat. 214 (1882). In a few cases over the next couple of decades, officials used the public charge provision to deport small numbers of individuals from jails and prisons. On use of economic grounds to deport people in U.S. jails and prisons, see United States *ex rel.* Freeman v. Williams, 175 F. 274 (S.D.N.Y. 1910). This section, however, concentrates on the focus of enforcement on institutions that cared for ill and indigent immigrants.

5. *AR-CGI* (1892), 12.

6. *AR-CGI* (1896), 15. A similar statement is made in *AR-CGI* (1897), 3–4.

7. *AR-CGI* (1913), 16.

8. Rule 39, *ILR*, 12th ed. (1911), 65.

9. Huntington Wilson, Acting Secretary of State, to the Ambassador John G. A. Leishman, May 27, 1912, File 150.06/4a, DS.

10. *AR-CGI* (1904), 124. See also a similar statement in *AR-CGI* (1913), 17.

11. *AR-CGI* (1898), 35.

12. *AR-CGI* (1896), 10.

13. *AR-CGI* (1897), 3–4.

14. As historian Michael B. Katz writes of the United States, "in colonial times, relief was a local responsibility, administered within a town, county or parish. In the nineteenth century, state governments tried to make the practice more uniform within their jurisdiction, but even then, a dazzling variety of local as well as state, differences remained." Katz, *In the Shadow of the Poorhouse: A Social History of Welfare in America*, 10th ed. (New York: Basic Books, 1996), x, 88–113. See also Walter I. Trattner, *From Poor Law to Welfare State: A History of Social Welfare in America*, 5th ed. (New York: Simon and Schuster, 1994).

15. *AR-CGI* (1898), 35.

16. Cybelle Fox, "Unauthorized Welfare: The Origins of Immigrant Status Restrictions in American Social Policy," *Journal of American History* 102, no. 4 (March 2016): 1051–74. Michael Katz explains, "A failure to classify inmates underlay the administrative problems of poorhouses. Critics throughout the [nineteenth] century complained that many poorhouses did not separate paupers by age, condition, sex, and color; allowed the worthy poor to mingle with the degraded; and failed to send the insane or other handicapped inmates to special institutions." Katz, *In the Shadow of the Poorhouse*, 30.

17. In international law, removal of an immigrant who had established ties to the community, except in times of war or extreme circumstances, was considered an unreasonable or inhumane act of governmental power. While, as shown in Chapter 1, U.S. lawmakers ignored this in Chinese exclusion, Congress wrote this understanding into national law by including time limits. Borchard, *Diplomatic Protection of Citizens Abroad*, 24, 51, 55, 91–94, 555–58.

18. Act of Mar. 3, 1903, § 20, 32 Stat. 1213 (1903); Hutchinson, *Legislative History of American Immigration Policy*, 133; Act of Feb. 20, 1907, § 20, 34 Stat. 898 (1907); Act of Feb. 5, 1917, § 19, 39 Stat. 874 (1917).

19. Act of Mar. 3, 1891, § 11, 26 Stat. 1084 (1891).

20. *AR-CGI* (1898), 34–35.

21. This was outlined in Rules 32 and 33. Rules 34 and 35 added additional instruction, stating that "Every immigration officer receiving a report in conformity with Rule 32, accompanied by a medical certificate that complies with either Rule 32 or Rule 33, shall communicate with the officer in charge at the port of entry and, if landing is verified from the official

records, shall make application for warrant in the manner provided by Rule 35. Such aliens will not be removed from the institution in which they are confined until after due hearing and after an order of deportation is issued, or unless special instructions for removal are incorporated in the warrant." Rules 33, 34, and 35, *ILR*, 12th ed. (1911), 59–60.

22. Rule 37, *ILR*, 12th ed. (1911), 63–65.

23. W. D. Scott, Superintendent of Immigration, to Frank Oliver, April 15, 1908, memorandum, vol. 513, file 800129, CAN.

24. J. H. Clark to W.D. Scott, Superintendent of Immigration, April 28, 1908, Immigration Branch, RG 76, vol. 513, file 800129, CAN.

25. Scott to Oliver, April 15, 1908; Clark to Scott, April 28, 1908.

26. Scott to Oliver, April 15, 1908.

27. Clark to Scott, April 28, 1908; Scott to Oliver, April 15, 1908.

28. A U.S. immigration officer noted, "There appears to be considerable objection on the part of the Provincial Authorities to the return to Canada of helpless aliens." J. H. Clark to L. M. Fortier, Acting Superintendent of Immigration, August 17, 1909, vol. 513, file 800129, CAN.

29. Assistant Provincial Secretary of the Province of Quebec to the Deputy Minister for the Canadian Department of Immigration and Colonization, Quebec, October 8, 1924, vol. 513, file 800129, CAN.

30. In 1924, the annual reports do not record the numbers of Canadians deported. They were recorded under the ethnic or national categories of the deportee. A Canadian of British heritage would likely have been recorded under the British category. A French Canadian would have been recorded as a French deportee. In 1924, immigration officials deported sixteen people of French heritage. *AR-CGI* (1924), 134–35.

31. *AR-CGI* (1913), 176.

32. Assistant Secretary, Department of Labor, to Secretary of State, Washington, March 22, 1922, File 150.06/162, File 55131/149, DS.

33. Fred K. Nielsen, Solicitor for the U.S. Department of State, to Charles E. Hughes, U.S. Secretary of State, April 22, 1922, File 150.06/162, DS.

34. Under the Naturalization Law of 1906, Americans who swore allegiance to another country lost their U.S. citizenship.

35. The State Department acknowledged that "it would be difficult for this Government to contend that persons of this class mentioned should be received by their native countries, upon deportation from the United States, unless it is in a position to [assure] the foreign governments concerned that former American citizens who have lost their American citizenship . . . would be admitted to the United States without regard to the exclusion provision of the Immigration Law." Hughes to Nielsen, April 22, 1922.

36. Seema Sohi, *Echoes of Mutiny: Race, Surveillance, and Indian Anticolonialism in North America* (New York: Oxford University Press, 2014), 8. On Indian migration, see also Chang, *Pacific Connections*; Nayan Shah, *Stranger Intimacy: Contesting Race, Sexuality, and the Law in the North American West* (Berkeley: University of California Press, 2011); Joan Jensen, *Passage from India: Asian Indian Immigrants in North America* (New Haven, Conn.: Yale University Press, 1988). For information on Sikh workers in the California citrus industry, see Garcia, *A World of Its Own*, 35.

37. Shah, *Stranger Intimacy*, 14–15; see also Takaki, *Strangers from a Different Shore*, 295.

38. Chang, *Pacific Connections*, 10, 90, 92–96.

39. Jensen, *Passage from India*, 105–7.

40. In 1907, the year before many of the restrictions were enacted, 2,415 Indians entered Canada. In 1909, 106 Indians migrated. Sohi, *Echoes of Mutiny*, 28. On executive exclusion, see Jensen, *Passage from India*, 105–7. See also Chang, *Pacific Connections*, 10, 90, 92–96.

41. McKeown, *Melancholy Order*, 206–7. For more on Canadian domestic policy, see Sohi, *Echoes of Mutiny*, 27–28.

42. Canada and India were both a part of the British Empire, but Canada asserted its own immigration policy when it came to colonial citizens of color. This legislation also enabled Canadian officials to limit the migration of people from the British Empire, based on the interests of those in self-governing sections of the empire. Officials used this class of law to interrupt the migration from British colonies to Canada or to variegate territories within the Commonwealth. McKeown, *Melancholy Order*, 198–99.

43. Jensen, *Passage from India*, 57–100. The Canadians also borrowed approaches from the Americans. In 1907, Theodore Roosevelt issued the Continuous Journey Order and Canada passed a Continuous Journey Order the next year. Both orders, Kornel Chang writes, "barred immigrants not coming directly from their country of origin. The technical language obscured its racist intent, as there was not a single steamship line providing direct service from India." They then cooperated in policing the U.S.-Canadian border and shared information. Chang, *Pacific Connections*, 124–47.

44. U.S. Department of Labor, *Reports of the Department of Labor, 1914: Report of the Secretary of Labor and Reports of Bureaus* (Washington, D.C.: Government Printing Office, 1915), 438.

45. Act of Mar. 3, 1891, § 1 & 11, 26 Stat. 1084 (1891); Hutchinson, *Legislative History of American Immigration Policy*, 102. In 1903, Congress extended the time limit on most deportable categories, including LPC, from one to three years. Public charges were deportable within two years after entry. Act of Mar. 3, 1903, § 21, 32 Stat. 1213 (1903); Act of Feb. 5, 1917, § 19, 39 Stat. 874 (1917).

46. Moloney, *National Insecurities*, 82–87; Gardner, *Qualities of a Citizen*, 87–95.

47. As Joan Jensen also points out, the commissioner of immigration noted that, while no "law excluded Indians as a race and that the bureau did not advocate exclusion of any race, there were nevertheless ways to exclude Indians . . . Indians were likely to become public charges on the basis of the poor physical condition and the inability to find jobs because of local discrimination." Jensen, *Passage from India*, 111. While this informal policy did not work perfectly, it was very effective in excluding most Indians by 1910. Jensen, *Passage from India*, 105–8, 111, 113.

48. U.S. Department of Labor, *Reports of the Department of Labor, 1914*, 438–39.

49. U.S. Department of Labor, *Reports of the Department of Labor, 1914*, 438–39. Historian Ronald Takaki noted that between 1908 and 1920, immigration agents "denied entry to some 3,453 Asian Indians, most of them on the grounds they would likely become public charges." Takaki, *Strangers from a Different Shore*, 297. For a very good, detailed examination of the exclusion efforts, which also overlapped with government efforts to crack down on Indian anticolonial activists, see Sohi, *Echoes of Mutiny*, 299–32.

50. Takaki, *Strangers from a Different Shore*, 132–76.

51. Erika Lee and Judy Yung, *Angel Island: Immigrant Gateway to America* (New York: Oxford University Press, 2010), 159.

52. Jensen, *Passage from India*, 116.

53. As historian Kornel Chang writes, "This principle hewed closely to the logic of a series of Supreme Court rulings, known collectively as the Insular Cases, which relegated the colonies to a 'liminal space' that fell 'both inside and outside of the boundaries of the Constitution, both "belonging to" but "not part of" the United States.'" Chang, *Pacific Connections*, 157. For more on the discussion in the Bureau of Immigration on these three years, see Sohi, *Echoes of Mutiny*, 118–24.

54. *In re Rhagat Singh*, 209 F. 700, 703 (N.D. Cal. 1913).

55. Sohi, *Echoes of Mutiny*, 122, 126.

56. Jensen, *Passage from India*, 147–48.

57. *In re Rhagat Singh*, 209 F. at 702.

58. *In re Rhagat Singh*, 209 F. at 701.

59. The records also refer to Sundar Singh as Sandu Singh. *Ex parte Moola Singh*, 207 F. 780, 781 (W.D. Wash. 1913); *In re Rhagat Singh*, 209 F. at 701.

60. As legal scholar Hiroshi Motomura writes, "Yamataya had announced this procedural exception to plenary power but gave it little content." Motomura, *Americans in Waiting*, 102.

61. Two key cases were *Low Wah Suey*, discussed in Chapter 1, and *Chin Yow*. On these cases, see also Salyer, *Laws Harsh as Tigers*, 174–87.

62. *In re Rhagat Singh*, 209 F. at 701.

63. *In re Rhagat Singh*, 209 F. at 704.

64. *In re Rhagat Singh*, 209 F. at 702.

65. *In re Rhagat Singh*, 209 F. at 702.

66. *In re Rhagat Singh*, 209 F. at 702.

67. *Healy v. Backus*, 221 F. 358, 364–65 (9th Cir. 1915).

68. Since part of their deportation also turned on the fact that the government was trying to hold them to rules revised after their landing in the continental United States, in this section of their defense they also argued that the government could not change the admission rules after the fact.

69. *In re Rhagat Singh*, 703.

70. *In re Rhagat Singh*, 704.

71. This case came from the U.S. Circuit Court of Appeals for the Second Circuit on a writ of habeas corpus from New York.

72. *Gegiow v. Uhl*, 239 U.S. 3, 8 (1915).

73. *Gegiow*, 239 U.S. at 8.

74. The decision continues, "unless the one phrase before us is directed to different considerations than any other of those with which it is associated. Presumably it is to be read as generically similar to the others mentioned before and after." *Gegiow*, 239 U.S. at 10.

75. *Healy v. Backus*, 243 U.S.; *Marshall v. Backus*, 243 U.S.

76. *AR-CGI* (1917), xviii–xix.

77. Act of Feb. 5, 1917, 39 Stat. 874 (1917); Motomura, *Americans in Waiting*, 125.

78. *AR-CGI* (1918), 299–300.

79. Act of Feb. 5, 1917, 39 Stat. 874.

80. *AR-CGI* (1917), xviii–xix.

81. *AR-CGI* (1918), 27.

82. Some officials were not convinced of the labor shortage. Assistant Secretary of Labor Louis Post wrote, "the farm labor shortage is two-thirds imaginary and one-third remedial."

Quoted in Philip Martin, *Importing Poverty? Immigration and the Changing Face of Rural America* (New Haven, Conn.: Yale University Press, 2009), 196 n. 7.

83. Zaragosa Vargas, *Labor Rights Are Civil Rights: Mexican American Workers in Twentieth-Century America* (Princeton, N.J.: Princeton University Press, 2005), 18.

84. *AR-CGI* (1901), 31–32, 52.

85. Act of Mar. 3, 1893, § 10, 27 Stat. 569 (1893).

86. Camille Guérin-Gonzales, *Mexican Workers and American Dreams: Immigration, Repatriation, and California Farm Labor, 1900–1939* (New Brunswick, N.J.: Rutgers University Press, 1994); Peck, *Reinventing Free Labor.*

87. *AR-CGI* (1911), 80–81.

88. *AR-CGI* (1911), 128–31; *AR-CGI* (1905), 45.

89. *AR-CGI* (1905), 45.

90. Garcia, *A World of Its Own*, 60, 88–90. See also Cindy Hahamovitch, *The Fruits of Their Labor: Atlantic Coast Farmworkers and the Making of Migrant Poverty, 1870–1945* (Chapel Hill: University of North Carolina Press, 1997). On the literacy test and its intent to curtail all immigration, especially European immigration, see John Higham, *Strangers in the Land: Patterns of American Nativism, 1860–1925* (New York: Atheneum, 1973), 300.

91. *AR-CGI* (1918), 17. The Immigration Act of 1917, in section 3, states, "That the Commissioner General of Immigration with the approval of the Secretary of Labor shall issue rules and prescribe conditions, including exaction of such bonds as may be necessary, to control and regulate the admission and return of otherwise admissible aliens applying for temporary admission." Act of Feb. 5, 1917, § 3, 39 Stat. 874 (1917).

92. Martin, *Importing Poverty*, 24. Mark Reisler, *By the Sweat of Their Brow: Mexican Immigrant Labor in the United States, 1900–1940* (Westport, Conn.: Greenwood Press, 1976), 27.

93. To provide incentive for the guest workers to return to their country of origin after the end of their contract, guest laborers deposited a portion of their wages in the U.S. postal bank, which they would then gain access to when they returned to Mexico. Martin, *Importing Poverty*, 24; Reisler, *By the Sweat of Their Brow*, 29.

94. Of these, 10,491 worked as farm laborers, 9,998 as railway workers, 89 as construction workers, and 65 as mining laborers. *AR-CGI* (1919), 12–13.

95. *AR-CGI* (1920), 8.

96. *AR-CGI* (1918), 16.

97. This was one part of a larger effort by the Canadian government to secure and control labor during World War I. It also, for example, released a number of Ukrainian prisoners from internment camps to meet labor shortages. John Boyko, *Last Steps to Freedom: The Evolution of Canadian Racism* (Winnipeg: Watson and Dwyer, 1995), 79.

98. There were no similar bilateral agreements or two-way worker migrations between the other countries contributing guest workers—between Mexico or the Bahamas and the United States. The documents are not explicit on why. One reason in the Mexican case was most likely that Mexican officials' focus after the revolution was on writing and ratifying a new constitution. For an excellent book on the history of Caribbean guest workers, including Bahamians, see Hahamovitch, *No Man's Land.*

99. By 1930, almost 1.5 million Mexicans lived in the United States; three-fourths of this population lived in Arizona, California, Colorado, New Mexico, and Texas. Vargas, *Labor Rights Are Civil Rights*, 16; Garcia, *A World of Its Own*, 60.

100. For the ways that Chinese workers built up California agriculture, for example, see Sucheng Chan, *This Bittersweet Soil: The Chinese in California Agriculture, 1860–1910* (Berkeley: University of California Press, 1989.)

101. Martin, *Importing Poverty*, 22.

102. On the broader racialization of Mexican immigrants, see Benton-Cohen, *Borderline Americans*; Haney López, *White by Law*; Vargas, *Labor Rights are Civil Rights*, Thomas Almaguer, *Racial Fault Lines: The Historical Origins of White Supremacy in California* (Berkeley: University of California Press, 2008); Garcia, *A World of Its Own*, 52–54; Foley, *The White Scourge*; Sánchez, *Becoming Mexican American*; Sarah Deutsch, *No Separate Refuge: Culture, Class, and Gender on an Anglo-Hispanic Frontier in the American Southwest, 1888–1940* (New York: Oxford University Press, 1987); Montejano, *Anglos and Mexicans in the Making of Texas*.

103. Torsten A. Magnuson, "History of the Beet Sugar Industry in California," *Annual Publication of the Historical Society of Southern California* 11, no. 1 (1918): 68–79.

104. U.S. Department of Labor, Inspector in Charge of Immigration at the Port of El Paso, American Beet Sugar Company at Oxnard, California; at Chino, California (2407); RG 85, Subject and Policy Files, 1893–1957, Box 2862, File 5426/202, INS.

105. *AR-CGI* (1916), 189.

106. *AR-CGI* (1919), 384.

107. *AR-CGI* (1919), 36.

108. *AR-CGI* (1913), 110–11.

109. *AR-CGI* (1914), 108–9.

110. *AR-CGI* (1919), 184–85.

111. *AR-CGI* (1920), 200–201. In 1921, the Bureau of Immigration deported 152 contract workers; 74, or more than 48 percent, of them were Mexicans. *AR-CGI* (1921), 120–21. Use of the contract labor provision to enforce the original intent during these years was still operational.

112. It is estimated that over twenty thousand left their contracts. Reisler, *By the Sweat of Their Brow*, 38.

113. *AR-CGI* (1919), 380.

114. *AR-CGI* (1919), 381.

115. Mark Reisler notes that in June 1921, after the program ended, more than 15,000 were still employed in the United States with the employers who brought them in. Another 21,400 had left their work contracts during the program, and they may also have remained in the United States. Reisler, *By the Sweat of Their Brow*, 38–42.

116. Reisler, *By the Sweat of Their Brow*, 39–41.

117. Act of May 26, 1924, § 15, 43 Stat. 152 (1924). See also Wen-Hsien Chen, "Chinese Under Both Exclusion and Immigration Laws" (Ph.D. diss., University of Chicago, 1940), 115, http://search.proquest.com/docview/301774542?accountid = 8065.

Conclusion

1. Robe Carl White, Assistant Secretary of Labor, to Secretary of State, November 18, 1925, 311.1224, DS; Harry Walsh, Consul, Nuevo Laredo, Mexico, to Secretary of State, August 10, 1925, 311.1224, DS. The records on the shooting are not precise.

2. Harry Walsh, Consul, Nuevo Laredo, Mexico, to Secretary of State, January 16, 1926, 211.12T63/6, DS; Memorandum, "Deportation to Mexico of Demetrio Torres by American

Immigration Authorities," February 19, 1926, 211.12T63/9, DS; "Translation: Item from La Prensa of San Antonio," January 31, 1926, DS.

3. Walsh to Secretary of State, August 10, 1925.

4. Sheffield to Secretary of State, October 23, 1925, 311.1224, DS; White to Secretary of State, November 18.

5. Walsh to Secretary of State, August 10, 1925, p. 5.

6. Walsh to Secretary of State, August 10, 1925, p. 4.

7. James R. Sheffield to Secretary of State, February 9, 1926, 211.12T63/23, DS.

8. Harry Walsh, Consul, Nuevo Laredo, to Secretary of State, February 4, 1926, 211.1263/22, DS, p. 3.

9. Harry Walsh, Consul, Nuevo Laredo, Mexico, to Secretary of State, August 25, 1925, Enclosures, 311.1224, DS.

10. White to Secretary of State, November 18, 1925.

11. White to Secretary of State, November 18, 1925; Hanson was not prosecuted. Charles H. Harris and Louis R. Sadler, *The Texas Rangers and the Mexican Revolution: The Bloodiest Decade, 1910–1920* (Albuquerque: University of New Mexico Press, 2004), 493.

12. Eric D. Weitz, "From the Vienna to the Paris System: International Politics and the Entangled Histories of Human Rights, Forced Deportations, and Civilizing Missions," *American Historical Review* 113, no. 5 (December 2008): 1334.

13. On the removals of persons of Mexican heritage after this period, see Francisco E. Balderrama and Raymond Rodríguez, *Decade of Betrayal: Mexican Repatriation in the 1930s* (Albuquerque: University of New Mexico Press, 1995); Guerin-Gonzales, *Mexican Workers and the American Dream*. See also Molina, *How Race Is Made in America*; Kelly Lytle Hernández, "The Crimes and Consequences of Illegal Immigration: A Cross-Border Examination of Operation Wetback, 1943–1954," *Western Historical Quarterly* 37, no. 4 (Winter 2006): 421–44; Vargas, *Labor Rights Are Civil Rights*.

14. Mark Mazower, "The Strange Triumph of Human Rights, 1933–1950," *Historical Journal* 47, no. 2 (June 2004): 384–85.

15. Kramer, "Imperial Openings," 322.

16. See Pliley, *Policing Sexuality*, 186, 211–15.

17. William Wilberforce Trafficking Victims Protection Authorization Act of 2008, H.R. 7311, 110th Congress, www.state.gov/j/tip/laws/113178.htm; Washington Office on Latin America, "Border Facts: Separating Rhetoric from Reality," http://borderfactcheck.com/ (accessed March 30, 2015); Pliley, *Policing Sexuality*, 154.

18. *Healy v. Backus*, 243 U.S. 657 (1917); *Marshall v. Backus*, 243 U.S. 657 (1917).

19. Colin Grant, *Negro with a Hat: The Rise and Fall of Marcus Garvey* (New York: Oxford University Press, 2008).

20. Marcus Garvey, President-General, Universal Negro Improvement Association, to the Secretary of State, December 20, 1927, 811.108, DS.

21. For example, while Garvey traveled in Costa Rica, a U.S. consular officer reported that Garvey had been raising money for the UNIA among United Fruit Company employees. Based on information from the general manager of the company and others, the consular officer reported that "the voluntary and continued subscriptions in favor of Marcus Garvey, of the negro employees of that Company in Costa Rica are approximately $2,000 monthly, and . . . that as a result of this personal visit he received over $30,000." Walter C. Thurston,

American Legation, San José, Costa Rica, to Charles Evans Hughes, Secretary of State, May 2, 1921, 811.108, Box 7351, DS.

22. Act of Mar. 3, 1891, § 11, 26 Stat. 1084 (1891); *AR-CGI* (1896), 10.

23. *AR-CGI* (1905), 102–3.

24. *AR-CGI* (1905), table 8, p. 24.

25. The Bureau of Immigration attributed this concentration to immigration flows; the *Annual Report* noted that about 90 percent of immigrants landed in the Northeast and Midwest, while only 4 percent went to the South and another 4 percent went to the Far West. *AR-CGI* (1905), 104, 106.

26. *AR-CGI* (1905), table 8, p. 24.

27. For a very good treatment of the reluctance before 1917 to make crimes on U.S. soil a deportable offense, see Angela M. Banks, "The Normative and Historical Cases for Proportional Deportation," *Emory Law Journal* 62, no. 5 (2013): 1243–1307.

28. Aleinikoff, Martin, and Motomura, *Immigration and Citizenship: Process and Policy*, 555.

29. *AR-CGI* (1961), 59.

30. *AR-CGI* (1927), 25.

31. Ngai, *Impossible Subjects*, 60.

32. *AR-CGI* (1926), 220.

33. *AR-CGI* (1930), 243.

34. Kelly Lytle Hernández, *Migra! A History of the U.S. Border Patrol* (Berkeley: University of California Press, 2010), 188–89, 194; Ngai, *Impossible Subjects*, 153; U.S. Department of Homeland Security, *Yearbook of Immigration Statistics: 2012* (Washington, D.C.: U.S. Department of Homeland Security, Office of Immigration Statistics, 2013), 103.

Index

Acknowledgments

I have many people to thank for their help and support while researching and writing this book. Starting with Peggy Pascoe, it is still hard to express how grateful I am to have worked with her. Several other people, including Francisco Balderrama, Choi Chatterjee, Matthew Garcia, Ellen Herman, Jim Mohr, Jeff Ostler, Daniel Pope, Elizabeth Reis, and Carole Srole, worked with me with such generosity and skill at the start of this project. Jim Mohr and Carole Srole—thank you for all that you have done over the years it has taken me to complete this project as well. Katie Benton-Cohen mentored me early in my career, and for that, I am very fortunate. Lorri Glover has been an invaluable mentor at Saint Louis University.

Scholars and friends commented on my work over the years and whether they read a chapter, the entire manuscript, or a conference paper, their feedback has been instrumental. They include Heidi Ardizzone, Jaime Aguila, Dirk Bonker, Christopher Capozzola, Deborah Cohen, Deborah Dinner, Tanya Golash-Boza, Polly Good, Justin Hansford, Kelly Lytle Hernández, Hidetaka Hirota, Madeline Hsu, Michael Innis-Jiménez, Daniel Kanstroom, Alan Kraut, Erika Lee, Daniel Margolies, Kate Moran, Jeanne Petit, Jessica Pliley, Jen Popiel, Regina Sullivan, Anders Walker, Theresa Alfaro-Velkamp, and Martin Valadez. Donna Gabaccia, Hasia Diner, Tyler Anbinder, and Deirdre Moloney fielded several questions, sometimes quite out of the blue, providing encouragement in addition to answers. Thank you to the editors of the special edition of the *Journal of American History*, Kelly Lytle Hernández, Edward Linenthal, Heather Ann Thompson, and Khalil Muhammad. Working with them helped me to write so that readers could better see the forest for the trees. My dear friends Beatrice McKenzie and Maddalena Marinari would read my work at the end of a day if I asked; they helped me keep going. The comments from many others, including the anonymous readers, also have been critical in the development of this book.

I have benefited greatly from the support of colleagues in St. Louis and, before that, at Roanoke College. At Saint Louis University I want to thank Stefan Bradley, Doug Boin, Flannery Burke, Nadia Brown, Pearl Ewing, Tom Finan, Phil Gavitt, Kelly Goersch, Claire Gilbert, Pauline Lee, Ben Looker, Emily Lutenski, Matthew Mancini, Filippo Marsili, Kate Moran, George Ndege, Hal Parker, Chris Pudlowski, Michal Rozbicki, Mark Ruff, Daniel Schlafly, Steve Schoenig, Silvana Siddali, Damian Smith, Daniel Smith, Katrina Thompson, and Luke Yarbrough. Graduate students Eric Sears and Beth Petitjean were excellent research assistants. At Roanoke College, Kirsten DeVries, Ivonne Wallace Fuentes, Ann Genova, Michael Hakkenberg, Karen Harris, Mary Henold, Whitney Leeson, Mark Miller, John Selby, Robert Willingham, and Stella Xu were all exceptional colleagues. Veta Schlimgen, Camille Walsh, and Bea McKenzie in the "Peggy group" were ever thoughtful and supportive. When I landed in St. Louis, two reading groups at Washington University in St. Louis added significantly to the intellectual community that has proved exceedingly helpful while writing. My thanks go to Lorena Estrada-Martínez for running the Latino reading group and all the members. Deborah Dinner and David Konig brought together faculty from the law schools and history departments of Washington University and Saint Louis University to form the Legal History Reading Group. The rigor of our discussions pushed me to ask different kinds of questions. My favorite of all was posed in the first meeting by Debbie when she asked whether this book was more history or legal scholarship.

Several archives and institutions have supported my research. The National Endowment for the Humanities, Mellon Faculty Development Grants, and the Dean's Travel Award from Saint Louis University provided funding for my research. The archivists at the National Archives and Records Administration in Washington, D.C., College Park, and Laguna Niguel made this project possible. Thanks also must go to people at the Library and Archives Canada. Saint Louis University librarians Jamie Emery and Rebecca Hyde found resources and supplied me with books. My work with Refugee and Immigration Services, Catholic Diocese of Richmond, in Roanoke, especially the opportunity to spend two years working on Violence Against Women Act (VAWA) cases, provided important perspective and insight. A very big thank you goes to the University of Pennsylvania Press and my editor Bob Lockhart, who helped strengthen the book in important ways. Thanks also to Erica Ginsburg and Jennifer Shenk as well as many others at the press who aided in my book's publication.

My dear friends and family not involved in academia provided unending support. My uncle Lewis and aunt Giorgina put me up in Washington, D.C., for weeks at a time over the years as I pored over the archives. Very important U.S.-based friends not already thanked are Alex Rasic, Steve Karlman, Conrad Rader, Janice and Bruce Stark, Jamal Adam, and Rebecca Wanzo. Last, I need to thank many Canadians. They include Erika Tyree, Jose Crisanto, Tara Mogentale, Clive Walker, Nadine Dillabaugh, Mark Philbrook, Vicki Drader and David Stewart, Noah and Casey Stewart, Robin Drader and Russ Smith, Kit and Dave White, Maureen and Ed Kochanuck, Elaine Little, Merilee White, Heather and Art Hester, George Baracos, Kim and Maurice Nesbitt, Kerry Hester, my mom and dad, Carole and Chuck Hester, my sister, Melissa Hester, and her husband, Donovan Hinch. Adam, my brother, went with me to Ottawa at a tough time in the research. None of these Canadians are in academia and they did not know when I signed up to write this book what I would ask of them or that they were going to be quite so integral to it. I am lucky to have them in my life.

Parts of this book were previously published in the *Journal of American History* and the *Journal of American Ethnic History* and are reprinted with their permission. Revised material from "'Protection, Not Punishment': Legislative and Judicial Formation of U.S. Deportation Policy, 1882–1904," *Journal of American Ethnic History* 30, no. 1 (Fall 2010), makes up part of Chapters 1 and 2. Portions of "Deportability and the Carceral State," *Journal of American History* 102, no. 1 (June 2015), are concentrated in the conclusion but are also in expanded form throughout the book.